The Good Quit

The Good Quit

Mastering the Fine Art of Giving Up

JEFFREY A. LOCKWOOD

UNIVERSITY OF WYOMING PRESS
Laramie

© 2026 by University Press of Colorado

Published by University of Wyoming Press
An imprint of University Press of Colorado
1580 North Logan Street, Suite 660
PMB 39883
Denver, Colorado 80203-1942

All rights reserved

 The University Press of Colorado is a proud member of Association of University Presses.

The University Press of Colorado is a cooperative publishing enterprise supported, in part, by Adams State University, Colorado School of Mines, Colorado School of Mines, Colorado State University, Fort Lewis College, Metropolitan State University of Denver, University of Alaska Fairbanks, University of Colorado, University of Denver, University of Northern Colorado, University of Wyoming, Utah State University, and Western Colorado University.

ISBN: 978-1-64642-806-9 (paperback)
ISBN: 978-1-64642-807-6 (ebook)
https://doi.org/10.5876/9781646428076

Cataloging-in-Publication data for this title is available online at the Library of Congress.

Cover photo: iStock / Liudmila Chernetska

To Josephine and Meredith,

May you develop the strength to persevere, the courage to quit—

and the wisdom to know when each is needed.

Contents

Acknowledgments ix

Preface xi

Introduction: Call Me a Quitter (but Not Too Loudly, Please) 3

SECTION 1: HOW DOES QUITTING MANIFEST? 17

1. Personal Endings: "I Can't Quit You" 19
2. Ending Work: "Take This Job and Shove It" 40
3. Quitting Conflicts and Contests: "Say 'Uncle'" 57
4. A Taxonomy of Quitting: Describing and Naming 72

SECTION 2: WHAT IS IT TO QUIT? 85

5. The Psychology of Quitting: Calculating the Incalculable 87
6. The Role of Free Will: Coerced Quits Aren't Quite Quits 106
7. Quasi-Quitting: Must We Give Up Completely? 126
8. Defining Quitting: Assembling the Puzzle Pieces 148

SECTION 3: PRACTICAL GUIDANCE 163

9. Quality Quitting: Cultivating Character 165
10. The Trifecta of Quitting: Why, What, and When? 183
11. How to Quit: Virtuosity and Virtue 200
Conclusion: A Few Last Words Before I Quit 216

Epilogue 231

Notes 233

Index 269

About the Author 275

Acknowledgments

In defiance of the "last but not least" rule of appreciations in books, I want to lead with my first and greatest expression of thanks to my wife, children, and grandchildren whose unconditional love and support foster a belief that I really should quit doubting that I'm a pretty darned good husband, father, and grandfather—whatever my inner critic says.

Now then, I would also like to express my gratitude to the University of Wyoming's Department of Philosophy and Religious Studies and the many colleagues who provided incisive and constructive critiques of my ideas—and to John Poland, who did a first-rate job of constructing the index. I'm also grateful to the Master of Fine Arts program in creative writing and those fellow writers who are models of perseverance. And I convey my thanks to the university's upper administration, the board of trustees, and the state legislature who both provided financial support for my work and contributed to my thinking about quitting.

I must also convey my deep thanks to the students in my honors course on the topic of quitting. These young people's intelligence, curiosity, dedication, and honesty reminded me of why quitting my work as a professor will be a most difficult decision.

I'm particularly grateful to the Wyoming Institute for Humanities Research at the university—a most stimulating association of scholars brought together through the clever and strategic use of meager institutional funding.

As for the University Press of Colorado, although the constant turnover typical of the publishing industry prevailed, they stuck with me. Darrin Pratt was an impressively responsive, encouraging, and professional editor.

Of course, I'm also indebted to the many thoughtful individuals in various fields—including business, climbing, counseling, gambling, law, martial arts, medicine, and military—who shared what amounted to more than 400 years of collective experience in realms where navigating the line between quitting and persevering is extremely difficult and profoundly important. They were wise and generous teachers.

Preface

There is growing interest among the general public (or at least that slice of society that still reads books) in "practical philosophy" and the overlapping field of "public philosophy."[1] These endeavors seek to engage thoughtful people in what too often has been the supercilious, even intellectually imperious, realm of academics. Philosophically relevant and culturally connected projects, such as the one I'm pursuing in this book, are concerned with how people can live well, not by following simple rules but by thinking deeply about what fosters (or impedes) their flourishing. In brief, the public philosopher genuinely respects his or her fellow citizens, believing they are most assuredly capable of critical thinking if complex concepts and arguments are presented in accessible ways without needless or unexplained jargon.

Perhaps my fondness for this kind of teaching resulted from having transformed fifteen years ago at the University of Wyoming from a professor of entomology in the College of Agriculture (a role I thoroughly understood) into a professor of natural sciences and humanities in the College of Arts and Sciences (an aspirational identity I admired but did not entirely grasp). This transition fostered my sympathy for "outsiders" trying to make sense of what seem to be terribly important matters (the nature of truth, reality, morality, justice, and beauty) that are often framed in frustratingly arcane terms. Instead of studying metamorphosis, I delved into metaphysics along with ethics and epistemology.

Even as a scientist, I was drawn to research—including some rather theoretical frameworks and esoteric models—that has ultimate applications to the real world. I pursued studies in which serious policies and tangible practices were at stake for actual people and ecosystems (e.g., effectively controlling pest populations while reducing the economic and environmental harm). So, I gave up being a scientist and now I'm contemplating throwing in the towel after nearly forty years as a professor. These endings entail disturbing but worthwhile revisions with regard to my sense of self—and they, along with other resignations, surrenders, and renunciations in my life, drew me into a practical, philosophical pursuit of the manifestations, meanings, and mastery of quitting.

By all appearances in modern life, quitting can be both very easy and extremely difficult. On the one hand, we seem to readily quit everything from relationships to religions to reality. On the other hand, we know the difficulty of quitting drugs, the challenges of divorce, and the trauma of suicide. While the US military was engaged in the agony of quitting Afghanistan, the big, unfolding story at home was the "Great Resignation" as people blithely quit work at unprecedented rates. Some interpret quitting employment by today's defiant workers as an admirable act of empowerment, while others contend it is nothing but a deplorable pursuit of self-indulgence. From battlefields to business parks, how can we understand such complexity and diversity with regard to individual and collective endings?

A life well lived involves masterful quitting, as this is among our most important, even momentous, decisions. Despite its ubiquity and difficulty, there are no rigorous, conceptual analyses of what quitting entails or how to cultivate excellence in this regard (notwithstanding the simplistic admonitions in self-help guides, or what I call "quit-and-grit lit," which make legitimately difficult decisions easy by offering simplistic, psychological pablum).

In pursuing an authentically "good life" (what the Greeks called *eudaimonia*), one ponders and pursues genuine fulfillment that resonates with the deepest values and aspirations regarding ourselves, as well as our family, friends, and community. This pursuit often delves into the virtues—character traits that foster a meaningful life, if not necessarily an easy or pleasurable existence (Jesus of Nazareth, Harriet Tubman, Jane Addams, Mahatma Gandhi, and Martin Luther King Jr. led profoundly admirable, but distinctly uncomfortable, lives). Many virtues have clear connections to daily life (e.g., gratitude and patience). But despite how much quitting well, indeed virtuously, contributes to a good life and shapes our identity—indeed, constituting many of our greatest triumphs and regrets—this practice has been neglected by scholars who, in the age of AI, can still offer genuine intelligence.

Human flourishing ultimately requires that we come to know why, when, and how to quit. Classical philosophers and theologians praised perseverance and tenacity while overlooking the reality that sometimes quitting is laudable. However, modern thinkers would do well to take a page from ancient sages. As we'll see, among the many virtues, *phronesis* or "practical wisdom"—the integration of book learning and street smarts—is the most vital capacity to cultivate in our lives, as it undergirds mastering the life skill of giving up.

Not known as the most sensitive or sagacious fellow, W. C. Fields offered a bit of curmudgeonly insight regarding whether to persevere or give up: "If at first you don't succeed, try, try again. Then quit. There's no point in being a damn fool about it."[2] He was right, of course, except it can take a lifetime to learn how many tries should come before quitting an endeavor. So, make no mistake: Quitting is conceptually complicated, emotionally fraught, and practically difficult—as it should be. But then so are love, forgiveness, tolerance, hope, loyalty, defiance, protest, and anger.

You won't find simple answers in this book, but I hope to have provided evocative exemplars, deep deliberations, and rigorous ruminations that will catalyze your own understanding of the often humbling, sometimes glorifying, feat of quitting.

A WARNING

This book is not intended to provide incisive perspectives on quitting with respect to the disciplinary concerns of individuals pursuing specific lines of research in particular fields of inquiry and practice. This project is analogous to cross-cutting, synthetic analyses of subjects that pertain in various ways to a diversity of fields, such as Routledge's long-standing series on the philosophy of concepts including agency, causality, collective responsibility, disagreement, emergence, evidence, imagination, information, luck, punishment, skill and expertise, and trust.[3] Or take, for example, the study of deception, which has diverse manifestations in economics, epistemology, ethics, evolutionary biology, game theory, law, marketing, military science, political science, psychology, religious studies, sports, and theater and film studies, among others. Perhaps a military historian might garner some clarity from understanding how a harmless species of butterfly fools predators by mimicking a toxic species, or a relationship counselor might glean an intriguing insight from considering the conditions under which lying is morally defensible, or a football coach might perceive how the Statue of Liberty Play could be improved by adapting principles of optical illusions. However, such cross-disciplinary insights would require the scholars and practitioners to engage in creative applications, novel extensions, imaginative linkages, intellectual curiosity, and metaphorical leaps. So it is with integrating an understanding of quitting into any given discipline or—as is the overriding concern of this book—any individual's life.

The Good Quit

INTRODUCTION

Call Me a Quitter (but Not Too Loudly, Please)

Throw in the towel,
    Raise the white flag,
        Put your tail between your legs.
A sobriety coin,
    A divorce decree,
        A tipped over chess king.
Roberto Durán says "no más" in the eighth round,
    Liz Carmouche submits in the first round of an Ultimate Fighting Championship title match,
        Simone Biles withdraws from the US gymnastics team.
On the deck of the USS *Missouri* in Tokyo Bay, 1945,
    On the rooftop of the American embassy in Saigon, 1975,
        On the tarmac of the Kabul airport, 2021.
Edward VIII abdicates as king of England in 1936,
    Richard Nixon resigns as US president in 1974,
        Mikhail Gorbachev steps down as president of the USSR in 1991.
Saint Paul converts to Christianity (Tom Cruise converts to Scientology 1,953 years later),
    Condoleezza Rice abandons the Democratic party for the Republicans,

      Mike Pence switches from being a Catholic Democrat to an evangelical Republican.

CEOs of Amazon, McDonald's, Peloton and Twitter bail,
    Presidents of Harvard, Columbia, MIT, and Dartmouth resign,
      And . . .
          since June of 2021, more than 4 million Americans have quit their jobs every month in what's been called "The Great Resignation."[1]

What are we to make of these historic and contemporary quitters—are they courageous or cowardly, virtuous or weak, savvy or lazy, admirable or despicable?

FIGURE 0.1. The Japanese surrender to Allied forces in World War II, aboard the USS *Missouri*, on September 2, 1945. Courtesy of the Naval Historical Center via Wikimedia Commons.

WHY ME? BOOK SMARTS, STREET SMARTS

A reader might well wonder whether I am a qualified guide into the world of quitting. While nobody has a doctorate in quitting (completing such a degree would be oxymoronic), I would suggest that I have the diverse credentials to plausibly undertake this interdisciplinary project. As a scientist-turned-philosopher at the University of Wyoming, I have the academic grounding for such an eclectic venture.

On the science side, I have studied animal behavior (mostly insects) and evolution (such as insecticide resistance) for many years. Insofar as quitting is an evolved behavior and humans are animals, I have the background to be a quitologist (not really a word).

On the philosophical side, I have worked extensively in the realms of environmental ethics and philosophy of science. As such, I've critically analyzed complex concepts such as our duties to future generations, the role of perspective in assertions of truth, and how political power is used to censor free speech. While quitting might initially seem conceptually straightforward, we'll soon see that it is a wondrous tangle of ideas.

How did a fellow with a doctorate in entomology become a professor of natural sciences and humanities, teaching courses such as natural resource justice, environmental aesthetics, and ecofeminism? Well, by quitting. Or at least through a metamorphosis. Some insects exhibit complete metamorphosis (e.g., a caterpillar becomes a butterfly), while others exhibit incomplete metamorphosis (e.g., a cockroach nymph repeatedly molts until it incrementally becomes an adult). My journey was more like the latter transformation, but there was a point at which I quit teaching courses such as insect anatomy and physiology, seeking grants for scientific research, mentoring graduate students in the sciences, and writing papers for research journals. Instead, I began delving not into the workings of nature but into the nature of knowledge, truth, goodness, and beauty.

But even if I have a foot in the worlds of both science and philosophy, a skeptic might say that to be a trustworthy guide through the thickets of quitting, practical experience is as important as an academic background. Who would want an expedition leader who studied maps but never trekked the countryside?

As a practitioner of quitting, my bona fides are solid if not exceptional. To be honest, I've ironically persevered in the sorts of endeavors that are commonly quit in the United States. I've never divorced, having been married since 1982. And I've worked for the same employer for thirty-nine years while switching departments internally and entertaining job offers at other institutions. And I admit to having unaccountably persevered in a plan to read 1,000 books between my fiftieth and sixty-fifth birthdays (the only book I came very close to abandoning was James Joyce's *Ulysses*).

With regard to my experiences of quitting, I began in my childhood by giving up on Santa Claus in the face of overwhelming contrary evidence. A memorably defiant quit in a rather demanding household was declaring that I was done with piano lessons. I became a modestly competent judoka as a teen but chose to pursue other ventures after advancing to the stage of being able to use choke holds, which meant learning when and how to submit (i.e., to quit). I had long dreamed of becoming a veterinarian, but I abandoned that plan while in college. During those years, I quit smoking pot after an acute panic attack, and I abandoned Catholicism after developing chronic skepticism. I've quit various secular organizations—everything from social action groups to a fantasy baseball league. I resigned as the director of creative writing after students vociferously doubted my alignment with their political causes. And like any other writer, I've euthanized many essays and stories, some during gestation and others after growing decrepit. Now that I'm half-retired (semi-quit), I might give up book-length projects after this one. Perhaps the most difficult quit in many ways was giving up on a grueling climb in Rocky Mountain National Park with my wife and son a few years ago, which meant admitting that I couldn't do things my younger self had done with ease.

Like others, I've had my share of vicarious experiences of quitting, with friends who have gone through messy divorces, ended addictions, and attempted suicides. Some years ago, a dear friend declared that he was quitting life as a man and transitioning to being a woman. And after my mother moved into an assisted living facility, I watched her struggle with dementia until she mentally surrendered but lived several months before her body consented to call it quits.

COPULATING, DYING, AND QUITTING: TABOOS THAT SHAPE OUR LIVES

Few decisions are as crucial to defining one's life, expressing one's values, or creating one's identity as quitting. Sure, the things we begin are important, as are those we endure and complete. However, many of these beginnings (e.g., a new job, relationship, or religion) are preceded by endings. Other quits are crucial to our selfhood simply by virtue of what is ended (e.g., renouncing citizenship, surrendering in battle, forsaking alcohol, rejecting meat, or choosing hospice). When thinking about how severing accretions from our lives shapes who we are, I'm reminded of the apocryphal answer Michelangelo supposedly gave when asked how he sculpted the famed statue *David*: "I just chipped off all the stone that didn't look like David."[2]

Despite its vital contribution to shaping our identity, quitting is typically viewed as a shameful act—and surely some, perhaps many, quits diminish our character through betrayal, cowardice, or laziness. We create euphemisms for those aspects of our lives that we avoid directly discussing in polite company, such as sexual intercourse (e.g., making love and rolling in the hay), urination (e.g., relieving oneself and answering nature's call), and death (e.g., passing away and meeting one's Maker). The same holds for quitting. Consider ending relationships, in which we: break up, go our separate ways, take things in a different direction, and (my favorite) consciously uncouple. But we avoid saying that we quit. The exception might be the line from *Brokeback Mountain* when Ennis tells his lover, "I wish I knew how to quit you."[3] But even here, the feeling is that of a man wanting to end an addiction—a socially sanctioned quit.

> THE WHITE HOUSE
> WASHINGTON
>
> August 9, 1974
>
> Dear Mr. Secretary:
>
> I hereby resign the Office of President of the United States.
>
> Sincerely,
>
> *Richard Nixon*
>
> The Honorable Henry A. Kissinger
> The Secretary of State
> Washington, D.C. 20520

FIGURE 0.2. Resignation letter of President Richard M. Nixon following the Watergate scandal. Courtesy of US National Archives via Wikimedia Commons.

Any number of famous people have disparaged quitting. There is, however, a tendency of talking the talk of this being an ignominious path but not walking the walk. To be charitable, perhaps it can be said that if one isn't sometimes a hypocrite, then one doesn't have very high standards or lacks the capacity for critical self-reflection.

From the world of power and politics, a year after he resigned the presidency, without evident irony Richard Nixon asserted that "a man is not finished when he's defeated. He's finished when he quits."[4] Although Douglas MacArthur proclaimed that "Americans never quit,"[5] when his views on military funding conflicted with those of President Roosevelt, MacArthur offered to resign as chief of staff of the United States Army—a seemingly un-American lack of true grit.[6]

The archetypal setting for disreputable quitting might well be athletic competition, in which individuals are encouraged to persevere as evidence of their character. Sports exemplify the high-profile, two-faced condemnation of quitting. Mike Ditka—who played professional football and coached the Chicago Bears to a Super Bowl victory—famously said "you're never a loser until you quit trying."[7] However, after twelve years of a difficult marriage, Ditka quit trying and divorced his first wife.[8] Jack Nicklaus, who won the Masters six times, admonished "resolve never to quit, never to give up, no matter what the situation"—apparently forgetting that he quit college to play professional golf.[9]

Female athletes also staunchly but speciously advocate perseverance, at least when it comes to their professional lives. Billie Jean King declared that "champions keep playing until they get it right."[10] But this courageous woman quit college, a marriage, a pregnancy, the consumption of meat, and a conservative Methodist upbringing.[11] While these might all be defensible, even admirable, decisions, they are forms of giving up. Likewise, Chris Evert pronounced "you can't give up! If you give up, you're like everybody else,"[12] but she gave up on three marriages, becoming like a million other people who divorce annually (although most don't quit three times).[13]

Women's tennis serves as a lens into our culture's growing ambiguity with regard to quitting. The conventional condemnation of those who don't persist in the face of difficulty has recently been challenged. The world's highest-paid female athlete from 2020 through 2022, Japanese tennis player Naomi Osaka, withdrew from the French Open in 2021 citing her struggles with depression and anxiety.[14] And less than a year later, the top-ranked women's tennis player, Ashleigh Barty, announced that she was emotionally spent and was quitting the sport.[15] While some have called these women courageous, others have criticized them as pusillanimous, emotional snowflakes. A cultural critic contended that cowardice had become the new courage: "We are now in the age where it is more admirable not to try. More heroic to quit."[16] It seems that in the culture war over what constitutes a virtue, quitting is a new battlefield.

From a psychosocial perspective, the negativity associated with quitting arises, at least in part, from the fact that any behavior becomes more readily performed with repetition. In positive terms, if you want to be a public speaker, then join a local chapter of Toastmasters. If you want to be a writer, then, in the words of legendary author Stephen King, "you must do two things above all others: read a lot and write a lot."[17] Or as the old joke goes: A fellow seeking to attend a concert in New York City spots a guy carrying a violin case and asks him how to get to Carnegie Hall, and the musician replies, "practice, practice, practice." We sense that the same can be said for vices and bad habits.

Conventional wisdom has it that one becomes a quitter through giving up repeatedly until quitting develops into a lifelong habit. Perhaps this character flaw begins with the individual trying to preempt the humiliation of losing a competition (being a loser may be the only opprobrium worse than being a quitter), and giving up becomes easier with each new occasion and context. First, the person throws in the towel during an amateur boxing match, then gives up on learning a new language, then resigns from a difficult job, and then leaves a spouse during a rocky patch in their marriage—nothing is too small or large to quit when the going gets tough.

Turning back to the development of laudable habits such as practicing the violin, in *The Nicomachean Ethics*, Aristotle contended that steadfast repetition is how one cultivates the virtues—a view supported by modern neuroscience.[18] But does the well-practiced musician find it merely less stressful to play the instrument, or do they become more skilled—and can one cultivate a kind of virtuosity when it comes to quitting?

LET NATURE BE YOUR TEACHER (OR NOT)

Shifting to a brief consideration of how we might understand quitting in biological terms—and why we might be well-prepared to perceive this behavior negatively—a case can be made that evolution favors persistence. A disposition for quitting may well have been a significant disadvantage in our past. Those individuals who gave up easily in the pursuit of food would not have fared well. After all, the animals we hunted had undergone natural selection to persevere with regard to resisting predators by flight and fight. Their quitters became our dinners. And our quitters became hungry hominids and perhaps meals for persistent, fierce carnivores.

A similar line of analysis would apply to acquiring mates. Those males and females who didn't persist in the seeking of a partner (or two or three, for those who were particularly unwilling to quit) didn't leave many offspring. This isn't to say that there is a "quitting gene," but there are surely psychological dispositions that are heritable, and it's not unreasonable to posit that gritty parents might have produced resolute offspring through both nature and nurture.

While the acquisition of resources would have entailed protracted struggle, a foolhardy persistence was costly. After repeatedly losing fights for dominance or territory, pursuing further conflict would only produce more wounds and fewer offspring. And, as we'll see, the practical challenge in the modern world is not so different. Knowing when to get off the canvas and when to throw in the towel—literally and metaphorically—is a difficult decision that doesn't neatly reduce to simple cost-benefit analysis given the incommensurable stakes of one's happiness, safety, wealth, and identity.

While we can posit that prehistoric quitters were destined to hunger and celibacy, scholars hold contradictory views as to whether persevering is in our nature. Some psychologists confidently assert "we now know that persistence is hardwired in the human species,"[19] while others maintain that "persistence requires overcoming the natural tendency to quit."[20] Even other species are inscrutable. While some evidence suggests that birds readily quit an unproductive task,[21] other studies report that our primate cousins don't seem adept at quitting when persistence continues to yield suboptimal results.[22]

We'll explore this stick-or-quit tension in much greater depth, but it's easy to appreciate both sides of the argument even at a personal level. On the one hand, we see ourselves and others as often acting with bullheaded persistence. We wonder why we stuck with a miserable job for so many years or why our friend wouldn't leave a dysfunctional relationship. Why are kids admonished to "hang in there" with piano lessons, math assignments, and athletic endeavors if doing so is an innate inclination? If we are truly hardwired to persist, US culture wouldn't need to have constructed a mythology of perseverance,[23] and there shouldn't be a market for children's books that encourage the little ones to "think they can" along with an anthropomorphized little engine[24] or for young adult books that valorize Katniss and her tenacity amid the Hunger Games.[25]

On the other hand, we find it easy to give up on a challenging puzzle, and my professorial colleagues shake their heads at how readily students withdraw from courses. But if quitting comes so easily, then why are there so many self-help books devoted to instructing people how to abandon various commitments? There is a cottage industry of "experts" advocating that we quit unfulfilling endeavors with advice such as "evaluate whether you might want to quit your good job in pursuit of a better one, leave your comfortable city and move to one with even bigger opportunities, and separate from a relationship that's pleasant but not inspiring or supportive of your dreams."[26]

So, is quitting a moral failing that needs to be overcome or a virtuous practice that needs to be cultivated? Which self-help general's battle plan should we select from the "grit-versus-quit lit" bookshelf?[27] Is it a psychobiological compulsion or a cultural creation? Should we opt for narcissistic quitting or Sisyphean persevering? Maybe the question is not that simple.

FOR EVERY SIMPLE QUESTION . . .

To paraphrase the inimitable social critic H. L. Mencken: For every complex problem there is an answer that is clear, simple, and wrong.[28] And when it comes to understanding the complex nature of quitting, there are three central problems that we'll explore in this book. For each, the solution will be complicated—not intractable or unassailable but appropriately challenging. I say "appropriately" because truly important problems of life rarely yield clear solutions. We wouldn't expect that an exploration of faith, justice, wisdom, or courage would be a simple journey, and the same holds for quitting.

In section 1, I begin with an investigation of quitting as a sociobiological phenomenon. The approach here is a voyage of discovery in which we explore the remarkably diverse forms quitting can take. I think of this as akin to an expedition I pursued with a colleague to collect insects in Amazonia for research and teaching purposes. We set up various traps to capture as many different crawling and flying creatures as possible so as to sample the full range of entomological diversity. After picking out specimens of research value for ourselves, we used the bulk of the material in our teaching laboratory and had students sort through the jumbled bodies and develop classification schemes based on patterns of insect anatomy (even to the inexperienced eye, beetles are distinct from flies, which differ markedly from ants). As for this anthropological expedition into the nature of quitting, after gathering marvelously varied accounts and organizing these observations systematically, the next challenge is to make sense of their essential features.

In section 2, I test out various hypotheses of what these diverse cases—ranging from military surrender, to mixed martial arts submission, to addiction withdrawal, to political resignation, to marital divorce, to religious conversion, to suicidal acts—have in common. Is there a fundamental nature that they all share? The shift from concrete cases to abstract concepts is crucial because without such a move, all we have is a series of psychosocial museum drawers filled with marvelous specimens of quitting and no deep or useful understanding. Famed physicist Ernest Rutherford arrogantly asserted that "all the science is either physics or stamp collecting."[29] To be charitable, he meant that without theory, a scientist has only a catalog of observations. And so, I'll attempt to derive a unified definition of quitting—a conceptual framework informed by the sciences (animal behavior, anthropology, economics, evolutionary biology, psychology, and sociology).

Section 3 is the payoff. Here I tackle the question that is likely to be most important and relevant to readers: What makes for a good quit? But, of course, we couldn't attempt a plausible answer unless we had already developed some conceptual grasp of quitting, just as we can't figure out what makes for good dances, fair fights, or justified lying without understanding what is meant by dancing, fighting, and lying. Figuring out the essence of a virtuous quit will entail delving into why, what, when, and how to give up. The reader should be warned, however, that there are no self-help, pop-psychology guidelines for the simple-minded. Rather, this is a book that respects the reader's intelligence and willingness to struggle with the truly important questions of life. One will not find easy answers, but one might discover how to ask better questions, including one of the most important and difficult decisions we make: Should I quit?

Before setting off on our voyage of discovery into the nature of quitting, it's necessary to provide a few caveats regarding the nature of this adventure. Most essentially, my concern is with the individual. There is surely much to be said for a more sociological approach to quitting in which we'd explore higher-level questions of how humans collectively prohibit, permit, or encourage quitting in a constellation of social contexts. But a journey is unlikely to get very far if every interesting detour is explored. I'm reminded of taking walks with my two-year-old granddaughter, which don't get much beyond the driveway if we pause to examine every intriguing flower, insect, and rock. That said, there will be some opportunities to at least broach questions such as whether our society is prone to quitting too readily or too reluctantly.

In focusing primarily on the individual, I'll mostly avoid the temptation to wander down the rabbit hole of cross-cultural analysis. There's no doubt that different cultures have different standards and practices when it comes to quitting. For example, the divorce rate in Maldives is twice that of Denmark, which is four times that of Qatar,[30] and the suicide rate in Lesotho is triple that of Russia, which is forty times higher than Barbados.[31] These sociological patterns are important to understand, but their complicated explanations would take us too far afield for the most part.

I'll also tread lightly through the thicket of gender, which is every bit as portentous and contentious as that of culture. In Western societies, quitting is typically viewed as weak and arguably associated with femininity. This gives rise to any number of complicated issues, such as the impression that women are judged more harshly than men when it comes to resigning from political office but not when seeking divorce. Interestingly, economic data suggest that women who quit their employment during "the Great Resignation" fared better in the job market than men who quit[32]—a phenomenon that combines gender and socioeconomics, which can be further complicated by taking into account whether quitting is a financial privilege.[33] All of this exemplifies why I'll largely avoid any attempt to explore the sociocultural aspects of quitting beyond what is necessary to inform our understanding at the individual level.

Finally, I should reiterate an important warning given in the preface (given how few people read prefaces, myself included). This project may disappoint those who have devoted their professional lives to delving ever more deeply and narrowly into their chosen fields. I have no objection to such dedication, and I genuinely admire many of those who have doggedly pursued such lines of inquiry (e.g., a colleague who spent more than fifty years studying the biology of Wyoming grasshoppers and made major contributions to entomology through his diligent investigations). However, such singularity of focus is not the only means of learning or teaching, notwithstanding contrary views among some of my academic associates. I'm reminded of this opposition by virtue of a reader's report provided during the early phase of this book's development, in which the very honest, if intellectually insular, commentator wrote: "I should state my bias against reading or writing academic books that are not in my area... I must say that I do not know in what field this manuscript intends to contribute" (the reader specialized in the subfield of employee turnover, which is surely an important, if rather narrow, concentration).

In a sense, a thoroughgoing grasp of quitting potentially contributes to virtually every field in the arts and humanities as well as the medical, behavioral, social, and natural sciences—but only if the specialist is able and willing to engage in intellectual extrapolation and creative curiosity. Perhaps one might think of an exploration of quitting as an exemplary case of transdisciplinary research that integrates traditional fields in a holistic manner.[34]

In the most immediate, personal, and practical terms, your having read this far leads to the question: Will you quit this book before completing it? For my part, I was tempted at times to quit writing; something like 97 percent of people who start to write a book never finish it.[35] As for readers, only about one-third claim to always finish what they start, while one in six give up in the first fifty pages.[36] Here's some balanced, perhaps even sage, advice from a comedy writer and avid reader: "Not enjoying that book you're reading? Quit. It's okay. You're allowed to do it. Just quit . . . I am not saying you shouldn't persist with a book because it's difficult at first. Sometimes overcoming that initial struggle is what makes a story beautiful."[37]

Should we be taking advice from a comedian? Sure. Notwithstanding my claim to scholarly competence, the quality of an argument is not necessarily a function of one's professional credentials (I'd also contend that comedians tend to be really smart people). Recall that the likes of Richard Nixon and Douglas MacArthur—public figures with significant gravitas—both vilified and instantiated quitting. Or perhaps we should consider the nuanced wisdom of Taylor Swift, a music icon who tweeted this insight: "Giving up doesn't always mean you're weak. Sometimes you're just strong enough to let go."[38] What does a country-turned-pop singer know about character compared to the likes of a president and a general? Perhaps a great deal, as we shall see.

SECTION 1

How Does Quitting Manifest?

Our understanding of an abstract concept such as quitting typically comes from knowledge of prototypical cases, along with a consideration of unconventional instances. For example, to understand what is ethical, we start with actions that strike us as intuitively moral (e.g., saving a drowning child) and then probe the conceptual boundaries by considering marginal cases (e.g., lying about the appearance of a friend's unsightly haircut), from which we develop a unifying and explanatory theory (e.g., you ought to do unto others as you would have them do unto you).

As such, this section of the book is devoted to gathering a wide range of case histories. We might imagine this venture as an expedition in which we collect a diversity of specimens in the tradition of natural historians such as Charles Darwin (a much more familiar and famous scientific adventurer than I). However, instead of pressed plants, pinned insects, and stuffed birds from the natural world, we'll gather varied samples of quitting from the civilized world.

One might wonder whether we ought to begin with a theoretical framework to organize our sampling. However, doing so presupposes an understanding of the concept and risks overlooking unusual and revealing cases of quitting. When I talk to people about quitting, they usually bring up marriage, work, and addiction, but they rarely think about poker, war, or hospice.

Starting with human experiences allows us to survey our lives without imposing a refined organizational structure. As Sherlock Holmes warned when Dr. Watson asked about the meaning of a mysterious event (in "A Scandal in Bohemia"): "I have no data yet. It is a capital mistake to theorize before one has data. Insensibly one begins to twist facts to suit theories, instead of theories to suit facts."

Of course, neither Darwin nor Holmes collected data willy-nilly. They needed some provisional notions of what might be relevant to their investigations. Likewise, the chapters in this section represent rough groupings along the lines of: personal endeavors (e.g., relationships, religion, and health), employment (e.g., jobs, careers, and education), and contests (e.g., military actions, combat sports, and board games).

A more familiar metaphor, given that most of us have little familiarity with nineteenth-century expeditions or mysteries, would be a journey to the grocery store. Imagine that you are going in search of salsa, an intriguing substance that you've heard about. So, you ask someone at the checkout stand where to find salsa. There is no uniquely "right" place for this condiment to be shelved, like chicken legs being in the meat department or avocados in the produce section. The cashier is confident that salsa isn't in the dairy case and suggests that you start in the Mexican food aisle; if it's not there, then try looking next to the tortilla chips or among the tomato and spicy sauces.

At this point, you are beginning to get a grasp of the nature of salsa. Indeed, you can infer its culinary origin, ingredients, and function. However, you should not to impose a hasty theoretical structure on salsa. If you defined it as a kind of tomato sauce, you'd exclude some of the important (and better, if you ask me) forms. I grew up in New Mexico, where red salsa is traditionally based on ripe chiles, not tomatoes. In addition, you'd omit salsa verde.

And so, let's begin our expedition and see what we find when we keep an open mind in seeking the flavors of quitting.

1

Personal Endings
"I Can't Quit You"

When considering the nature of quitting, perhaps the first thing that comes to mind is the ways individuals give up on personal commitments or associations. In this regard, we'll explore four types of quits that reflect our personal lives, keeping in mind that they may overlap with other forms in later chapters (e.g., quitting a team can be understood as a personal ending, but it may also constitute abandoning a social contract with teammates).

First, we'll explore a type of quitting that has almost surely been experienced by everyone reading this book—the ending of personal relationships. Romantic breakups, whether formalized by marriage or not, are the most familiar, but we also give up on relationships with partners, friends, children, and parents in various ways.

Next, we'll consider religious quits, which are also common, as many readers will have left the faith community of their childhood. An explicit renunciation, a gradual transition into disbelief, or a move to another religious community are all unique dynamics, but each of these changes entail quitting one practice to take up another.

Third, we'll examine various socially sanctioned quits, which include less public cases (e.g., letting go of a resentment) and more apparent instances (e.g., embracing voluntary simplicity). There are also psycho-medical quits that society has come to quietly affirm (e.g., ending life in hospice) or openly celebrate (e.g., ending addictions).

And finally, we'll need to compassionately but directly consider the socially stigmatized forms of quitting, including those that are in the gray area of cultural acceptance (e.g., physician-assisted death and euthanasia) and the most difficult to confront—suicide.

BREAKIN' UP AND BREAKING HEARTS

When I was a little kid, budding romancers were teased with a chant: "Jeff and Nancy sitting in a tree, k-i-s-s-i-n-g, first comes love, then comes marriage, then comes Nancy pushing a baby carriage." Of course, this sequence is hardly de rigueur in the twenty-first century, but it identifies the conventional stages of relationships from which an individual might exit. I'll focus primarily on quitting romantic partners, but a few words about the baby carriage are in order.

In terms of pregnancy, we might not typically think of abortion as a kind of quitting, but there is a plausible sense in which a woman ends a biological and emotional relationship. Once a child is born, a woman (and often her partner) may decide to quit parenthood and terminate parental rights—a decision that typically happens within days of the birth. However, a minor child can be relinquished at any age (by surrender either to a sanctioned agency or to consenting, adoptive parents), as can be attested by my wife (a social worker who began her career in child and family services). To avoid the negative valence of quitting, it is deemed preferable to refer to "placing a baby for adoption" rather than "giving up a baby."[1] Adoption might well involve another manifestation of quitting if the adoptive parents have given up trying to have a biological child. Of course, an adult child can be "disowned" or, in more legal terms, disinherited. And we ought not to forget that the reverse is also possible: a child can quit his or her relationship to parents and renounce all financial and personal associations.

Relationships used to end with breakups, but the new euphemism is "romantic disengagement," which has the advantage of including relationships beyond those with other people, as we shall see. I admit to being somewhat bewildered by the self-help advice that begins with "if you happen to be in one of those no-strings-attached relationships"[2] in that I can't quite fathom how such an association qualifies as a relationship. Let's assume for our purposes that there are strings—emotional, physical, social, financial, or whatever—and severing them constitutes a form of quitting. Indeed, relationship counselors might well contend that everything that provides human meaning entails connections.[3]

Intimate bonds are typically ascribed to relationships between two people who engage in sexual or sensual intimacy with interdependencies of emotional and material support.[4] Although there is a distinction to be made, we can also have deep, even romanticized, relationships with jobs and places, as what we do professionally and where we connect ecologically can be vital to our identity. Leaving a career or a homeland can be a kind of quitting that entails a sense of loss—an emotionally traumatic disengagement. We might well say "I love my job" or "I love this town" and find our identity as intimately linked to these as to a life partner.

Relationships may also develop with objects, as when a quilt, bracelet, or tool is imbued with memories. I'm reminded of a colleague who is on the cusp of retirement, and moving from Laramie to New York City will involve shedding possessions, including keepsakes from her mother that are of great sentimental value.[5] Having moved my nonagenarian in-laws from their home of fifty years into a senior apartment, I well know that chairs, dishes, and artworks can be infused with family stories. So, it appears not to overly extend the concept of "romantic disengagement" to include beloved objects.

Given the pain of quitting relationships, people understandably seek assistance in mitigating this trauma. Although much can be lost when a relationship ends, the costs of staying together may be greater than the emotional and material costs of leaving. As a relationship deteriorates, individuals begin to understand that emotional detachment is a gradual process, more like incrementally removing stiches than yanking off a Band-Aid. However, they tend to seek therapy when they are well on their way to calling it quits, which accounts for a therapeutic success rate of about 50 percent in terms of sustaining relationships.[6] Indeed, therapists recognize that they are often consulted at the end of the process of separation, when recommending relationship skills is less helpful than facilitating disengagement.[7] They are, in effect, relationship hospice counselors.

Hollywood's version of divorce is glamorized in such movies as *Eat Pray Love* and *Under the Tuscan Sun*, so a more realistic overview is in order.[8] In the early 1900s, along with the rise of industrialization, urbanization, and women's suffrage came increasing divorce rates. The solution to what was perceived as a societal problem became one of professional counseling to prevent ill-advised marriages. In the 1920s and 1930s, psychologists next argued that divorce was a consequence of interpersonal conflict that could be mitigated with couples therapy. In the 1940s, divorce rates dropped during World War II and rose immediately after, as people struggled to resume pre-war roles. After a dip in the 1950s, divorce rates rose in the 1960s through the 1980s as all institutions, including marriage, were questioned and people felt free to abandon dissatisfying relationships. In subsequent decades, divorce rates slowly declined.

Today, about 40 percent of all first marriages end in divorce, peaking 2.5 years after the wedding.[9] The US divorce rate is higher than that in other industrialized nations, which might be explained by a focus on satisfying individual desires.[10] By amalgamating risk factors, the least likely to divorce are well-educated, religious, older individuals who don't suffer from an anxiety disorder or alcoholism and whose spouse is faithful and children are healthy.[11] That's a tall order.

Describing the process through which married couples ultimately decide to call it quits has become something of a cottage industry in psychology.[12] Cost-benefit theories propose that people engage in a quasi-quantitative analysis of their relationships, although this may not be explicit or rational, while process models specify the stages of divorce. Perhaps the most detailed theory describes a cumulative process with

FIGURE 1.1. Marilyn Monroe sitting in a courtroom with her attorney during the high-profile divorce proceedings from Joe DiMaggio, her second of three divorces. Courtesy of the *Los Angeles Times* via Wikimedia Commons.

more-or-less identifiable stages in which typically one of the married parties amasses dissatisfactions as courtship illusions give way to unfulfilling marital realities.[13] The couple may try to discuss or resolve specific complaints, with the woman often taking responsibility for problems while the man withdraws or intensifies controlling behaviors. The shift from overlooking desirable traits to magnifying negative behaviors in one's partner generates anger, which gives way to disaffection and disengagement. This process instantiates the insight that the opposite of love is not hate but indifference.[14] The growing detachment, which might be analogized to the excision of a leaf in autumn, often culminates in a relatively brief, if decisive, event, but this moment is the endpoint of a systemic and chronic condition. In effect, quitting is a months- or years-long process. Much less is known about the dissolution of same-sex marriages, but it is not unreasonable to expect similar dynamics.

Neil Sedaka was right when he sang that breakin' up is hard to do. Along with financial costs comes the potential collapse of our identity and social network. If an individual's sense of self is tightly woven into a marriage, then divorce may entail quitting one's identity—a potentially devastating transformation.[15] Indeed, divorce has been described as a crisis and mourning process that evokes a sense that a person's selfhood has perished.[16]

Even if the depth of engagement is not so profound as to shatter an individual's identity, the emotional toll of divorce is substantial. According to attachment theory, many couples form interdependencies that sustain them and their relationship.[17] Between 50 percent and 60 percent of couples are characterized as "securely attached" such that severing this bond is psychologically painful.

When a marriage is deteriorating, the tendency of men to withdraw emotionally should not be taken to mean a lack of angst, given that men experience more problems than women when initially separated from their spouses. Indeed, recently divorced men are much more likely to continue the process of quitting until the ultimate, existential endpoint is reached. Their suicide rate is six times greater than that of married men, while there are no differences between the rates for divorced and married women.[18]

A relevant digression into the philosophical considerations that attend divorce might further explain why people find this form of quitting to be so fraught. Eddy M. Zemach has argued that momentous institutions, such as marriage, cannot be blithely abandoned because admission into these institutions involves promising to behave according to their rules.[19] Couples typically vow to stay together for better or worse, and breaking a promise is a moral failure. Contrary to those who assert that quitting is ethically neutral and individuals should have no compunction in abandoning whatever is not serving their interests,[20] at least some quits—such as those involving weighty institutions, including marriage—are morally problematic. While Zemach's line of reasoning may not be explicitly in individuals' minds, there may well be a deeply troubling, inchoate sense that divorce breaks a solemn promise made in front of an authority and witnesses—often in association with a religious tradition, which leads us to the next form of relational quitting.

If a rich and meaningful life is built on relationships and both forming and breaking these bonds plays an important role in shaping our identity, then surely deciding to leave a religious community is a form of quitting that merits consideration.

CONVERSION VERSIONS

Before exploring how quitting is manifest in the renunciation of one's religion, let's briefly consider the ways quitting can deepen commitment. Religions provide ample opportunities for the faithful to quit, at least temporarily, behaviors that impede piety. Various Christian denominations require fasting for an hour before communion, abstaining from meat on Fridays, and forgoing an earthly indulgence during Lent. Muslims stop eating, drinking, smoking, swearing, gossiping, and having sex between dawn and dusk during Ramadan. Shakers gave up sexual intercourse entirely, and ascetics in various traditions renounce all sorts of bodily pleasures. Indeed, faith itself can entail quitting, as exemplified by the Knight of Infinite Resignation in Søren Kierkegaard's *Fear and Trembling*.[21] The most extreme examples of quitting while remaining within a religious tradition involve martyrs who give up their lives rather than betray their faith. The list of martyrs is long and includes essentially all religions, which is unsurprising given the power struggles between communities of faith and political states.[22]

While few of us will become martyrs, many people will change faiths or simply quit religion altogether. In the most straightforward terms, conversion means acquiring a new system of religious beliefs and relinquishing a previous framework,[23] which bears a conceptual and perhaps emotional similarity to divorce and remarriage. Indeed, some nuns wear wedding rings to symbolize their devotion to Jesus Christ. And like the dissolution of a relationship between two people, conversion is typically a gradual process of quitting as a believer becomes increasingly dissatisfied until there is a break from that which no longer meets their needs.[24] In the early twentieth century, William James famously described conversion as a process "by which a self hitherto divided, and consciously wrong, inferior, and unhappy becomes unified and consciously right, superior, and happy in consequence of its firmer hold upon religious realities."[25] In 1933, the psychology of religious conversion was further elaborated by Arthur Darby Nock,[26] who referred to a "deliberate turning from indifference or from an earlier form of piety to another, a turning which implies a consciousness that a great change is involved, that the old was wrong and the new is right." After decades of relative disinterest, there is growing curiosity about conversion among anthropologists, with a recent focus on the interplay between religion and identity,[27] along with a complexification of the earlier notion that conversion was simply the exchange of one worldview for another.[28]

In the twentieth century, the most common form of conversion worldwide was moving from tribal religions to Christianity, Islam, Buddhism, or Hinduism.[29] At the same time, the number of atheists and agnostics increased from virtually zero in 1910 to 15 percent of people worldwide in 2000, meaning that about a billion people gave up (or grew up without) religious beliefs.[30] Today, nearly half of US adults do not belong to their childhood faith, including about one in six who have switched denominations.[31] If recent trends in disaffiliation continue, Christians will make up about 40 percent of the US population in 2070, dramatically down from 64 percent in 2020 and 90 percent fifty years ago.[32] Most individuals make the change before age twenty-four, with more than 95 percent of former Catholics and Protestants disaffiliating by age thirty-five.³³ The most common motivations for drifting away from an earlier religious faith were reported to be growing intellectual doubt and moral criticism, with a diminishment in the meaningfulness of religious experiences also playing a role.³⁴

Perhaps the best-known conversion was that of Saint Paul, who underwent a dramatic "come to Jesus" moment on the road to Damascus (Acts 9:3–9). There are contemporary case studies of Pauline transformations, such as the woman who walked into a Catholic Church, which was taboo for her, and "all of a sudden I could feel God ... Within a week I moved out of my home. I left my family, friends, job; all were Jehovah's Witnesses, the only world I knew."³⁵ She renounced her former faith, sold her possessions, and took another leap of faith to become a Benedictine nun.

Despite such drama, modern studies describe conversion as a typically gradual process.³⁶ Various models propose incremental stages that involve dissatisfaction, disappointment, and doubt—leading to crisis, exit, and search, then culminating in encounter, transition, and acceptance.³⁷ With regard to the psychology of quitting, the crucial stage is disillusionment in which belief is disrupted and cognitively challenged, leading to rejection.³⁸

Social context may powerfully shape personal dynamics,³⁹ as the religious community that is renounced may view the quitting as a defection or apostasy in judging that the leave-taker is aligning themselves with an oppositional religion. Openly contemplating conversion may evoke expulsion, which is akin to being sacked from a job insofar as a religious leader or group rejects the individual in a kind of "you can't quit, you're fired" tactic.

The conventional formulation of conversion suggests that upon quitting, an individual slides smoothly into another religion. But of course, many people remain unchurched for a period of time, in what is termed deconversion (disaffiliation without reaffiliation).⁴⁰ About 11 percent of Americans have deconverted, which can be further classified as secularizing or heretical exits, depending on the nature of the disbelief (e.g., agnosticism or atheism).⁴¹

Other forms of conversion might not constitute full-blown quitting, as when an individual switches to a closely aligned denomination or joins a religion that is more accommodating and inclusive without requiring the individual to abandon most or perhaps any of their previous beliefs (e.g., Unitarian Universalism is exceptionally open to such possibilities of theological accretion rather than requiring a full-blown paradigm shift). Further, simply being part of a religious community does not necessarily entail "true belief," as it is possible for one to be socially within a tradition and eventually convert fully to its creedal strictures.[42]

Having grown up Catholic, quit this religion to spend my college years unchurched, and then become Unitarian Universalist, my own story of conversion reflects a trajectory that is common, if not entirely embraced culturally. Generally speaking, fidelity to people and communities is more valued than mate or church swapping. So, let's turn to forms of quitting that are socially approved.

CONGRATULATIONS ON HAVING QUIT

Some forms of quitting are admirable, while others are acceptable or at least not condemned. For the most part, praiseworthy quits involve giving up something that is plausibly bad, although what society deems worthy of quitting changes with time (e.g., quitting smoking was not widely advocated or admired a hundred years ago).

Various forms of dietary quitting are respectable, even commendable. Giving up meat is often viewed positively, as it is generally accepted that vegetarians have good reasons for repudiating meat, such as physical health, environmental concerns, and animal welfare. Veganism is also seen as a virtuous, if perhaps extreme, renunciation. Giving up industrially produced foods or consuming only organic produce or humanely raised meat is likewise sanctioned, given what are presumed to be morally sound principles. While religious prohibitions (e.g., not eating pork by Jews and Muslims) are generally respected, the religious rationale makes the abstinence more dubious and less admirable for many non-believers.

When it comes to gender, how we judge quitters is more complicated but increasingly affirmative as society becomes more tolerant of diversity.

When an individual stops conforming to their gender assigned at birth, most Americans might not find this particularly laudable, but a plurality believe that society hasn't gone far enough to protect people who are transgender.[43] I have a dear friend who quit being Dan and started becoming Kate nearly twenty years ago, when such transitions were less common, particularly for someone in their fifties—and the courage and grace with which she managed this conversion were profoundly admirable.[44] A generally more private quitting (the exception being those who join various religious orders) is voluntary celibacy, which has been increasing in recent years for a conglomeration of reasons.[45] Many would deem such a decision to be acceptable, and the self-discipline might well be seen as commendable.

Other forms of quitting that are both praiseworthy and often invisible involve the decision to renounce certain mental states or habits, perhaps with the assistance of a therapist. For example, a person might give up listening to that internal, critical voice (the one demanding perfection and condemning inadequacies), wallowing in shame (I'll consider the possible upside of regret in a later chapter), expecting to control one's life (clinging to the "way things should be" and refusing to accept that things sometimes just happen), and hating or resenting someone who harmed them (perhaps forgiveness entails an element of quitting). We'd likely admire an individual who relinquished a debilitating and irrational fear (e.g., arachnophobia) or quit comparing themselves to cultural ideals of wealth and beauty. And we might notice and affirm relatively subtle quits, such as a friend who stops cursing or a co-worker who ceases biting their nails. The estimable willpower needed to break a bad habit brings us to the most socially celebrated form of quitting.

Addiction pervades the modern world, with nearly one-third of Americans over the age of twelve chemically dependent on a chemical substance, including nicotine (50 million), alcohol (15 million), opiates (2 million), and other drugs such as cocaine, heroin, marijuana, inhalants, and barbiturates (collectively, 23 million).[46] But quitting is also relatively common, as the half-life of substance abuse ranges from four to six years (cocaine and marijuana), to sixteen years (alcohol), to thirty years (tobacco).[47]

The conventional view is that addiction is a chronic disease, remission being a temporary state at best with individuals invariably and chronically tempted to relapse. As such, the clinician who counsels the addict is analogous to an inhaler an asthmatic uses regularly to keep symptoms at bay.[48] In effect, addiction and quitting are never-ending processes.

In contemporary terms, individuals have a "substance use disorder" (SUD).[49] Not only does "addiction" have a negative moral valence, but the condition is not recognized in the *Diagnostic and Statistical Manual of Mental Disorders* (DSM-5, the authoritative compendium for mental health professionals).[50] Extensive research does not support the earlier notion that SUD is a lifelong disease. Rather, this condition has one of the highest remission rates of any mental disorder. While some individuals use drugs throughout their lives and others fit the quit-and-relapse pattern, many people successfully quit on their own after a few years.[51]

Along with SUDs, there are BUDs (behavior use disorders), such as gambling, video games, sex, and other activities that are working their way into the DSM. A very successful professional poker player who admitted that he had a "gambling problem" equated the intense highs of winning and lows of losing with drug hits.[52] What all of these use disorders have in common is that they are problematic compulsions—and quitting is both difficult and admirable.

—

My interviews of SUD therapists provided unanticipated perspectives on quitting.[53] Contrary to my naive expectations based on movies and novels, quitting may not require total abstinence. Rather, the question for the client is: What are the negative consequences of using the substance that diminish the quality of life? For example, an alcoholic might want to quit getting into drunken brawls. So, the personal, contextualized goal might be to reduce consumption such that the individual stops becoming violent. The therapists hastened to note that for some individuals, it is necessary to entirely forgo the problematic substance (the classic all-or-nothing framework) to achieve the desired result.

Psychologists refer to "making a meaningful change" rather than "quitting," which evokes a standard of absolutism such that any lapse feels like a failure and implies a return to the original condition. Lapses are considered typical and are analogized to having a flat tire on a trip. When a tire loses air, one doesn't go home and start over but fixes the flat and continues the journey toward Quitville.

As for whether therapy is efficacious, various studies provide conflicting conclusions. At least for illegal drugs (alcohol and tobacco potentially having other issues), addiction is primarily a disorder of youth, such that the typical user quits six to eight years after the onset of dependence—often without therapy. However, a significant minority persist beyond age thirty. Seeking treatment for SUDs is something like signing up for an aerobics class. Some people have the wherewithal to exercise on their own, but lots of couch potatoes are more likely to quit indolence when guided by a professional.

Not all people have the same prognosis with regard to quitting a substance. After amalgamating predictive features, the best bet is on a white, wealthy, well-educated, married man who is worried about being arrested and damaging his health while using an illegal drug.[54] Education increases susceptibility to science-based information regarding the hazards of drug use, and legal drugs, such as alcohol and nicotine, are more available so remission rates are substantially higher.[55] The minority stress model suggests why women and non-whites, who struggle against social pressures, fare more poorly.[56]

In the end, people with an SUD have a tough choice to make.[57] They don't choose to be miserable and addicted, but the option of quitting is brutally difficult and even agonizing. We are not wired to accept, or practiced at accepting, immediate, short-term suffering in exchange for the promise of a better, distant future that might seem on the verge of impossibility. But there are other quits that can be even more psychologically, if not physically, traumatic.

WHEN ENOUGH IS ENOUGH

There are socially condoned forms of quitting within the realm of medicine. When a person is near death, ending resuscitation or life support is culturally acceptable for the most part. To better understand these situations, I interviewed a pair of pediatric critical care physicians with a combined six decades of experience in deciding whether to "pull the plug" in cases of prolonged life support and to "end a code" in cases of acute resuscitation.[58] Although the issues of quitting also pertain to adult patients, the stakes seem more vivid in the case of children.

Not surprisingly, the doctors were averse to the term *quitting*, viewing it as pejorative and preferring "concluding" to describe the rational termination of a medical intervention. Any competent physician won't pigheadedly continue to do what isn't working in support of a patient's meaningful life, whether that is a course of antidepressants, infusions of chemotherapy, a heart-lung machine, or cardiopulmonary resuscitation. But knowing when to give up exemplifies the complex mix of art and science in medicine.

When a patient's heart stops, a nurse or doctor "calls a code" and a team arrives with a designated leader. Resuscitation continues until the leader, in consultation with the team, decides enough is enough.[59] The decision is a combination of objective information and subjective experience, taking into account complex factors (e.g., duration of the arrest, the chances of a quality life post-resuscitation, and preexisting conditions).[60]

Inside their medical bubble, physicians in general and pediatricians in particular used to "go to the wall" to prevent death, but there's increasing awareness that a child is part of a family.[61] Today, parents are allowed to witness a code, with the support of a medical professional. Resuscitation can be violent, with breaking ribs and bleeding lungs. Often, the parent sees that it's time to quit before the physicians do: "Please stop, I just want to hold her."

In chronic cases, there is more time for gathering information, attempting prognoses, pondering values, and ultimately deciding if medical interventions are simply prolonging suffering and delaying death.[62] Our society's diminishing trust in science and expertise makes such quits increasing difficult as parents have begun to doubt physicians' knowledge, functionally unmooring the decision from rationality. Of course, feelings matter, but as the only factor, emotions leave much to be desired. And while cost should not determine when to give up, keeping a patient with a condition that will never improve in an intensive care unit takes resources from a system with limited capacity.[63]

The critical care pediatricians also did not see palliative care (i.e., relieving the suffering without treating the underlying cause) as quitting but as affirmatively making life better while you have it.[64] In the United States, hospice care is not quite fifty years old. However, the choice to forgo further life-prolonging medical interventions has become widely accepted despite terminological confusion (e.g., "comfort care," chosen by Barbara Bush, typically means opting out of respirators and CPR but allowing medicines to ease breathing or diminish pain).[65]

The spiritual director (and licensed clinical psychologist) at the hospice in my community described his facility's mission as helping individuals "find the path to a good quit."[66] Indeed, Dr. Lou Farley's position is that the highest form of quitting is renunciation, which he takes to be "withholding or withdrawing from medical interventions for the purpose of personal, social, and communal well-being or enrichment."[67] Ultimately, renunciation and resignation allow one to be at peace and experience a contented dying.

Hospice is a form of quitting but should not be equated with suicide. Dr. Farley has no problem with self-euthanizing, which is an active, reasoned decision to engage in a non-violent act that brings one to a state of peace. However, he views suicide as "a rotting away of the will to live" or the spiritual equivalent of an aggressive, incurable cancer that strips a person of agency and dignity. To be sure, suicide is not among the socially approved forms of quitting, which we'll consider next.

THE ULTIMATE QUIT

Let's turn to our final forms of quitting, which fall into the realm of suicide—a socially stigmatized form of giving up that is more complicated than quick and easy condemnation would suggest. Suicide has been defined as death caused by self-directed injurious behavior with the intent of lethality.[68] However, it is often difficult or impossible to know someone's intentions,[69] as when a person engages in dangerous behaviors that suggest an unconscious "death wish."[70]

What we do know is that in the United States, suicide claimed the lives of nearly 46,000 people in 2020, about twice the homicide rate.[71] For reasons psychologists can't explain and despite efforts to reduce suicides, the rate has generally increased in the twenty-first century,[72] with a tripling among youth in the last forty-five years.[73] Women are more likely to attempt suicide,[74] but men are nearly four times more likely to kill themselves. With respect to age, suicide is the second or third leading cause of death in age cohorts between ten and thirty-four years.[75] My home state, Wyoming, leads the nation in suicide deaths, with 30.5 per 100,000 people, perhaps due to the Western mythos of fierce, manly independence that eschews asking for help.[76]

We have a cultural fascination with suicide, along with a deep ambiguity as to whether we should praise or condemn the deaths of Vincent van Gogh, Ernest Hemingway, Sylvia Plath, Hunter S. Thompson, David Foster Wallace, and Virginia Woolf. In the context of philosophy, Albert Camus wrote: "There is but one truly serious philosophical problem, and that is suicide. Judging whether life is or is not worth living amounts to answering the fundamental question of philosophy."[77] For Socrates, the answer was demonstrably "no" as he willingly drank hemlock out of respect for the law when the Athenian court decreed him guilty of impiety and corruption of the youth. Hamlet was rather less certain when Shakespeare had his eponymous character contemplate "to be, or not to be, that is the question"—a question Romeo and Juliet answered with poisoning and stabbing. In my youth, two movies used dark humor to ponder suicide: *Harold and Maude* (a cult classic) and *M*A*S*H* (a popular blockbuster with five Academy Award nominations and a catchy theme song about suicide). In opera, women variously and bravely leap to their death (Puccini's *Tosca*), commit ritual suicide (Puccini's *Madama Butterfly*), and poison themselves (Verdi's *Il Travatore*). The list goes on in literature, theater, and film, with readers and audiences often left to ponder whether the individuals are admirable, pitiable, or contemptible.

To set the stage for discussing the common or typical acts of real-world, modern-day suicide, let's start with versions that are in the gray area of social judgment—those ways of ending life that can be acceptable, maybe even virtuous. To begin, martyrdom is sometimes heroic, as when a religious believer defies state authorities (e.g., the apostles Peter and Paul were crucified and beheaded, respectively, under Emperor Nero) or a soldier throws himself on a grenade to save his buddies. In World War II, twenty-seven United States Marines were decorated in the Pacific theater for this act of self-sacrifice,[78] while on the other side, Japanese kamikazes demonstrated the depth of their devotion—as did the hijackers of planes on 9/11. Suicide missions can be morally messy, but they are simply deplorable when carried out against non-combatants (a conceptually complex status in today's economically and politically entangled world), as with suicide bombers in public spaces. Conversely, we might admire, if not fully endorse, the self-immolation of the Buddhist monk at a busy intersection in Saigon in 1963 as a way of protesting persecution by the South Vietnamese government.[79]

While sacrificial exits are unlike standard suicides insofar as the former have an element of other-regarding behavior,[80] there is a further gray area of self-interested but somewhat socially countenanced quitting—physician-assisted death (PAD). Jack Kevorkian is arguably the most (in)famous advocate of a patient's right to die with the help of a medical doctor.[81] Today, various forms of voluntary euthanasia are legal in ten states and the District of Columbia, with typical provisions being that the individual is eighteen or older, mentally sound, within six months of dying from a terminal illness as affirmed by two doctors, and able to self-administer the lethal drugs.[82]

FIGURE 1.2. Jack Kevorkian, physician and euthanasia proponent who assisted in the suicides of at least 130 terminally ill patients. Courtesy of Greg Asatrian via Wikimedia Commons.

The American Association of Suicidology has attempted to draw a bright line to distinguish between suicide and PAD, although many of the distinctions between these forms of quitting are less than convincing. For example, the association asserts that the suicidal individual experiences unrelenting psychological pain and despair (which conceivably accompanies terminal illnesses in those seeking PAD), acts impulsively (there are clearly exceptions), and is unable to assess the situation objectively (surely the decision of an individual with a terminal illness is heavily laden with subjectivity in contemplating PAD).

The most socially acceptable form of euthanasia is provided to animals, but even in these cases the procedure is decried if employed for the wrong reasons (e.g., a healthy animal is killed because the owner has become bored or inconvenienced). A psychologist in Colorado State University's College of Veterinary Medicine and Biomedical Sciences who specializes in human-animal interactions considers "quitting" a justifiable description of euthanasia, but the negative connotations lead her to prefer the euphemistic phrase "giving up on what is not working" (not unlike the critical care pediatricians mentioned earlier).[83] There is a range of defensible reasons for euthanizing a companion animal, the foremost being to put an end to untreatable suffering, with less compelling rationales being the owner's inability or unwillingness to care for a chronic condition and the animal's irredeemable behavior problems.

For the most part, regret arises from a sense that the choice of euthanasia was selfish, particularly if finances are an issue or the owner feels they let the animal suffer too long because they couldn't bear its loss. Knowing the "right time" to call it quits is enormously difficult, although there are quasi-objective, quality-of-life factors that can be helpful (e.g., asking the owner to keep track of good and bad days and whether the animal still enjoys eating or going outside)—and some owners believe their pet lets them know.[84] However, it does not appear that any animal other than humans is aware of its mortality—and the full meaning of giving up on life.[85]

When subjected to stress, some non-human animals engage in aberrant behaviors (e.g., refusal to eat and self-injury) that may culminate in death. Perhaps most dramatic, when a bee stings, the individual is lethally eviscerated. However, it appears that suicide—intentionally taking one's life—is a uniquely and universally human phenomenon.[86] While other animals feel helplessness, we know hopelessness.[87]

My consulting suicidologist, Dr. Carolyn Pepper, at the University of Wyoming (a disturbingly apropos locale given the state's suicide rate), set me straight on terminology. A person is no longer said to commit suicide but to die by/of/from suicide. Rather than the language of crime, psychologists use the language of disease.

The psychological recipe for suicide begins with a large measure of hopelessness. Next, add a mixture of misery and depression along with a dash of burdensomeness. Then, combine these with the capacity to act. In brief, people quit when the reasons for living are less compelling than those for dying. And there can be plausible reasons for this judgment.

According to Dr. Pepper, an individual can be rationally hopeless. Suicide notes make this evident with phrases such as "for the last year I have been in agony day and night," "there is just this heavy, overwhelming despair," and "the pain has become excruciating, constant, and endless."[88] A friend who's a Jesuit priest once told me that the greatest sin was despair, as it was a giving up on the goodness and power of God—a kind of religious quitting that can be entangled with an emotional-cognitive despondency.

Setting aside the theological implications, there is a temptation to imagine suicide as an understandable response to a crushing problem, but "the normal mind, although strongly affected by a loss or damaging event, is well cloaked against the possibility of suicide."[89] Indeed, if our society was composed of only so-called normal minds, almost nobody would give up on life.

While years-long, untreatable, and soul-crushing depression might provide a cogent basis for suicide, the impulsive self-destruction of young people who lack the perspective of time is heartbreaking.[90] In school settings, contagion is a real concern, although there are strategies to check the spread of suicidal behavior.[91]

Factors that diminish the likelihood of an individual giving up on life include religiosity, social support, financial security, and physical health.[92] Older men are at particular risk due to their losses of a social network, familial role, and meaningful employment.[93] Chronically grim socioeconomic conditions go a long way to explaining why non-whites are also prone to suicide.[94] And so perhaps the one thing we really must not quit is the effort to understand and reduce the frequency of suicide.

LET'S CALL IT QUITS

Having journeyed into the impressively diverse realm of personal quitting, we've encountered cases that range from the admirable to the despicable, the heroic to the tragic, and the understandable to the unfathomable. This foray into one province of quitting has provided diverse raw material for a systematic classification of this phenomenon. However, there are two other realms of quitting to consider.

Next, we'll explore a domain of resignation that is familiar to almost everyone—a kind of quitting that is often seen as constructive and even necessary with regard to creating opportunities. But, as we shall see, these qualities don't mean that pulling the plug on employment or education is necessarily simple, easy, or praiseworthy.

2

Ending Work
"Take This Job and Shove It"

The word *employment* entered the English language 250 years before the first mention of *unemployment*.[1] Perhaps this timing reflects Western culture's early, practical emphasis on labor: Without working, one might well starve. Simply put, a job generates the money necessary to meet basic needs. And when it comes to quitting, anyone who's ever been employed for a paltry hourly wage can appreciate the bitter sentiment of the 1977 country music song "Take This Job and Shove It." However, quitting a career is another matter.

A career is a long-term pursuit of personal ambitions and professional goals. Such an endeavor is part of one's identity.[2] According to Thomas L. Dumm, a professor of political ethics, leaving a career can be tantamount to losing part of oneself: "A resignation ... is a giving up of something—one's life, one's being, one's soul ... The resignation letter similarly requires a signature to mark the breaking of the seal or sign of the honorable commitment."[3] In less overwrought terms, researchers have investigated the nature of "voluntary employee turnover"—the professional euphemism for "quitting." Scholars have developed a slew of models to understand how and why individuals decide to quit.[4] And the last few years have provided an abundance of data from those leaving both jobs and careers.

QUITTING TIME IN AMERICA

Even before a wave of quitting that became known as "the Great Resignation" captured headlines in 2021, Americans were becoming steadily less committed to their employers. Consider that college students who graduated between 1986 and 1990 averaged 1.6 jobs in the five years after schooling, while those who graduated twenty years later averaged nearly twice as many jobs.[5] The long-term trend has been for changing jobs more frequently with each generation.[6] On average, workers ages fifty-five to sixty-four stick with a job for nearly ten years, while those twenty-five to thirty-four last less than three years. Workers ages forty-five to fifty-two have held an average of 1.9 jobs, compared with 4.5 jobs among twenty-five- to thirty-four-year-olds.[7]

At the beginning of 2021, more than 40 percent of workers were reportedly thinking about leaving their work. This turned out to be no quixotic dream or idle threat. Starting in April and continuing for more than a year, about 4 million people—nearly 3 percent of all workers—left their employment every month, the highest rate of resignations in US history.[8] Between April and September 2021, retail apparel experienced the highest attrition rate at 19 percent, with the internet seeing 14 percent and airlines 5 percent.[9] This wave of quitting swept across both blue- and white-collar workers, with jobs and careers abandoned at unprecedented rates. Analysts suggested that managers could reduce the attrition rate by creating lateral career opportunities, allowing remote work assignments, sponsoring social events, and providing predictable schedules, but nothing seemed to work when it came to keeping people employed. The millennial generation embraced "fluidity,"[10] which could be taken to mean an admirable capacity for adaptation to novel opportunities or a deplorable lack of commitment to any sustained endeavor.

All told, more than 38 million workers quit in 2021, a trend that peaked in 2022 at 50.6 million and then declined to 39.6 million in 2024.[11] Some of the quitters are switching jobs, while others may be moving to the employment sidelines—the latter surely a major tactic given that there are more than 10 million unfilled jobs in the country.[12]

The Great Resignation has been described as the culmination of decades of workers trying to quit their way to happiness—or so they imagined. Perhaps millennials saw how little joy their parents derived from careerism in a vicious cycle of dissatisfaction leading to ambition, generating consumption, and returning to dissatisfaction.[13] Even prior to 2021, 91 percent of millennials expected to change employment every three years, their career path shaped by the pursuit of freedom and leisure time rather than a long-term dedication to a line of work.[14] Does a shift to the viability of quitting represent wisdom beyond their years as they grasp that there's more to life than work, or does it reflect a sense of entitlement to be given their dream job? Put another way, is the mantra "delay of gratification" a sucker's bet to keep employees laboring in unfulfilling work or a mature understanding that short-term sacrifices are necessary for long-term gains?

Ethnographer, social critic, and business consultant Simon Sinek maintains that millennials "have grown up in a world of instant gratification" and cultural conditions that have ill-prepared them for the arduous, long, and difficult efforts needed for meaningful careers and relationships. According to Sinek, when these impatient young people don't make an immediate impact in the workplace, they become disheartened and quit.[15] Maybe so, but there is surely more to the wave of resignations that swept up a much wider demographic of workers.

Let's consider the six most plausible explanations for the Great Resignation. First, we have Covid-19. More than 90 percent of people who quit at least two jobs since March 2020 said "the pandemic made them feel life is too short to stay in a job they weren't passionate about." And one of the top five predictors of employee turnover in organizations was a poor response to the virus.[16] Dissatisfaction might explain why people change jobs, but it doesn't explain the overall decrease in the number of people who are employed.[17] In short, people were forced to confront their mortality in starkly honest terms. They evidently realized that they were exchanging their lives for money in a world in which death could come indiscriminately (the efficacy of predisposing conditions, masks, and vaccines notwithstanding). This pandemic-induced reflection might also explain "goblin mode," which was chosen by the public as the 2022 Oxford word of the year. In this mode, an individual quits caring about social norms and expectations and defiantly lapses into a kind of slovenly self-indulgence.[18]

Next, quitting became a positive feedback system. That is, as workers left, employers increased wages and benefits to attract new workers, who might then be drawn away by even better offers elsewhere—and so on. Thus millennials are actively, if unwittingly, achieving advancement through quitting, with 36 percent expecting to work for a different organization in the next year (versus 21 percent of non-millennials).[19] The bottom line for businesses is that half of their millennial workforce doesn't see a future with them—a turnover rate that costs the US economy $30.5 billion annually.[20] But it's not all driven by the employees. For example, my interview with an owner of a startup company revealed that he encourages ambivalent workers to "consider whether your work is meaningful to you and beneficial for the company"—a strategy intended to challenge employees to get off the fence and either leave voluntarily or deepen their commitment.[21]

The decision to quit or commit is one many workers ponder without the frank confrontation of an employer. And so, the third explanation of the Great Resignation is the struggle with the quality of the working environment and how it supports or undermines individual flourishing. As one would expect, companies with a reputation for a healthy culture experienced less turnover during the Great Resignation. Somewhat surprisingly, more innovative companies manifested higher rates of attrition. The thrill of working for a cutting-edge firm is offset by greater demands imposed by a fast-paced industry.[22] Managers are advised to design jobs that are enjoyable, use people's strengths, and allow career development[23]—fine sentiments, although sometimes work is not fun, weaknesses must be overcome, and advancement is not assured.

Popular psychology offers particularly commiserative analyses that represent perspectives increasingly held by American workers.[24] Self-help guides ask whether what an individual is doing at work fits one's long-term goals, discounting the possibility that sometimes a person has a good-paying job rather than a career. The individual is prompted to ask whether their value as a worker isn't appreciated by their employer, a rather self-aggrandizing question that presumes the absence of the Dunning–Kruger effect in which people with low expertise in a field tend to overestimate their ability or knowledge.[25] The proto-quitter is encouraged to consider whether they've remained in their position out of a "misplaced sense of moral duty," which implies that one has no ethical obligations to an employer or fellow employees and that loyalty is not a virtue. This raises the further question of what, if anything, workers owe to their employer in an exploitative, capitalist market; however, delving further into this moral thicket will take us too far afield.

Another factor in deciding to quit that seems like a stretch is contemplating that although the disgruntled individual is competent in their less-than-ideal position, their persevering blocks some other, unspecified person from being hired into their dream job. But, of course, this reasoning would apply to any sort of work if we presume that someone might flourish if given a chance to haul garbage, shuffle papers, or placate clients. Finally, these sources ask the would-be quitter whether they are following an autonomous life plan that provides thrilling results, as if work was a kind of socio-emotional amusement park. These various questions are certainly valid considerations, but the pendulum seems to have swung from self-abnegating grit to justify persistence to self-indulging entitlement to rationalize quitting.

Grit (or its lack) is at the core of the fourth explanation of the Great Resignation: mental health. Psychologists have contended that each generation of Americans, for social and cultural reasons, has grown up less tenacious than the one before.[26] Researchers defined grit as perseverance and passion for long-term goals, and it was measured using a questionnaire with statements such as: I finish whatever I begin; I often set a goal but later choose to pursue a different one; and I have achieved a goal that took years of work. Grit was the best predictor of who would make it through endeavors as diverse as completing the initial training at West Point and reaching the higher rounds of the Scripps Spelling Bee.[27]

Grit would seem to be the antidote to burnout, which has been proposed as a main culprit in the ongoing wave of resignations, with one-quarter of remote workers in a 2021 study citing this psychological state as one of the top factors in their dissatisfaction (the other factor was work-life balance, which seems confounded with a feeling of burnout).[28] Chronic stress and fierce competition for recognition have been cited as fueling burnout in academia.[29] To quit for the sake of mental health is reasonable, but doing so because a workplace has "high expectations and uncertain prospects"[30] seems idealistic or even naive. Such appeals echo the earlier sense that work should not be difficult or demanding.

The fifth explanation of the mass exodus from work shifts the rationale from victimhood to empowerment. Quitters are collectively driving businesses to change their practices to benefit workers. The "politics of resignation" led American corporations to initially deny the problem, then to offer token accommodation, and finally to pursue strategic engagement.[31] According to this view, widespread discontent represents a tipping point with regard to social change that will eventually benefit both employers and workers.

Finally, although I am skeptical of the woe-is-me justifications of quitting that emerged during the Great Resignation, I appreciate the weightiness of work-life balance and mortality. I've advised graduate students as they navigate their careers to reflect on the fact that they are literally exchanging their lives for answers to the research questions they ask. As such, to justify perseverance, a line of inquiry had better be pretty damned important—whether in the short or long term, locally or globally, tactically or strategically, personally or socially. I used to doubt whether my admonitions mattered to young minds, but what an aging professor might not have been able to accomplish, it appears a pandemic was able to achieve.

Having spent nearly forty years in universities, I cannot resist a few words about recent trends among academics with regard to quitting. Even though the pressure of publishing is among the reasons for giving up, academics have managed to produce a new genre of writing with which to build their vitae.[32] "Quit lit" consists of impassioned and often narcissistic expositions of faculty calling it quits, in which individuals bemoan worsening labor conditions as "universities became market enterprises characterized by a neo-liberal governance, stakeholder expectations and a culture of entrepreneurship."[33] I am sympathetic to the assertion that universities have come to view themselves as corporate structures, eroding intellectual rigor and scholarly integrity to fill coffers with grant dollars and classrooms with students.

That said, the justification for quitting can seem like the whining of an entitled elite—at least to workers who do not enjoy the privileges of university faculty. Few American workers can empathize with professors who contemplate quitting because they cannot find "the space for fantasy, for play, for the unexpected, for the surprising"[34]—as if the workplace was a playground for self-indulgent toddlers. Emotional fragility is manifest with complaints that competition and criticism are too much to bear such that academia is no longer a "labor of love."[35]

When faculty bemoan the "array of measured, meaningless, and bureaucratized tasks that fill their lives,"[36] people employed by organizations of any size would likely reply "welcome to my world. Wanna trade salaries, responsibilities, freedoms, and flexibilities?" Of course, the situation is particularly grim for unbenefited adjunct and part-time faculty who administrators treat as fungible resources that can be liquidated in lean times. With a quarter of these faculty enrolled in public assistance programs,[37] not quitting reflects the sort of grit many American workers can appreciate (assuming they're not caught up in the Great Resignation).

University administrators are much more concerned with students quitting than with faculty resigning, except for the small number of professors—almost entirely outside the arts, humanities, and social sciences—who bring in more grant and contract overhead dollars than they cost in terms of salary. If a university was a restaurant (perhaps more accurately, a vending machine for credentials), the owner would be less worried if the strolling violinist or cannoli chef threw in the towel than if paying customers kept leaving after buying the appetizer course and eating free breadsticks. So, there is serious concern that 30 percent of university students drop out after their first year and only 41 percent graduate in four years.[38] It's even worse in two-year colleges, where just 5 percent of students graduate on time, the inverse of the 95 percent of high school students who eventually matriculate.[39]

During my time as a student, dropping a course was seen as an embarrassing lack of academic grit, while today quitting is a pro forma process requiring nobody's permission and coming at little academic cost. The percentage of US university students who say they drop a class because "I did not like the course" (21%) is almost the same as the return rate of online purchases.[40] With a business-and-buyer mentality prevailing at universities, students quitting a degree program or a course is on a par with consumers returning a product of the wrong color or size.

POWER QUITS

Many of the most exemplary (or at least the best documented and most ballyhooed) quits occur when individuals in positions of power relinquish their roles. In the modern world, walking away from fame and fortune—which are generally taken to be the epitome of achievement—is noteworthy in a "man bites dog" sort of way. Of course, regular folks make dramatic changes in their careers that entail quitting one professional and personal commitment to take on another. However, journalists didn't flock to interview the Unitarian Universalist ministers who came to serve my fellowship after leaving careers in chemical engineering and computer science; nor did the press cover the story of my friend who retired early as a professor of electrical engineering to become a nurse. Rather, the resignations of political, business, and religious leaders have captured the attention of the media.

FIGURE 2.1. Cartoon lampooning Secretary of the Interior Richard Ballinger who resigned in 1911 following accusations of scandalous favoritism of extractive industries. Courtesy of Hennepin County Library via Wikimedia Commons.

Politicians can also achieve infamy by refusing to quit, as when Donald Trump refused to concede the 2020 presidential election, which catalyzed the insurrectionist assault on the United States Capitol.[41] The peaceful transfer of power began with George Washington stepping down in 1797, and this gracious act of political surrender had been a part of American culture that many took for granted in local, state, and national elections.

Admitting defeat was so woven into US politics that Al Gore conceded twice to George W. Bush.[42] Gore initially conceded on election night, then retracted his decision as the Florida votes became muddled, and finally conceded five weeks after the election. He expressed sharp disagreement with the United States Supreme Court but quit his contestation for the good of the nation.

High-ranking bureaucrats also quit, sometimes under pressure and other times to make a political statement. In 1946, Interior Secretary Harold Ickes very publicly resigned to draw attention to an egregious breach of principle when President Harry Truman nominated Indiana oilman Edwin Pauley to be the undersecretary of the navy. Pauley had tried to get Ickes to drop federal claims to offshore oil deposits in exchange for a large campaign contribution.[43]

Military and political interests provide rich fodder for bureaucrats to quit when things don't go their way. John Sullivan resigned in 1949 as secretary of the navy in protest of the defense secretary canceling support for a super-carrier, which Sullivan interpreted as a move to eliminate the United States Navy's air capacity; he feared the next step would be to disband the United States Marines and thereby take away the navy's land forces.[44] This was part of the "Revolt of the Admirals" under the Truman administration, which involved several other resignations to protest a shift of funding from the navy.

More recently, pundits have second-guessed Secretary of State Colin Powell's decision to persevere and implicitly support President George W. Bush during the invasion of Iraq, the prisoner abuse scandal at Abu Ghraib prison, and the controversy over policies and practices at Guantanamo Bay.[45] Critics speculate that had Powell quit in protest, his action might have galvanized public opinion and forced the Bush administration to end a disastrous occupation.

Not all political resignations are about military actions and funding, although war provides a powerful context for principled exits. But just as often, bureaucrats step down to protest domestic policies and decisions. For example, in 1973, Attorney General Elliot Richardson and Deputy Attorney General William Ruckelshaus resigned from the Nixon administration rather than follow the president's order to fire Archibald Cox, the special prosecutor for the Watergate investigation. These resignations contributed to a firestorm of public outrage that forced the president into a political retreat and eventually led to his own resignation.[46]

Such strategic quits don't necessarily yield political results. A wave of resignations in protest over President Trump's instigation of the January 6 riots and insurrection had no discernible effect on the course of the president's subsequent words and actions. The highest-profile quits came in the immediate aftermath of the violence, with the departures of Secretary of Transportation Elaine Chao and Secretary of Education Betsy DeVos. The exodus soon included the deputy national security adviser, a senior director at the National Security Council, a deputy assistant secretary of commerce, an assistant secretary of the Department of Health and Human Services, an assistant attorney general, a batch of Federal Aviation Administration officials, and a top economic adviser, along with the deputy press secretary and the White House social secretary. However, eighteen months later, only the chief of staff to the first lady agreed to speak on the record about their decision while expressing persistent concern about personal and political retaliation.[47]

Political resignations are most assuredly not the exclusive purview of Americans, as dozens of other nations provide examples of people quitting government positions. For example, British ministers have a far greater propensity for resigning in protest of the government than do their American counterparts.[48] One might say that political quitting is built into the British government with the principles of "collective responsibility" (ministers must leave the government if they cannot support the Cabinet's position) and "individual responsibility" (ministers are expected to take the blame for their department's egregious errors, as well as their own).[49]

British royalty are far less likely than elected or appointed officials to give up their power. The abdication of Edward VIII in 1936 so he could marry a divorced American socialite created a tremendous cultural kerfuffle, not to mention a constitutional crisis. Only three other British kings and queens have abdicated in the nation's long history.[50]

Although most of us are substantially less powerful than even low-level politicians, anyone can quit their country by renouncing their citizenship either explicitly or de facto. Henry David Thoreau's brazen exit of Concord, Massachusetts, for the tranquility of Walden Pond and his refusal to pay taxes in protest of the Mexican-American War have been characterized as "expressive exits"[51]—a form of quitting echoed a century later as 570,000 young men became "draft offenders" (evaders and resistors),[52] with 80,000 leaving the United States to avoid the Vietnam War. And in effect, about a million Confederate soldiers renounced their citizenship by fighting in the US Civil War. Indeed, imminent and ongoing war is the most common catalyst for citizens quitting their countries, including such luminaries as Theodor Adorno, Hannah Arendt, Willy Brandt, and Albert Einstein who left Germany during the rise of Nazism.[53]

In the modern world, corporations are arguably more powerful than governments—and in many cases it appears that a chimeric corporatocracy is calling the shots.[54] Even so, consumers can engage in collective quitting to alter business practices, as exemplified over the last sixty years by the boycotts of Canada Goose to stop selling fur, the Body Shop to end animal testing, Staples to force the sale of environmentally responsible paper products, Pepsi to withdraw its products from military-controlled Myanmar, Nestle to end marketing of baby formula in developing countries, and grape growers to reach a collective bargaining agreement with the United Farm Workers.[55]

On the other side of the power coin, CEOs have been quitting in droves since 2020, with the pandemic forcing even corporate heavyweights to reflect on their priorities; over 80 percent of high-level executives rate mental health as more important than career.[56] And they're walking the walk (out the door), with more than a thousand high-profile departures exemplified by Bill Gates and Jeff Bezos, along with resignations of the CEOs of Disney, Groupon, IBM, Kickstarter, Mastercard, Pinterest, Salesforce, Southwest Airlines, Starbucks, T-Mobile, Tinder/Match, and Under Armour. A few resigned under duress (e.g., the CEO of Credit Suisee was caught stalking a former employee through a private investigator), but most were fed up or worn down.[57] A countervailing consideration is the eccentric glamour that comes with quitting in the technology field (e.g., Mark Zuckerberg and Dustin Moskovitz dropped out of Harvard and became industry moguls).[58]

Along with government and business, religion forms a trifecta of power—and so, quitting by spiritual leaders is a big deal. The world's 1.4 billion Catholics were taken by surprise in 2013 when Pope Benedict XVI became the first pontiff in 600 years to exit the papacy by retirement instead of death. The idea of there being two popes (one emeritus and the other in office) was both intriguing and troubling for the faithful—and there was the possibility of three pontiffs.[59] Pope Francis broached the possibility of stepping down, which might have made quitting the papacy more the rule than the exception in coming decades.

To bring together quitting in government, business, and religion, we have the story of "the Great Renunciation" from 533 BCE. The son of a raja, Prince Siddhārtha Gautama lived in luxury as his father shielded him from all forms of suffering—until he wandered away from one of his three palaces and witnessed human misery in the forms of aging, disease, and death. So moved was the young man by these sights that he renounced his life of privilege, abandoned his wife and newborn son, became a wandering ascetic, and was known as Gautama Buddha. After years of meditation, the Buddha died upon reaching *parinirvana*—the ultimate quit in Buddhism whereby one escapes from the cycle of rebirth and suffering.[60] Given the cardinal importance of non-attachment, Buddhism could be understood as a spiritual discipline grounded in tactical quitting.

This venture into the realm of power quits serves to exemplify the many ways giving up can manifest. Adding these cases to our collection

FIGURE 2.2. Pope Benedict XVI during his visit to Berlin, Germany, eighteen months before he resigned the papacy. Courtesy of WDKrause via Wikimedia Commons.

provides a rich basis for developing a coherent and comprehensive classification of quitting. Even among the forms explored so far, it is apparent that politicians, CEOs, and religious leaders may abandon their paths but these can be very different behaviors, manifesting in variable ways and arising from diverse motivations—all of which will be considered in due course.

HALFWAY QUITTING

Even within a given workplace, quitting can come in degrees, which will feed further into our robust analysis of this phenomenon. There are options between stoic perseverance and "take this job and shove it," such as my status as semi-retired (teaching only in the spring semesters, which might constitute a *quasi-quit*).[61] To be honest, it's rather difficult to completely quit a career, although I have colleagues who, on their last day, lock the office door and never look back, work on another manuscript, or read another institutional email. But being semi-retired is something like living next to your ex or maybe being "friends with benefits"—the physical and emotional detachments can seem misaligned. However, semi-quits are also increasingly popular among younger people in the workplace.

So-called quiet quitting is typically an early-career strategy.[62] Coined by an economist in 2009 to describe diminishing ambitions in Venezuela, a form of "quiet quitting" arose in China in 2021 with *tang ping*, or "lying flat," as a counter-cultural movement in opposition to overworking.[63] The strategy was popularized in 2022 via TikTok,[64] although American workers were already adept at this approach without its being named, as evidenced by a Gallup poll which found that about half of US workers were well-practiced quiet quitters.[65]

Defenders of this tactic maintain that quiet quitters justifiably set reasonable boundaries by not working harder or more than required (e.g., not answering emails after the end of a workday for which one is compensated). Members of Gen Z are not villains but merely want to see the direct link between extra work and extra pay. Advocates find "quiet quitting" an offensive label insofar as they aren't abandoning their responsibilities as employees but enacting their autonomy and performing only the labor for which they are contractually obligated.[66]

Critics of quiet quitting contend that this practice is a pseudo-principled guise for willfully and selfishly underperforming without regard to the effects on other workers. In its most degenerate form, such minimalism represents a kind of passive-aggressive revenge toward a purportedly abusive employer. In response, companies are "quiet firing" workers to avoid the legal and emotional strife of dismissing an employee by making their job increasingly unpleasant and unrewarding so as to induce a "voluntary" resignation.[67]

Quiet quitters should explicitly recognize that they are stepping off the path to promotions, raises, and other forms of compensation that will be garnered by those able and willing to go above and beyond. And if the employment picture shifts from underemployment to downsizing, quiet quitters are likely to be first workers laid off.[68] But then, this may be an acceptable price to pay for having maintained a healthy work-life balance during the good times. Having disconnected their identity from their work, the emotional toll of a person losing a job may be nominal whatever the financial cost.

QUITTING IS HARD WORK (SOMETIMES)

Whether job or career, partial or complete, politician or citizen, quitting work allows us to escape unhealthy situations. However, there is also a risk if escape is too easy, hasty, or cowardly. I've argued elsewhere that we are defined by our duties,[69] drawing on Viktor Frankl's contention that our obligations to people and projects allow us to persist under the worst of conditions.[70]

In short, our identities are shaped by our commitments rather than our liberties. Of course, many of our freedoms (including the right to quit speaking upon arrest, to abandon religion, and to end life support) have been secured through hard-fought battles—both literal and metaphorical. Indeed, this phrasing illustrates that no category of quitting involves greater emotional intensity than human conflicts.

In understanding the working world, we infuse our concepts and headlines with the language of war (e.g., "HUSKY ENERGY VOWS TO BOOST DOWNSTREAM OUTPUT IF IT WINS MEG HOSTILE TAKEOVER"[71] and "'NUCLEAR OPTION': GUNSTOCK MANAGEMENT TEAM RESIGNS"[72]), combat sports (e.g., "UNITED AIRLINES THROWS IN THE TOWEL ON SAN FRANCISCO–PAINE FIELD ROUTE"[73] and "IBM THROWS KNOCK-

OUT PUNCH AT SCO"[74]), and serious games (e.g., "UNION BOSS MAY HAVE LIRR IN CHECKMATE"[75] and "POKER-FACED FORREST PLAYS HIS HAND, BUT MARKET CALLS BLUFF"[76]).

And so, we now turn to the final realm in our journey of discovery and collect forms of honorable and shameful quitting that are woven into human competition—from a soldier surrendering on the battlefield, to the fighter submitting in the mixed martial arts octagon, to the player resigning in a chess tournament.

3

Quitting Conflicts and Contests
"Say 'Uncle'"

My first course in animal behavior around forty years ago drove home what I knew intellectually but hadn't fully processed—the bestial nature of *Homo sapiens*. Humans are social animals, and living in groups (e.g., families, tribes, or nations) has considerable advantages in terms of shared defense, childcare, shelter, hunting, farming, industry, and education. However, close association also entails conflicts that may manifest in brutal altercations or ritualized contests.

When individuals of a social species have the capacity to kill one another, the group's viability requires the evolution of behaviors to communicate submission on the part of the weaker individual to terminate potentially lethal clashes (e.g., a subordinate wasp lowers its head, a defeated rat rolls onto its back, and a submissive chameleon abruptly darkens its coloration).[1] We represent a particularly intriguing sociobiological case given our technological capacity to wage war and our cultural ability to create ritualistic combat. And the role of quitting is vital to understanding these diverse realms of human struggle.

WHITE FLAGS AND TURNCOATS: WHEN SOLDIERS QUIT

In the course of military conflict, there are at least four distinct ways for a soldier to terminate participation. An individual can choose to die, surrender, desert, or defect; each of these forms of quitting has its own physical, psychological, and moral complexities.

The most direct exit from battle comes with an act of suicide, which can take a couple of forms. As noted earlier, a soldier might sacrifice himself or herself, such as falling onto a live grenade to save their comrades.[2] A less spontaneous death comes with a soldier accepting a "suicide mission" in which the chances of survival are diminishingly small. In either case, martyrdom is viewed as an honorable death that turns quitting—insofar as choosing to die constitutes a renunciation of life—into a moral virtue.[3]

While suicidal acts might be debatable as constituting quitting by a soldier, surrender would seem to be the archetypal case of giving up. However, in some branches of the US military, this tactic is not an option. For example, members of the United States Special Forces promise "I will never surrender though I am the last." Such extreme commitments are aspirational and can't account for every circumstance in the course of violent conflict.[4] That said, all members of the United States Armed Forces are held to a Code of Conduct, and these rules permit a soldier to surrender when facing overwhelming odds or obeying a superior's lawful order.[5] While an individual is required to never quit opposing the enemy, a soldier is not expected to mount suicidal opposition.

Throwing down one's weapon and raising one's hands in submission are not viewed as quitting by the military when done in accordance with the Code of Conduct. A captured soldier is not permitted to give up entirely but must "continue to resist by all means available." As such, it is possible for a prisoner of war to serve honorably by taking care of comrades, costing the enemy resources, and attempting to escape as portrayed in war films (e.g., *The Great Escape* and *Bridge over the River Kwai*).

FIGURE 3.1. German soldiers surrendering in Cisterna, Italy, to the US 3rd Division infantry in May 1944. Courtesy of Signal Corps Archive via Wikimedia Commons.

While a US soldier voluntarily joins the United States Special Forces and in so doing chooses to forgo the option of surrender, the situation was markedly different with the Soviet Union in World War II. During the Axis invasion in 1941, Joseph Stalin issued Order no. 270, which required the Red Army to "fight to the last."[6] Indeed, surrender was a capital offense, viewed as tantamount to desertion.

The classic cases of refusal to surrender involve soldiers of the Imperial Japanese Army, who continued to hold out long after the end of World War II. Most famously, Second Lieutenant Hiroo Onoda hid in the mountains of the Philippines for twenty-nine years, engaging in guerrilla attacks and shootouts with local police while waiting for orders from a superior officer. Finally, his former commander located Onoda and formally relieved him of duty in 1974.[7]

Determined duty can devolve into pigheaded persistence, but at the other extreme we have draft evasion and desertion—a third mode of escape from military conflict. During the Vietnam War, as many as 100,000 young men avoided the draft by fleeing the United States,[8] while others used creative tactics such as pretending to be homosexual.[9] Whether these evasions were based on moral principles or selfish cowardice is difficult to resolve and surely varied among individuals. In addition to draft dodgers, about a thousand enlisted soldiers quit the war by deserting to Canada.

Perhaps the most gut-wrenching case of desertion from the US military was that of Private Eddie Slovik in 1944. He survived a terrifying artillery attack, begged to be reassigned to a rear unit, was ordered to return to the front, and then ran away. Slovik was just 1 of more than 21,000 American soldiers who were convicted of desertion in World War II, including 49 who were given death sentences. However, he was the only one to face a firing squad, the first US soldier to be court-martialed and executed for that crime since the Civil War.[10]

Quitting in the midst of war can come in degrees, as seen during recent military conflicts. First Lieutenant Ehren Watada considered Operation Iraqi Freedom to be an illegal war and refused deployment to Iraq, but he offered to serve in Afghanistan. The United States Army, unappreciative of the nuance, pursued a court-martial and eventually issued an "other-than-honorable" discharge. This case contrasts with that of Specialist Aidan Delgado of the 320th Military Police Company who could not square his Buddhist beliefs with his service at Abu Ghraib prison and declared himself a conscientious objector while still serving, which the army recognized with an honorable discharge.[11]

Finally, we come to the soldier who abandons their side and joins the enemy—a kind of quitting with parallels to some religious conversions (e.g., an infidel who turns from Islam to atheism or from Catholicism to Satanism). In the classic case, Benedict Arnold became disheartened with the squabbling of the Continental Congress and being overlooked for promotions during the Revolutionary War. This turncoat became a brigadier general in the British Army.[12] Two hundred years after Benedict Arnold gave secrets to the enemy, Edward Snowden leaked classified information from the National Security Agency. Whether he was a hero or a traitor depends on seeing his decision as a virtuous quit or a vile betrayal.[13]

OPERATIONAL WITHDRAWALS AND *DIDI MAO*: WHEN ARMIES QUIT

Just as an individual soldier has various ways of quitting, groups ranging from platoons and battalions to armies and nations can give up the fight in different ways. Some of these tactics parallel individual decisions (both a soldier and an army can surrender) while others are uniquely collective (only a nation can agree to an armistice). Before we consider the various coordinated approaches used to stop killing the enemy, let's consider a form of collective quitting that initiates deadly combat.

In a manner analogous to a contested divorce, proto-nations can "break up" with their controlling government.[14] In political terms, rebellion can be understood as an act of mass treason. Best known to Americans and British is the Declaration of Independence, which asserted: "When in the Course of human events, it becomes necessary for one people to dissolve the political bands which have connected them with another . . . it is the Right of the People to alter or to abolish it." Quitting a government entails military action, as nations are loathe to allow portions of themselves to become separate entities. Exemplar cases in the history of the United States include the Revolutionary War, when the colonies declared their independence from Britain, and the Civil War, when eleven states seceded to form the Confederate States of America. The difference in terminology—revolutionary or civil war—reflects whether the quit was successful (some Southerners called their secession the "Second American Revolution" but they lost, so the name faded into obscurity).

Once a military conflict is under way, a group of soldiers can abandon the fight through retreat. This tactic is often employed to buy time and avoid a decisive defeat, which is why military leaders refer to these temporary quits with euphemisms such as "operational withdrawal" or "evacuation to reorganize."[15] For example, during World War I, when the Allies were poised to encircle their enemy, the Germans retreated forty miles before engaging in the First Battle of the Aisne, which devolved into a four-year stalemate of trench warfare.[16] Perhaps the most famous military retreat was the evacuation of Dunkirk in World War II, when British, Belgian, and French troops avoided imminent defeat in the north of France. Over the course of ten days, a flotilla of military and civilian merchant ships transported more than 338,000 Allied soldiers across the English Channel to reorganize and continue the war.[17]

———

A decisive and enduring retreat takes the form of wholesale withdrawal, typically by an invading force that has failed to defeat the enemy. In recent times, the US military terminated a nine-year campaign in Iraq and a twenty-year occupation of Afghanistan—endings that are painfully and honestly described as quits by at least some military officers.[18] After the first two years in Iraq, US Secretary of Defense Donald Rumsfeld insisted that "we don't have an exit strategy, we have a victory strategy"[19]—a lack of planning that became disastrously evident. This political failure was repeated when the United States launched an invasion of Afghanistan. In this case, the eventual quit was surely justified given the staggering costs of the occupation (900,000 lives and $2 trillion),[20] but the frantic exit was horribly bungled, leaving behind hundreds of American citizens and Afghan allies.[21]

These endings evoke memories of Vietnam War, an act of foolish perseverance in which escalating casualties led to a situation that was foretold by the US secretary of state in the summer of 1965: "Our involvement will be so great that we cannot—without national humiliation—stop short of achieving our complete objectives."[22] The images of the panicked evacuation of Saigon convey a national-scale version of *didi mao* (the Vietnamese expression that US soldiers understood as "let's get the fuck out of here"). At long last, there is growing recognition of the necessity to decide when, why, and how to quit before launching a military venture.[23]

Of course, unpopular withdrawals are hardly new or unique to the US military. In the second century, the Roman emperor Hadrian, not unlike Presidents Barack Obama, Donald Trump, and Joe Biden, inherited an unwinnable war in the Middle East. Over his generals' strenuous objections, the emperor ordered the withdrawal of his armies from a decades-long conflict with the distant Parthian Empire. This quit allowed Rome to devote resources to improving domestic conditions—a lesson for modern politicians.

Forms of quitting that are more political than military include a range of options, such as negotiating a truce or ceasefire. Setting aside the complicated legal nuances, a truce is more formal and binding, but both approaches are typically transitory cessations of hostilities.[24] By contrast, an armistice means that military operations cease indefinitely, although the agreement does not ensure peace. While the two sides quit killing one another, they might well pursue other forms of political and economic aggression. For example, in June 1940, France signed armistice agreements with Germany and Italy to avoid imminent defeat. Henri-Phillippe Petain's government transformed into Vichy France and worked closely with the Nazis, who occupied more than half of the country.[25] More recently, the Korean War ended in 1953 with an armistice agreement that terminated military hostilities "until a final peaceful settlement is achieved," which has yet to happen, as the US continues hostilities through various sanctions of North Korea.

Finally, a military conflict can end with surrender. The option of so-called peaceful surrender is used to avoid annihilation before warfare begins. This version is exemplified by Genghis Kahn's strategy of amassing overwhelming forces outside a city and allowing an enemy to preemptively capitulate, knowing the reputation of the Mongols to mercilessly slaughter those who refused to submit.[26] A classic case of submission by military defeat is Germany's unconditional surrender after Berlin fell to the Soviets. A hybrid case might be the surrender of Japan in World War II, which was preceded by the loss of several major battles while maintaining the capacity to fight on home soil. However, given the atomic bombings and an impending Allied invasion by more than a million troops, surrender was chosen to avoid a bloody and complete defeat.[27]

THE ATHLETIC QUIT: THROWING IN THE TOWEL

In January 1913, the *Fort Wayne Journal-Gazette* reported, "The crowd importuned referee Griffin to stop the fight and a towel was thrown from Burns' corner as a token of defeat."[28] This was the first published account of a boxing match being ended by throwing in a towel. Previously, tossing a sponge into the ring was the standard method of conceding defeat. The towel likely became more popular as it evoked the use of a white flag, which had been a symbol of military surrender since the first century.

Warfare and combat sports have developed customs of quitting to avoid deadly outcomes, notwithstanding that since the introduction of the Queensbury Rules in 1884, nearly 2,000 boxers have been killed in the ring.[29] The recent emergence of mixed martial arts (MMA) has also been associated with lethal consequences.[30]

The two most iconic quits in boxing—the "No Mas Fight" and "The Thrilla in Manila"—represent the greatest difference in how the public perceived the fighter who gave up. After Roberto Durán defeated Sugar Ray Leonard in June 1980, Leonard plotted his revenge.[31] Knowing Durán's penchant for indulging himself with bacchanalian excesses after a victory, Leonard pushed for a rematch as soon as possible to exploit his nemesis's inevitable weight gain and subsequent necessity to quickly shed pounds. Just five months after their first fight, the two boxers met in New Orleans. Rather than trading punches with Durán, this time Leonard used his movement and speed. As Durán wore down, Leonard began taunting and humiliating his out-of-shape opponent. In Round 8, although repeatedly pummeled but not at risk of being knocked out, Durán muttered "no mas" (no more) to the referee, turned away from Leonard, and simply quit. Giving up in this manner permanently damaged Durán's reputation as a boxer.

FIGURE 3.2. Rachid Haz, a mixed martial arts fighter, forces his grimacing opponent to submit by inflicting the pain of an arm bar. Courtesy of Nestor22ns via Wikimedia Commons.

By comparison, in their third meeting, Muhammed Ali and Joe Frazier (each having won a previous fight by decision) exhibited phenomenal grit.[32] In the Philippine Coliseum, they exchanged punishing blows for fourteen rounds. Before the final round, Frazier's corner-man, Eddie Futch, knew his fighter could barely see. Futch directed the referee to stop the fight despite Frazier's impassioned protests. This boxer is celebrated for when and how he quit. As for Ali, he would later say that this was as close to dying as he'd ever been, telling his biographer, "Frazier quit just before I did. I didn't think I could fight anymore."[33]

My own experience with martial arts came from practicing judo in my youth. While judo includes submissions, throwing and pinning your opponent are far more common tactics. Likewise, taekwondo and karate can involve submission, but the ultimate discipline in this regard is Brazilian jujitsu, with thirty-seven different chokes and joint locks to inflict unbearable pain.[34] Put in such a position, a fighter can "tap out" before serious damage is done, at least in principle and usually in practice.

In MMA, competitors use a variety of disciplines to defeat an opponent. About 40 percent of Ultimate Fighting Championship matches end by knockout, with submissions accounting for a quarter of all endings (the rest are victories by decision).[35] Some MMA aficionados maintain that refusing to tap out constitutes unsportsmanlike disrespect of a superior opponent.[36] However, others view submission as dishonorable, and some fighters refuse to tap out—such as Jorge Gurgel, whose knee was shattered in a leglock by Masakazu Imanari in 2003, and Tim Sylvia, whose radius and ulna were broken in an arm bar by Frank Mir a year later. In combat sports, what makes a champion is often a constitutional inability to quit, which means others must protect them from themselves—and rarely, if ever, does a corner-man feel he's thrown in the towel too soon on behalf of a fighter.[37]

According to Thomas Erik Angerhofer, an experienced sensei who teaches mixed martial arts, knowing when and how to submit is the first thing to be addressed with new students, who learn from the experience of escalating discomfort.[38] But Angerhofer doesn't shy away from saying that submission is quitting. His students are taught that submission is an acknowledgment of defeat from which one has the opportunity to learn. The fighter is expected to reflect upon the mistake that created a potentially painful, teachable moment—and whether escape might have been possible.

―

Combat sports are not the only competitions in which quitting is a contentious choice by athletes. Runners, like fighters, can make dreadful decisions to persevere. For example, Siobhan O'Keeffe ran through the pain of a broken fibula during the 2019 London Marathon, ignoring the recommendations of medics to quit the race. She completed the last eighteen miles in agony while risking permanent injury so as to not disappoint her supporters.[39]

Most (in)famously, Simone Biles quit the US Olympic gymnastics team in 2021, when she decided that a case of the "twisties" (a mental condition that causes a person to lose their sense of space and control of their body) would not allow her to compete without physically endangering herself and harming her team's performance. Notwithstanding her specious assertion that she didn't quit, most sports analysts defended her decision to leave the competition.[40] Some even went so far as to implausibly assert that Biles didn't owe anyone an explanation despite the very considerable social resources that had been dedicated to her training.[41] A few others were far less sympathetic, such as a high-profile conservative pundit who tweeted: "Simone Biles just said sitting out the big competitions shows how strong you really are. That's like saying soldiers who run away from battle are courageous."[42] For our purposes, what matters is that quitting, despite compelling justification, can generate tremendous emotional reactions in our culture—even when the stakes are quite frankly as low as an athletic competition.

Contrary to combat sports, in team sports a much stronger contestant may be expected to quit scoring as a display of sportsmanship. For example, a coach might put in second- or third-string players to avoid humiliating the other team. Indeed, some high school athletic organizations have rules against blowing out opponents. So when a Connecticut football team was up 49–0 in the fourth quarter and the coach left his starters on the field, a refusal to quit resulted in his suspension.[43] Even greater sanctions were imposed in California following a final score of 106–0.[44]

Merciless domination is not unique to high school football. Lisa Leslie is a basketball legend, having accrued four Olympic gold medals, two WNBA championships, and three MVP awards. When playing professionally, a no-holds-barred approach might be understandable. But in the first half of a high school game, Leslie once tallied 101 points while the other team managed just 23—and she later attempted to justify her refusal to quit humiliating her opponents. When the other team's coach decided not to bring his players to the floor for the second half (he had only four players since two had fouled out trying to guard their vastly superior opponent), Leslie asked him to put his depleted team on the court long enough for her to score three more baskets and set a fatuous national high school record. However, his team had no interest in being further embarrassed to feed the ego of an athlete who didn't know when to quit.[45]

RESIGNATIONS: NO DISHONOR IN TURNING BACK OR GIVING IN

Let's now consider what many people would judge to be the extreme forms of human struggle in terms of physicality and mentality—the mountaineer and the game player. Whether courageously enduring hypoxia while climbing at 29,000 feet or sustaining phenomenally intense focus at the chess board, quitting lurks as a possible end to the toil.

According to Mark Jenkins, a world-class mountaineer who has summited Mount Everest, quitting is an acquired and vital skill in which thinking must override emotion.[46] When working with beginning rock climbers, Jenkins finds it necessary to discourage quitting because success comes only if one can overcome an innate fear of falling and push through adversity, including pain. But as expeditions become more serious, even expert climbers can fall prey to their passion of reaching a summit (cascades of testosterone are sometimes as dangerous as avalanches of snow). In his decades of mountaineering, Jenkins has found that people become increasingly exhausted and vested in summiting with each passing hour, and rational judgment must increase accordingly to achieve the ultimate goal: returning to base camp alive.

Because we are human, emotions can't be eradicated but neither can they be allowed to dominate if one is to make good decisions, which is at the core of mountaineering. Knowing the hazards of peer pressure and self-delusion, before a climbing team makes a final push for a summit, they typically commit to a turnaround time—the point at which, no matter how close they are to success, the plug is pulled. This tactic recognizes that the worst time to make a decision is when you're "in it."[47]

According to Jenkins, a good quit on the mountain comes with having done your best, honored commitments to your partners, and owned your decision. In this regard, he refers to a climb in Bolivia. When some team members fell prey to severe altitude sickness and the summit was another thousand feet higher through hip-deep snow, resignation was the wisest choice. Although he doesn't shy away from saying that being a "good loser" is a life skill, Jenkins fudges a bit when it comes to whether he has truly quit a climb. In his mind, he hasn't given up on a peak when he turns back, as long as he keeps open the possibility of returning—and succeeding.

Although games lack the life-or-death qualities of mountaineering, chess is fiercely competitive and includes highly stylized elements of combat, including the contentious element of quitting. To resign, a player can lay down the king or extend a hand to the opponent (there are similar ritualistic expressions of submission in Go, involving the placement of playing pieces or a verbal resignation). But when and whether one should resign is a matter of considerable debate.[48] Some players contend that resignation conveys respect, acknowledging that one's opponent has achieved a position from which victory is assured. However, it is possible, if very rare, for even highly accomplished players to resign prematurely, overlooking a strong or even winning position.[49] While resigning as soon as a player recognizes a virtually unwinnable position is gracious, waiting until a move or two before being checkmated is seen as stubborn rudeness, obviating the opponent's chance to make a killing blow. For other players, resignation is never admirable, as it reflects a lack of character bordering on cowardice. Quitting before checkmate is like a gladiator committing suicide rather than courageously and defiantly facing death. And no matter the situation, defeat is never inevitable: "Chess is a battle, a fight . . . Many a boxer knocked down in the first round comes back to win."[50]

The game in which masterful resignation has arguably the greatest importance is poker—at least if we consider folding as a kind of quitting (perhaps similar to punting in football). Indeed, knowing when to fold has been described as the skill that separates the elite players from the wannabes.[51] While a professional plays no more than a quarter of the starting two-card combinations in Texas Hold'em, amateurs stick with their cards more than half the time. Craig Varnell, a top money winner who pulls down from $200,000 to $1 million annually, considers folding to be like retreat in warfare—it allows one to live to fight another day. A player must be willing to lose a battle to win the war. As with mountaineering, Varnell insists that vanquishing emotion is essential: "You have to be dead inside."[52] Analytical rationality, including the ability to read one's opponent, must drive a decision to quit because in the short run "luck is real," but in the long run skill prevails. He advises new players to leave their ego and stubbornness at the casino door.

Beyond the manifestations of warfare, sports, and games, there are surely many other forms of conflict and competition that involve opportunities for quitting well or badly. I'll very briefly finish with a familiar social institution. Although attorneys might object to calling the practice of law a game, there are good reasons for doing so.[53] After all, a game is a competition that involves skill and knowledge while following a fixed set of rules to defeat an opponent, and this seems to be a rather plausible description of lawyering.

Attorneys most assuredly grasp the strategic value of quit-like maneuvers such as settling a case, seeking a plea bargain, filing for bankruptcy, and pleading nolo contendere (no contest).[54] Ultimately, the client makes a decision whether to persevere or relent, but the attorney can present the best- and worst-case scenarios. Unlike a casino, however, the courtroom is a gambling venue without fixed probabilities, given the variability of juries and judges. However, sometimes the prosecution has overwhelming evidence, and a plea bargain becomes analogous to peacefully surrendering to Genghis Kahn in which one tries to work out the best possible deal for a client in the face of imminent defeat.

A MATRIX OF POSSIBILITIES

How might we understand quitting in contexts as wide ranging as military surrender, MMA submission, and chess resignation? One approach is to consider a 2 × 2 matrix, in which deciding to quit can be easy or hard and instantiating a quit can be easy or hard—and then seeing how the varied forms of conflict and contest exemplify the four resulting possibilities (table 3.1). When it comes to a hard decision but an easy enactment, we have Eddie Futch's throwing in the towel for Joe Frazier. As for an easy decision that is hard to implement, there's reaching the turnaround time on Mount Everest and descending in a howling blizzard. With regard to an easy decision easily performed, we have folding when dealt a two of diamonds and seven of clubs in Texas Hold'em. Finally, it appears that it was both hard to decide and hard to enact the withdrawal of the US military from Afghanistan and Vietnam.

Table 3.1. A simple 2 × 2 matrix illustrating the conceptual possibilities of quitting

Instantiating a Quit	Deciding to Quit	
	Easy	Hard
Easy	Poker player having been dealt a weak hand	Manager seeing their fighter bleeding and battered
Hard	Mountaineer reaching the turnaround time	President contemplating a protracted military conflict

Our next challenge is to consider the full diversity of cases—relationships, religions, addictions, lives, jobs, wars, competitions, and games—and consider whether they can be gathered into a coherent, conceptual framework and if there is something unique about these cases that makes quitting different from other life changes.

4
A Taxonomy of Quitting
Describing and Naming

Given my academic background in the life sciences and my philosophical affinity for the importance of metaphor,[1] I think of our journey into the human experience in search of diverse forms of quitting as a kind of (un)natural history expedition. If one wants to know the nature of organisms, it makes sense to wander the landscape and see what sorts of creatures crawl, leap, fly, and swim across one's path. One cannot sit comfortably by the fire and merely speculate about what kinds of beings might be found in terra incognita. Charles Darwin boarded the HMS *Beagle* as the expedition's naturalist and conducted the world's most famous collecting trip in an effort to know what species existed—and from their similarities and differences to infer the sum and substance of life.

And so, having filled the drawers and cabinets of the Museum of Quitting with specimens, my next task is to organize the collection. Some of this framework is implicit in the rough grouping of cases in the previous chapters, but here I'll make explicit both the place of quitting in the larger context of human experience and the relationships among the varied species of quitting by adapting a hierarchical system familiar to biologists.

ORGANIZING OUR COLLECTION: PUTTING QUITS IN THEIR PLACE

The nested structure used to organize the diversity of living beings is Kingdom, Phylum, Class, Order, Family, Genus, and Species. Technically speaking, biological taxonomy is rooted in an underlying theory that explains the relationships among taxa.[2] That is to say, scientists hope that the species within a genus share an evolutionary history with one another to a greater degree than they do with those in another genus. This aspiration is likely met at lower phylogenic levels (e.g., species and genera), while higher levels are more arbitrary, reflecting conceptual convenience rather than phylogeny.[3] The particular forms of quitting are not "natural kinds" as opposed to biological species that exist independently of human perceptions and our desire to categorize things. As such, the systematic framework for quitting is most properly termed a classification rather than a taxonomy.[4] However, I trust that the reader will understand the metaphorical value of thinking in the familiar terms of science (table 4.1).

To begin, I propose there being a kingdom of "human experience." Another kingdom might be what philosophers call "a priori knowledge" (i.e., what we know without empirical evidence, such as logical deduction via pure reason). Within human experience lies the phylum "intentional acts." There are, of course, other phyla, such as accidents, reflexes, instincts, and physiological functions. Going further down the organizational framework, within intentional acts is found the class "life changes." This excludes life's constancies (another class, not shown) in which we choose to continue some venture, and it includes such events as marriage, education, employment, travel, and—of central concern—the order called "quitting."

This brings us to the three families of quitting (personal, work, and contests). To get a sense of the scheme without going deeply into each of these, let's consider the genera within the family of personal quitting, which consist of relationships (species include divorce, adoption, and abortion), religion (species include conversion, martyrdom, and

Table 4.1. A Classification Scheme of Human Experiences Following the Conventions of Biological Taxonomy, with a Particular Focus on the Manifestations of Quitting

A Classification of Human Activities

KINGDOM = Human experience
  PHYLUM = Intentional acts
    CLASS = Life changes
      ORDER = Quitting
        FAMILY = Personal
          GENUS = Relationships
            TYPICAL SPECIES = Divorce
          GENUS = Religion
            TYPICAL SPECIES = Conversion
          GENUS = Mental health
            TYPICAL SPECIES = Addiction
          GENUS = Bodily health
            TYPICAL SPECIES = Diet
          GENUS = Ultimate
            TYPICAL SPECIES = Suicide
        FAMILY = Work
          GENUS = Employment
            TYPICAL SPECIES = Resignation
          GENUS = Politics
            TYPICAL SPECIES = Abdication
          GENUS = Academics
            TYPICAL SPECIES = Drop out
        FAMILY = Contests
          GENUS = Military actions
            TYPICAL SPECIES = Surrender
          GENUS = Sports and games
            TYPICAL SPECIES = Submission
          GENUS = Law
            TYPICAL SPECIES = Plea bargain

forsaking), mental health (species include forgiving others, breaking habits, and ending addictions), physical health (species include diet, gender, and celibacy), and ultimate acts (species include hospice, suicide, and euthanasia). Of course, we could further subdivide species in subspecies; diets would include ending the consumption of meat (vegetarianism), animal products (veganism), and industrially produced foods (organic diet). Similarly, ending addiction would include the subspecies of substance use and behavioral disorders, with the former including the strains of quitting alcohol, tobacco, opiates, and the like. And this would eventually come down to individual specimens, such as my friend having been sober for five years.

A FIELD GUIDE TO QUITTING

In biology courses, students learn about the character traits that unite a taxon (in phylogenetic terms, these are called synapomorphies). For example, mammals have fur, produce milk, and exhibit an erect gait—features that distinguish them from other vertebrates such as reptiles and amphibians. In field guides to plants and animals, the descriptions often refer to the distinguishing traits shared by members of a taxon, such as individuals within a species or species within a genus.[5]

So, are there features of quitting shared among its various kinds? There are certainly some traits common to particular manifestations. For example, both veganism and vegetarianism eschew animal flesh, both martyrdom and suicide put an end to one's life, and both tipping over a chess king and tapping out in martial arts signal defeat. However, vegans are not pursuing their own demise, and chess players often enjoy a good steak. So, if there are fundamental traits, they must be rather more abstract or conceptual to manifest in all aspects of a vegan martyr submitting to a chokehold.

Before we delve into quitting's prevalent characteristics, note that none of these qualities is unique to this phenomenon (in science-speak, such would be an autapomorphy). The same may be true in biology of traits such as milk production, which we associate with mammals, but various insects, spiders, fish, and birds also secrete fluids for nourishing

FIGURE 4.1. *On the Road: Death of a Migrant* (1889) by Sergey Ivanov, a Russian artist who depicted the brutal resettlement of peasants. Courtesy of the Tretyakov Gallery via Wikimedia Commons.

their young.[6] So, while all mammals produce milk, not all animals that produce milk are mammals. Likewise, all quits are endings, but not all endings are quits. Which leads us to the first of our five features.

To begin, quitting occasions the cessation of some state or process. But as just noted, not every situation comes to an end via quitting. One could resign from a job, but it's also possible to be fired. But do all intentional life changes entail quitting, which would seemingly undermine quitting as a unique concept? If I choose to learn Spanish, I quit being monolingual, just as if I get married, I quit being single. However, this semantic trivialization merely reflects that any condition can be defined in antonymic terms without the individual intending to terminate some existing condition. My goal is to learn Spanish, not to cease being monolingual, or my objective is to become a husband, not to quit bachelorhood. So quitting entails a targeted or purposeful cessation.

Second, quitting involves ambiguity. Arguably, all of its species have a nebulous quality. Even considering the apparent clarity of monarchical abdications, Edward VIII gave up the throne, but he did not forgo royalty insofar as he was given the title of Duke of Windsor and called a Royal Highness. Perhaps suicide could be proposed as a form of quitting without marginal cases, but there are twenty-five suicide attempts for every suicidal death,[7] and about 1 in 100 adults age fifty-five and over harbor a death wish.[8] As such, quitting is polysemic, having a variety of meanings such that context matters greatly. To declare "I quit" has different implications depending on whether one is referring to an arm bar, a marriage, or an addiction.

Third, quitting involves an element of struggle. It may be hard to decide (e.g., quitting a high-paying job), hard to enact (e.g., quitting smoking), or both (e.g., quitting a solo climb of Half Dome).[9] Even when the process is quantitatively incremental, there is often a qualitatively distinct commitment constituting a difficult leap (e.g., gradually cutting back on social media until one finally and fully terminates their Facebook account).

Fourth, quitting affects an individual's identity to a substantial extent. Philosophers have recently been struggling with the question of what makes a reason genuinely compelling for individuals—something that you truly ought to do. One very plausible answer is that such normative reasons are grounded in our identities, which are shaped by what we are unwilling to give up.[10] This view suggests that one's character is changed by quitting, such that a memory of before-and-after persists. Neither a soldier nor a nation forgets surrendering. Indeed, a competitor can learn from submitting to an opponent only if the fighter remembers what led to the resignation. There is a psychological scar, even when quitting marks the onset of a better condition. Leaving a bad marriage is a good thing, particularly if one avoids making the same mistake again. And this leads us to the final trait.

Fifth, quitting comes with an element of hopefulness. We quit in the expectation that we are relinquishing something less desirable for a change to a better condition—whether it is a job, lover, boxing match, or legal settlement.[11] Sometimes, perhaps often, this hope is realized, although self-help gurus promote the absurdity that every quit will lead to something better.[12] The alternative may not be well defined insofar as some quitting may be a kind of escape from an awful situation into the unknown, based on the belief that "anything is better than this."

QUITTER, LOSER, FAILURE: WHAT'S IN A NAME?

Once a biologist has figured out similarities and differences among a group of organisms, the scientist names them, generally alluding to an abiding quality. For example, we are called *Homo sapiens*, or the "wise man." However, wisdom has been called into question as a central or actual quality of the human species. And so, with a desire for greater descriptive accuracy, other names have been proposed by scientists, scholars, futurists, philosophers, and writers, including *H. adorans* (worshipping man), *H. deus* (Godly man), *H. economicus* (economic man), *H. interrogans* (questioning man), *H. narrans* (storytelling man), and *H. technologicus* (technological man).[13]

As for our explorations, I've been calling the taxon of ceasing some state or process "quitting." But perhaps this is too facile, even insensitive. The negative valence associated with quitting is apparent from various perspectives. First, a cultural stigma exists at a gut level for most of us. Consider the immediate feeling that is evoked if you are confronted with the question "did you quit?" Implicit in this inquiry is a judgment of your character. Your divorce, resignation, or surrender requires some explanation to defend your decision, other than a lack of courage, grit, or dedication. Next, the negative undertone is evidenced by individuals' tendency to simply deny what is even an undeniable quit. Simone Biles, the Olympic gymnast, wrote, "For anyone saying I quit, I didn't quit." But of course she did and for a good reason, as she went on to explain: "My mind and body are simply not in sync as you can see here [in reference to a video of her athletic struggles]."[14] Instead, Biles said that she "withdrew"—and this leads us to the most common strategy for sidestepping the negativism of being associated with quitting.

FIGURE 4.2. Simone Biles at the 2016 Olympic Games, where she won a gold medal in the women's team competition. Courtesy of Agência Brasil Fotografias via Wikimedia Commons.

Much of the effort to avoid the negative aura of quitting has been focused on rephrasing this phenomenon in upbeat terms. There's something to be said for a New Year's resolution phrased as "start being kind" rather than "quit being mean." But most rhetorical efforts are more convoluted.

Those in the self-help industry who are enthusiastic proponents of quitting provide a rich array of terms to take the edge off of quitting. Rather than quitting some endeavor, they suggest that we can "pivot" to another pursuit.[15] Or instead of giving up on an aspiration, we are advised that "sometimes, a goal needs to be adjusted to accommodate other priorities."[16] This is reminiscent of how someone in the public eye explains that they didn't really quit their position as CEO or senator (a negative action) but that they simply decided to "spend more time with family." Maybe they really did want to reallocate their time toward their children, but more often this is a way to provide a positive gloss on quitting their current job for some unsavory reason.

A TAXONOMY OF QUITTING

Then there is the move to transform quitting into not merely neutral terms but a positive personal success.[17] The alleged problem is that quitting is confused with failure, which is, most assuredly, a lack of success. The solution, we are told, is to redefine success. So the self-helpers aver: "If you quit your job without ever making it to upper management, but your new job is one you love that is still able to support you financially, that sounds like success to me."[18] This is all well and good, unless your new job is grim and pays poorly, but the quitting advocates presume that people can always find a way to frame the consequences of quitting in upbeat terms. And perhaps this is possible given our potential to imaginatively conjure up a world in which having persevered would have been more miserable than whatever came after quitting.

An arguably more plausible strategy is to reframe quitting as "settling," in which a person decides that some aspect of life is suboptimal but good enough and therefore not worth further effort.[19] Notwithstanding the glib assertion that settling is "suicide of the soul,"[20] settling can be a calculated (re)allocation of time to more important endeavors. However, the stark reality is that settling entails quitting something in order to, often quite defensibly, strive for other things.[21]

Many of the people I interviewed avoided references to quitting in their fields of expertise. Martial artists "bow out" to superior opponents,[22] physicians "conclude a medical intervention,"[23] and military leaders "tactically retreat."[24] Even when quitting is socially affirmed, professionals try to avoid the stigmatizing connotations, such that addiction counselors replace "quitting" with "achieving abstinence, recovery, or sobriety."[25]

—

Perhaps the lurking disgrace of "quitting" can be obviated by finding a single, less negative synonym. We could abandon, abdicate, abjure, abscond, abstain, cease, change, concede, decamp, depart, desert, desist, disappear, drop out, egress, embark, escape, evacuate, exit, forgo, give up, leave, let go, migrate, refrain, relinquish, renounce, resign, retire, retreat, send off, surrender, terminate, transition, valedict, walk out, withdraw, or yield. The difficulties here are that some of these potential synonyms sound no better than quitting (e.g., conceding, giving up, retreating); others pertain to rather specific occasions of quitting (e.g., surrendering and deserting have a military connotation, migrating and evacuating have spatial associations, abdicating and resigning have professional implications), and a few are weirdly unfamiliar (e.g., abjuring, decamping, and valedicting).

Without analyzing every possibility, I suggest that the best of the lot is perhaps "escape" insofar as quitting moves one (literally or figuratively) from a less desirable condition to a better situation (or at least this is the intention). There's also a sense that escape entails being drawn toward what is left behind (e.g., escaping the pull of gravity) or perhaps even a strong resistance (e.g., escaping from prison). This counteracting force often manifests in emotional terms with regard to the familiarity, comfort, and security of the status quo.

As for my quitting experts, Mark Jenkins alluded to fellow alpinists as having the feeling of being emotionally trapped in their ascent. Even storms from which climbers struggle to escape are often ascribed malevolence, despite nature's utter disinterest in the human condition.[26] And suicidologist Carolyn Pepper said that although therapists don't refer to quitting, clients might well view suicide as an escape from an intolerable existence, even a release from oneself.[27] Lou Farley, the hospice counselor, wasn't keen on "escape" but allowed that escaping could be a courageous act.[28]

Ultimately, the search for a neutral or even positive synonym for quitting is probably futile. It has been argued that every word has a unique meaning and there is no such thing as a true synonym.[29] The exception to this rule might be the scientific and common names for an organism (*Homo sapiens* and humans), but even in these cases there may be contexts in which the use of one or the other conveys a different meaning. Some people claim that other pairings are fully interchangeable (e.g., fall and autumn, sofa and couch, smell and odor, fat and obese, flammable and inflammable).[30] But each of these supposed synonyms can provide a distinct sense: Autumn is more poetic than fall, sofas are fancier than couches, odors are more offensive than smells, lips can be fat but only people are obese, and flammable liquids seem more dangerous than inflammable substances. Furthermore, words of Germanic origin seem cruder than their more sophisticated Latin synonyms, such as piss versus urinate or spit versus expectorate. I maintain that any presumptive synonym paired with "quit" would also fail to convey the same meaning or to cover the same range of events.[31]

A solution to the negative valence of quitting comes by conceptually separating the act from the actor. Perhaps one murder makes you a murderer, but does a single sin make you a sinner? If a person tells a lie on occasion (and who doesn't?), should we call them a liar? In referring to socially countenanced acts, it would be odd to claim that you're a teacher just because you once taught a child to tie their shoes, that you're a runner because you dash from your office to your car when it rains, or that you're a gardener because you plant a few petunias next to the mailbox. Mikaela Shiffrin, who is arguably the best skier of all time, disappointed her fans by failing to medal during the 2022 Olympics. But she quite convincingly said, "You can fail and not be a failure."[32] Likewise, one can quit without being a quitter.

Although Vince Lombardi's famous assertion that "quitters never win and winners never quit"[33] might one day replace "In God We Trust" on American currency, the curmudgeonly football coach would be hard pressed to defend this claim (at least the bit about "winners never quit") had he lived long enough to see Simone Biles, seven-time Olympic medalist (including four golds, along with twenty-five world championships), quit the 2021 Olympics. The problem for the Lombardian view is that having quit once is not sufficient grounds to call someone a quitter, any more than winning a game on occasion makes one a winner.[34]

We tend to call someone a quitter if we don't support their decision,[35] and that was certainly evident in the use of this label by those who found fault with Biles's decision.[36] However, calling someone a quitter suggests a pervasive tendency that amounts to a contemptible character flaw.[37] Quitters give up whenever the going gets tough. They readily, even blithely, abandon projects, jobs, relationships, organizations, lessons, and contests. We cannot count on these weak-willed wimps.[38] Of course, few people are utterly gutless and untrustworthy in all contexts, but neither are many of us invariably persevering and dependable.

THIS IS NO TIME TO QUIT!

In sum, quitting is a remarkably diverse taxon, and the term *quitting* should be interpreted in the context of whatever is being ended. Perhaps we could find or invent a term for every set of circumstances or add a plethora of adverbs (e.g., she quit willingly, happily, reluctantly, defiantly, cravenly, or courageously). Clearly, this is not a viable solution. I'll stick with "quit" for the balance of this book. As for "quitter" however, one should use this term only in reference to an individual who has demonstrated a chronic disposition for giving up readily and so warrants the deprecatory attribution.

We now have an organized collection of quitting specimens. From these varied cases, we are getting a sense of how this psychosocially diverse taxon is manifest. However, a cabinet filled with drawers of bird skins neatly arranged and cleverly named does not reveal the nature of birds. Their inner workings, what makes one a hummingbird and another an eagle, might be hinted at by their appearance (e.g., a thin beak or curved talons), but in most cases discerning the essence of the species requires observing how it functions in the world. From the body of a starling, nobody would imagine the shape-shifting murmurations of these birds in flight. Nothing about the appearance of a bowerbird suggests that the males build and decorate elaborate structures to attract mates. Who would guess that the drab, plump African gray parrot possesses cognitive abilities on par with those of a five-year old child?

In a sense, we are at the point of the ancient Greeks when it came to describing the human species as "featherless bipeds" (a pair of qualities that was amended to include "having broad, flat nails" after Diogenes brought a plucked chicken to Plato's Academy and declared "Behold! I've brought you a man").[39] A couple thousand years later, our species was named for our sapience rather than our anatomy, gait, or appearance.

We've collected, organized, and described diverse species of quitting, but that is like gathering up people from various locales and saying that we understand what it is to be a human by noting that all of our specimens walk on two legs and lack feathers, rather than realizing that these humans are also capable of thinking as well as worshipping, self-aggrandizing, bartering, questioning, storytelling, and tool using. And so, our next task is to delve more deeply into the inner workings of quitting and to move toward a definition rather than a mere description of this phenomenon that is so important to us naked bipeds.

SECTION 2

What Is It to Quit?

Imagine that you are a researcher trying to understand the nature of fundamental human actions, such as belonging, caring, fighting, playing, working, and worshiping. Let's say you decide to study belonging and, in particular, what is means for a person to be associated with a religious community. In conducting your investigation, you interview Lanny, who professes to be a Methbyterian (a fictional Christian denomination). You begin to fit his account into a straightforward hypothesis that joining a church is a matter of cost-benefit analysis. So you ask Lanny about the downsides of his affiliation (e.g., tithing 10% and praying two hours/day) and the upsides (e.g., entry into Heaven and potluck dinners). You quickly realize that the costs and benefits appear to be incommensurable. What are the socioeconomics of belonging?

Exploring further, you discover a variety of incentives and impediments to Lanny's belonging to a church that entail both rational and emotional considerations (e.g., the value of a social safety net versus the loss of time that could be spent advancing his career and the comfort of a familiar setting versus the anxiety of forgoing other affiliations). What is the psychology of belonging?

Given the complex psychological factors, you question Lanny more deeply and find that he became Methbyterian because his wife threatened to leave him if he didn't join the church and he worried about the possibility of eternal damnation. You wonder whether he truly belongs to this religious community or whether his membership was coerced. What is the role of intentionality in belonging?

From an outside, objective perspective, Lanny seems to belong to the Methbyterian faith. However, he admits that he doesn't really pray for two hours daily and that he often plans his upcoming week during Sunday sermons. He's certainly more allied with his church than are non-believers but less so than fully committed members. What is the possibility of partially belonging?

Section 2 is devoted to understanding the nature of quitting—a fundamental human action that profoundly shapes our lives. The chapters in this section raise the sorts of questions one might have with regard to belonging in the case of Lanny's religious affiliation. The challenge becomes finding the psychological and philosophical threads that are woven through the varied manifestations of quitting we explored in section 1. Without conceptual clarity—at least to the extent possible for a complex phenomenon—our ultimate task is stymied. That is, we can hardly hope to figure out what makes a good quit (section 3) if we don't have a grasp of what constitutes quitting itself (this would be like trying to argue that you've written a good symphony without understanding the nature of music).

The three fundamental perspectives in this section are the psychology, intentionality, and partiality of quitting. In these regards, we'll delve into the constraints of behavioral economics (e.g., is quitting rational—and should it be?), the requirements of free will (e.g., is quitting a voluntary decision—and to what extent?), and the continuous or partial nature of quitting (e.g., is genuine quitting an all-or-none matter—and must it be a permanent act?). The synthesis of these perspectives will culminate in an analytically sound working definition of quitting.

5

The Psychology of Quitting
Calculating the Incalculable

When we struggle to decide whether to give up or persist, we are wrestling with tradeoffs. The chorus of the classic punk rock song "Should I Stay or Should I Go" by the Clash distills the problem of quitting into the stark terms of a cost-benefit analysis: "If I go, there will be trouble / And if I stay it will be double." In the four decades following this song of romantic angst, popular books have fueled the debate with quitting questors publishing titles such as *Quit: The Power of Knowing When to Walk Away* and *Quitting: A Life Strategy*, along with *Quitting: Why We Fear It—and Why We Shouldn't—in Life, Love, and Work* and recently *Quitting: A Life Strategy*. Perseverance promoters have countered with the likes of *The Power of Determination* and *The Will to Persevere: How to Develop Unshakeable Willpower and Determination*, along with *Grit: The Power of Passion and Perseverance*.

While both sides claim to offer empowering advice, the conflicting guidance reflects the state of socio-behavioral science, which is theoretically tangled and often reductionistic. Given the complexity of quitting, let's sift through the apparently contradictory arguments to see if this phenomenon can be understood in psychological terms that will inform our pursuit of a coherent, conceptual framework and viable definition.

Nobody would suggest that we should never quit any endeavor, no matter how miserable, difficult, and degrading the conditions might be. Further, no reasonable person would contend that we should never persevere in any undertaking that presents the slightest difficulty, challenge, or discomfort. This pair of responses (persevere versus quit) can be framed as manifestations of the classic, if somewhat oversimplified, fight-flight choice. We ought to struggle/persevere in the course of a grueling wrestling match and flee/quit in the midst of a tear-gassed protest. The heart of the matter is making a sound judgment of when to stay and when to go, and this struggle gives rise to two, opposing generalizations about people: We persist too long versus we quit too readily. In either case (and surely the truth depends on the type of endeavor in question), we would lead more fulfilling and meaningful lives if we understood our psychological propensities and mitigated unwittingly adverse tendencies.

A SOCIETY OF TENACIOUS TROOPERS OR DIFFIDENT DEFEATISTS?

To explore the nature of quitting, let's begin with the hypothesis that we're inclined to persevere. In evolutionary terms, those who quit easily in the pursuit of food and mates or those who readily fled when others came into their territory didn't leave as many descendants as did their tenacious comrades. Hence, it has been argued that "persistence and staying put are the default settings for human behavior" and even that "persistence is hardwired."[1] In particular, psychologists have found that individuals who desire control and success while also possessing high abilities and emotional hardiness are most likely to doggedly persist.[2] World-class mountaineers navigate a fine line between glory and disaster, understanding that "humans are designed to hang in," and this quality can—and perhaps must—be cultivated to produce the Type-A, iron-willed bulldogs who summit the world's most perilous peaks.[3] Or die trying. This latter possibility of figurative if not literal fatality has led to

FIGURE 5.1. Climbers ascending Ullu-Tau Range in the Caucasus Mountains on the Russia-Georgia border. Courtesy of Jann Kunnap via Wikimedia Commons.

the assertion that maximizing happiness "means doing more quitting."[4] However, this advice is founded largely on anecdotes, heuristics, and dubious studies.

Perhaps the most famous study-of-sorts regarding whether we persist to our detriment was conducted by economist Steven D. Levitt, who put up a website where people pondering big life decisions (e.g., divorcing, resigning, dropping out) could flip a virtual coin to determine whether they would persist or quit.[5] Thousands of people ostensibly made their decision in this manner, and those who quit reported higher levels of happiness afterward, which has been misinterpreted to mean that "people are generally quitting too late."[6] The findings are extremely questionable, given that the participants represented a biased, self-selected sample of people who were probably inclined to favor quitting and wanted to outsource responsibility for the decision (why else would someone seek such a website?). Setting aside the flaws of the study's design, we must still wonder why even those who evidently favored quitting didn't simply do so without the aid of a techno-scapegoat (surely an actual coin would have been sufficient if the individual was truly ambivalent).

A pair of widely shared personality traits corresponds with a tendency to persist in the face of adversity. First, those who persevere have an ample dose of pride, which comes down to a belief that they or their actions are socially valued.[7] When someone is esteemed for achievements in some domain, the person is motivated to pursue endeavors with greater devotion than an individual who doesn't feel particularly accomplished in that regard.[8] This incentive to persevere may yield success, thereby creating a kind of positive feedback such that pride becomes a serious impediment to giving up, even when the task becomes onerous or impossible. Moreover, genuinely disengaging from a goal toward which one has made admirable progress—and which has thus become entwined with one's identity—is psychologically difficult or even traumatic.[9]

The other personality trait associated with potentially excessive perseverance is self-esteem, which is less domain-specific than pride. Self-esteem can arise from a history of success, so that when an individual with this pervasive trait encounters some difficulty even in a novel domain, they expect to prevail with continued effort.[10] Indeed, researchers have found that subjects with high self-esteem persist beyond the point of fruitful effort. For example, given an unsolvable puzzle, those with high self-esteem persevere even when explicitly informed of inevitable failure.[11] Thus their expectation of imminent success yields worse performances than those of low self-esteem subjects who give up on tasks where persistence and performance are unrelated.[12] It has been argued that "high self-esteem can mean delusionally conceited as easily as low self-esteem can mean pathologically insecure."[13] And outside of the laboratory, responding to failure by increasing effort through groundless optimism may lead to tragically deleterious results in such diverse realms as warfare, sports, and investments.[14] In today's everyone-gets-a-medal world where people may accrue unwarranted self-esteem, the misery of persisting in endeavors for which individuals are objectively inept would seem inimical to happiness. In harsher terms, if our society is generating individuals whose subjective confidence greatly exceeds their objective abilities, then perhaps we are not just unproductively steadfast but ineffectually pusillanimous.

Let's turn now to the hypothesis that humans are natural-born (and sociobiologically conditioned) quitters. In evolutionary terms, those who fled from danger and hardship lived to fight (and mate) another day. From this premise, scientists have reasoned that "persistence requires overcoming the natural tendency to quit."[15] According to this view, humans are natural-born quitters because standing one's ground had serious downsides. In pathologizing this psychobiological foundation for turning tail, repeated retreats can lead to learned helplessness in which one gives up agency altogether—a condition that can be therapeutically overcome through persistence training.[16] Indeed, maladaptive risk aversion is manifest even in the presumptively gutsy world of sports, with football coaches choosing to punt far more frequently than is rational.[17] And so, the challenge is not to encourage quitting but to cultivate the gritty perseverance that goes against our proclivity to punt in all aspects of life.

A compelling line of evidence for our having a natural tendency to quit is the abundance of children's literature devoted to inspiring perseverance, which wouldn't be necessary if this were a strong evolutionary inclination. One would look long and hard to find stories encouraging kids to give up versus Watty Piper's classic *The Little Engine That Could*, which is approaching its centenary. Recent books include titles such as *She Persisted* by Chelsea Clinton, *Manjhi Moves a Mountain* by Nancy Churnin, and *I Am Courage: A Book of Resilience* by Susan Verde. Modern culture also provides adults with countless messages encouraging perseverance, such as the admonition of Calvin Coolidge: "Persistence and determination alone are omnipotent. The slogan 'press on' has solved and always will solve the problems of the human race."[18]

Ancient literature takes a severely negative view of quitting, with tales of misery following decisions to give up.[19] For example, there is a Platonic dialogue that heaps shame on those who abandon family and friends in times of trouble.[20]

Our proclivity for quitting one endeavor and moving on to another is furthered by an often unfounded optimism that constitutes what I call the *greener grass fallacy* (as in the ancient proverb that the grass is always better on the other side of the fence). Through this mistaken reasoning, people believe that abandoning a difficult endeavor will likely, if not certainly, lead to a better set of conditions. The self-help genre is filled with advice along these lines: "By not quitting, you are missing out on the opportunity to switch to something that will create more progress toward your goals . . . Anytime you stick to something when there are better opportunities out there, that is when you are slowing your progress."[21] Indeed, quit advocates explicitly play on the fear of missing out (FOMO) by (mis)applying scientific principles: "This brings us to another economic concept . . . called 'opportunity costs' and it refers to the cost of what you are missing out on if you stay in your current situation."[22] While life coaches criticize individuals who stick with an unpleasant venture as overly optimistic that things will get better, unwarranted hopefulness is not applied to the belief that quitting will improve one's life. Any inherent proclivity to quit via evolutionary predilection is fueled with the contemporary social message that delay of gratification (i.e., perseverance) is a quaint anachronism and inimical to happiness.

Complementing efforts to put quitting in a positive light is the human capacity for post hoc rationalization. As one woman claimed: "Each time I quit something, the next door was allowed to open up. Each successive situation I entered into was a better next step in my personal development."[23] Others frame their quits in the melodramatic language of "life or death" to justify decisions that clearly did not involve such stakes.[24] The ability to reframe events in intensely favorable terms (e.g., "If I hadn't given up on my previous relationship, I never would have found the fulfillment I've experienced with my new partner") is a form of protective self-justification that defends the psyche from objectively adverse consequences.[25] So central is this form of rationalization to our mental serenity that it has been called our psychological immune system. By telling ourselves a silver-lining story, particularly if we're not cognizant of doing so, we make quitting feel good in a way that is much more challenging than with persevering.[26]

—

So, there you have it. We somehow manage to both persist too long and quit too readily. At least some of this contradictory impression arises from the *availability heuristic* in which we give particular weight to evidence that is readily accessible. Some contend that this phenomenon leads us to accept the "myth of persistence," which is reinforced through tales of athletes and inventors who achieved fame by overcoming setbacks (e.g., Michael Jordan didn't make his high school varsity basketball team and Thomas Edison's first patented invention was a dud). However, the competing "myth of resignation" is substantiated by well-known accounts of entrepreneurs who dropped out of college and then struck it rich (e.g., Bill Gates, Steve Jobs, and Mark Zuckerberg).

If one were to ask whether humans fight too readily or flee too easily, the answer would surely be: "It depends." Whether a person rationally stands up to a robber or bolts from the scene would depend on who is armed, if the proto-victim is trained in martial arts, if the thief is a weakling, what valuables are at stake, whether an escape route is readily accessible, how fast the individuals can run, and similar factors. And although perseverance may be key to business success early in a venture, financial performance declines when companies stick with initially fruitful, but eventually outdated, strategies.[27] The conclusion is that quitting and persisting are tactics or tools that must be applied judiciously. The question therefore becomes how one knows when to stay and when to go. And the answer is math—or so economists would have us believe.

HOLD 'EM OR FOLD 'EM? JUST RUN THE NUMBERS (YEAH, RIGHT . . .)

Imagine that I'm a shortstop playing for a minor league team, and the Blue Sox pay me $25,000 a year. My agent tells me that the Jankees will pay me $75,000 to play for them. But breaking my contract with the Sox will require that I pay my current team a onetime $50,000 penalty. Should I quit? If I jump ship, I'll benefit by $50,000 in the coming season, an amount that will cover the cost of the penalty, and thereafter I'll pocket the entire $75,000 every year. So, a calculation of benefits ($50,000 yearly) and costs ($50,000 once) means that I'm entirely rational to quit the Sox.

One could contend that the theoretical framework for quitting is the direct, rational application of *cost-benefit analysis*—at least when outcomes are assured.[28] Continuing with our example, the benefit-cost analysis would get fuzzier if the penalty was $100,000, given that it would take two years to pay off this expense and it's possible that I could be injured in my first season with the Jankees. Life involves uncertainties, but even these are subject to statistical analysis (e.g., major league fielders suffer an injury rate of < 4/1,000 players and a tiny fraction of these injuries are career-ending).[29]

We are now in the realm of what's called *expected value*. Simply put, an expected value is the difference between expected benefits and expected costs. An expected benefit is the probability of receiving a particular gain times that gain's value, and the expected cost is the probability that a particular loss will be incurred times its cost.[30] In the baseball example, let's assume there's no penalty for breaking the contract, but imagine that the minor league lacks financial stability such that the Jankees have an 80 percent chance of going bankrupt by next season (given how much they're willing to pay mediocre players like me), while the Sox have a 90 percent chance of continuing. So, the expected value of sticking with the Sox is 0.9 × $25,000 = $22,500 and the expected value of quitting the Sox and joining the Jankees is 0.2 × $75,000 = $15,000. So, it would not be reasonable for me to quit my current team.

Expected value as a heuristic for quitting is plausible when the probabilities of future events are known, as with flipping a coin or playing poker[31] or in the highly unlikely case in which there are no benefits to persisting.[32] Sure, we should quit while we're ahead in a game that's stacked against us in the long run,[33] but what about the tournament of romance or the game of hospice? Psychologists offer the obvious and unhelpful recommendation that we should persist when the chance of realizing a goal is favorable and quit when a goal is unreachable.[34] But how can we know if a goal is unattainable unless we persist (e.g., a fulfilling career or a gold medal)? Moreover, who can assign probabilities to whether you'll find a better mate if you break up with your current one or whether you'll be better off if you drop your music major and pursue a theology degree?

—

The standard economic model of human behavior assumes that we are fully rational, informed, competent, and self-interested. Now there's a theoretical framework that's worth abandoning! Challenging just one of these assumptions, the field of behavioral economics emerged in an attempt to try to understand why people don't act rationally. In particular, there are some intriguing explanations of why we steadfastly refuse to quit, even when doing so would be to our benefit.

Perhaps the best-known phenomenon that accounts for headstrong persistence is the *sunk cost effect*. In strictly rational terms, economists contend that we should make our decisions based on what is likely to happen in the future without regard to the past. However, when we have invested considerable money, time, energy, or emotion into a venture, there is a tendency to reflect on these expenditures when contemplating the possibility of quitting, even though we can't get back these sunk costs.[35] And so, the sense of not wanting to have wasted one's resources fuels an emotional state in which the individual continues to invest in an endeavor as if doing so could somehow salvage all that's already gone into the romantic relationship, professional career, beloved avocation, military battle, college major, construction project, or financial plan. In

FIGURE 5.2. The *Concorde* was a supersonic airliner estimated to cost $88 million in 1962, but the price escalated to $2.5 billion by 1976, when the plane entered commercial service. Courtesy of Eduard Marmet via Wikimedia Commons.

a sense, persistence becomes a positive feedback system such that the longer we sink resources into a venture, the more resistant we become to quitting.[36]

The most (in)famous case of the sunk cost fallacy is known as the "Concorde Fallacy,"[37] which began in 1962 and unfolded over nearly forty years as the British and French continued to pour funds into building and marketing the *Concorde* long after it was apparent that the supersonic jet was a financial money pit. With costs rising to thirty times the original estimate, the governments couldn't bring themselves to terminate the program and see billions of dollars go for naught.[38] A similar case is seen with California's continuing pursuit of a high-speed bullet train system, which is an ongoing, too-big-to-quit losing venture.[39]

Both small and enormous examples abound. At one end of the spectrum, the sunk cost fallacy plays out continuously in casinos among recreational gamblers who continue to bet at poker tables where they are demonstrably outmatched.[40] The most tragic instances of the sunk cost fallacy have been in the context of war. As lives and money were poured into Vietnam, Iraq, and Afghanistan, leaders could not bring themselves to call it quits and accept that continuing the fight would not restore what had already been lost.[41]

Humans are not the only pigheaded species prone to the irrationality of trying to recoup lost resources by bullheaded persistence, contrary to claims that other animals aren't burdened by such notions.[42] Although pigs and bulls haven't been found to exhibit this tendency, laboratory experiments have shown that the sunk cost fallacy may manifest in capuchin monkeys, rhesus macaques, mice, rats, pigeons, swallows, sparrows, and bluegills[43] (some experimental psychologists offer alternative interpretations).[44]

Our familiarity with the sunk cost fallacy has led to this phenomenon being used as an easy, go-to explanation of complex decisions that don't appear to be rational. Most famously, a study of professional basketball players revealed that first-round picks were allotted more playing time and stayed both with a team and in the league longer than did lower picks with equal performances; similar patterns have been found with regard to draft order and compensation of football players.[45] The expenditure of a very valuable high draft selection is a sunk cost, and this has been used to explain the continuing commitment to players despite their early performance being no better than that of lower-rated teammates. However, this simple interpretation overlooks other, equally or more plausible explanations. For example, previous performance may well be a reasonable predictor of future gains (notwithstanding investment warnings against this extrapolation). Draft picks are based on perceived potential, which may not be fully realized early in a player's career and must be assessed with playing time. And it is not irrational to stick with a proven player (at least prior to the draft) during a slump longer than one might persevere with an unproven athlete exhibiting the same performance. Moreover, allocating time to a first-round draft pick might well draw larger crowds and greater ticket sales or foster a sense of hope within the team.

Another problem in hastily applying the sunk cost fallacy to explain seemingly unreasonable persistence is the assumption that the probability of desirable results is constant. While past expenditures cannot be recouped, it doesn't follow that these investments of time and energy do nothing to make future, desirable outcomes more likely. While a couple's history of dysfunction might generate emotional costs that fail to justify sticking with a bad relationship,[46] past struggles conceivably enhance future expectations. A couple who works their way through difficulties expends emotional capital that is unrecoverable, but in doing so they might be increasing the expected value of the relationship by having mutually demonstrated that they are reliable, devoted, and supportive mates.

Here's a further concern regarding the potential misapplication of the sunk cost fallacy, which is sometimes allied with the gambler's fallacy. In this version, one believes that a random event becomes increasingly (un)likely as a function of repeated trials (e.g., after flipping heads five times in a row, one believes there is a greater or lesser chance of the coin being heads on the sixth toss). Likewise—or so it could seem—one might believe that after having been passed over for promotion five times, the chances are better the next time. However, the gambler's fallacy pertains only if each chance at a promotion is independent of all earlier decisions by the employer. That might be the case, but it's entirely possible that continued efforts and loyalty impress one's superior such that the events are statistically dependent and the probability of a promotion increases with each opportunity.

Finally, to utterly dismiss past investments of resources and base decisions based solely on future, expected value can constitute its own irrationality. For example, a student cannot recover the time or money spent in the first seven semesters pursuing an undergraduate degree in chemistry. Now, what if the student who's going into their final semester decides to quit majoring in chemistry because science is not as fulfilling as majoring in dance might be, without regard to their full-ride scholarship paying for a total of only eight semesters? That would hardly be reasonable—despite this avoiding the sunk cost fallacy (even self-help cheerleaders for quitting cannot bring themselves to entirely ignore accrued debt).[47]

If you had to bet on whether a person would quit when contemplating a challenging situation, the smart money would be on that individual doubling down. A psychological package of subconscious phenomena augments our reluctance to relinquish sunk costs. Rather than turn tail, we tend to dig in thanks to the influences of a panoply of misperceptions and biases that, as we'll see, might not be quite as explanatorily potent as advocates of quitting imagine. Let's consider these complementary phenomena in isolation, even though they are conceptually entangled.

When someone pursues a goal but obstacles and failures seem to continually drive the possibility of success further into the future, a rational person might simply give up. However, it's often the case that the struggle itself makes the goal appear ever more valuable, such that repeated frustration fosters a deepening of resolve.[48] Such *escalating commitment* can become a cyclical process, making a decision to quit increasingly difficult.

This phenomenon is seen across a wide range of settings, including jobs, relationships, investments, mountaineering, and even sticking with dull movies and tedious books.[49] Escalating commitment is particularly intense when the individual feels personally responsible for the persistent adverse results.[50] The most tragic instances of this incapacity to quit a losing venture are manifest in the perpetuation of wars. The classic cases blend into the sunk cost fallacy, as when US Secretary of State George Ball issued a darkly prescient warning to President Lyndon Johnson regarding the Vietnam War: "Once large numbers of U.S. troops are committed to direct combat, they will begin to take heavy casualties in a war they are ill-equipped to fight in a non-cooperative if not downright hostile countryside. Once we suffer large casualties, we will have started a well-nigh irreversible process."[51]

In contrast, escalating commitment can be a fruitful tactic. For example, setting goals increases commitment and thereby provides motivation to overcome obstacles in pursuit of worthwhile, difficult objectives.[52]

An intriguing pair of complementary tendencies can further impede our willingness to give up. In what's called the *endowment effect*, we place greater value on something we possess than on the same thing that we have yet to acquire. And in the case of *loss aversion*, the displeasure of losing what we already possess is much greater than the joy of acquiring something of exactly the same objective value.[53] Indeed, for the identical resource, the negative emotional impact of loss is about twice the positive feelings of gain. Along similar lines, we can sympathize with *sure-loss aversion* in which people resist turning an abstract or "paper" loss into a tangible, concrete failure (e.g., you don't lose money in a bear market until you actually sell your stocks). It's easy to understand how the endowment effect and (sure) loss aversion conspire to augment escalation of commitment, thereby creating a mutually supporting system of perceptions that inhibit quitting.[54]

Experimental psychologists and behavioral economists have demonstrated these phenomena in capuchin monkeys using tokens redeemable for various foods[55] and in humans with everything from chocolate bars to coffee cups. These studies can be extrapolated to virtually all of our possessions,[56] with notable exceptions given what can happen at garage sales and flea markets where assets may be sold for less than their objective value.

It has been argued intriguingly that even our ideas are prone to the endowment effect, such that we cling to our beliefs.[57] However, we should not hastily ascribe irrationality to those who resist giving up a belief even when the evidence seems to undermine their position. Our beliefs are typically interdependent, such that quitting one may precipitate a collapse of many others in a kind of house of cards that could be tremendously costly to one's identity and worldview. As such, epistemic conservatism has philosophical and psychological merits.[58]

—

Take a heaping spoonful of sunk costs, add a generous dash of endowment effect along with a dollop of loss aversion, and you have the recipe for what's been termed *status quo bias*. In this way of thinking, the familiarity of one's current path or situation—even if unpleasant ("the devil you know")—is preferred to the unknown consequences of changing direction. Laboratory experiments and field studies have shown that even when changing course generates a higher expected value, people tend to stick with their current circumstances.[59] However, the popular heuristic that "a bird in the hand is worth two in the bush" constitutes justifiable perseverance in some situations, given the validity of discounting future value based on an uncertainty.

Another version of this phenomenon is *omission-commission bias*, in which we tend to favor passively accepting present conditions rather than taking action. This is apparent in the famous "Trolley Problem"—a thought experiment in which some individuals find it preferable to allow several people to die rather than taking responsibility for directly causing the death of a single person (hence, the "doing harm versus allowing harm" distinction).[60] The presumption of quit advocates is that quitting entails doing something, while persisting is merely a matter of allowing the status quo to continue, so the latter becomes our default.[61] However, it is entirely possible to quit passively or by omission (e.g., terminating a service by allowing a contract to expire or "ghosting" a romantic partner by not communicating).

APPLES AND ORANGES: WHEN TO QUIT USING SPREADSHEETS

The analysis of when we ought to quit—and the explanation of why we don't—has become largely the province of behavioral economics. The basic concept seems plausible: If we can quantify the costs and benefits of quitting (and persevering), then rationality will lead to optimal decisions.

Consider this "natural experiment" of weighing pros and cons. The resignation of a cabinet member from either the US or the British government is big news and typically arises because the individual cannot countenance or hope to change a repugnant policy. However, British politicians are almost ten times more likely than Americans to resign in loud protest.[62] The explanation is simple. While politicians from both nations quit to preserve their personal integrity, a public declaration by a British leader has the added benefit of potentially swaying public opinion without the cost of being driven out of politics. British cabinet members are typically chosen from, and return to, the ranks of Parliament after resigning, while US cabinet members have no such safety net with regard to their political careers.[63] As such, political quitting illustrates the explanatory power of cost-benefit analysis.

A spreadsheet approach is particularly viable when managers use monetary accounting to assess which decision is likely to yield the greatest profits. If persisting with product A, which has been the company's mainstay for decades, means continuing to spend $1 million to get $2 million in returns while switching to newfangled product B is expected to cost $2 million but provide $5 million in sales, then by all means quit manufacturing product A and go with product B—at least if that's the entire story.

Perhaps adopting product B would infuse a sense of excitement into new employees and elevate the company's morale, but what if abandoning product A—a long-term source of company pride—would produce heartbreak among those who devoted their lives to crafting this product and push some old-timers into deep depression or even suicide? This scenario comes much closer to the complexities of quitting in real life, where there are no common units of measure that allow a spreadsheet to reveal the greatest net return.[64]

As fascinating and informative as natural, laboratory, and thought experiments are and as much as they allow researchers to isolate specific elements of human (ir)rationality while revealing biases and fallacies in the context of the objectively best decisions, quitting in the real world is fraught with incommensurable costs and benefits.[65] Robert Goodin, a distinguished professor of philosophy and social and political theory who has delved deeply into how humans make decisions, has argued: "People are not merely bundles of beliefs and desires. They also have (and want to have, and are better off and better people for having) sympathies and commitments to people, principles, and projects. Those commitments specify what a person cares about."[66]

In addition, beliefs and desires are not independent aspects of one's life. Quitting a particular endeavor may entail giving up any number of other elements of a meaningful life with which it is entangled.[67] Even giving up on what seems to be an isolated effort may well have ramifications that extend to an individual's sense of identity. Former Ultimate Fighting Championship (UFC) middleweight champion Michael Bisping explained his refusal to quit under the extreme duress of what's called a rear, naked choke: "I wouldn't tap. I'd worked too hard for this title. Everything went fuzzy, then black."[68] In that fight, Bisping lost his title but retained his identity: "'A fighter,' was always a statement of who I was, what I was, earlier than my occupation. Martial arts had defined me."[69] Likewise, in cultures that place tremendous value on honor, quitting is contemptible, while a combatant who is defeated or even killed in battle may well be considered a hero.

When it comes to dying or, more precisely, quitting life-preserving medical interventions, individuals in hospice engage in a complex and deeply personal set of incommensurable tradeoffs. What are the odds of a miraculous cure; what is the quality of one's remaining life; what are the effects of rejecting further treatments on one's family; what are the financial costs of continuing medical procedures; what are one's religious beliefs about the value of life, whatever its character; and what can I teach my loved ones about dying and dying well?[70]

In less dramatic terms, a plea of "no contest" in a criminal case may be understood by the defendant as a kind of surrender to the legal system but not an admission of guilt. In this way, the individual preserves their dignity, exchanging a potentially long prison term for the ability to preserve a "self" that never admitted to the crime.[71] There is, of course, no way to convert an individual's personal identity to years of imprisonment that would allow a cost-benefit calculation of whether it is rational to quit fighting prosecution.

And so, the most difficult framing of cost-benefit analysis is not that complex external factors impact one's life (e.g., the financial cost of divorce, the territorial cost of surrender, the gain of professional status with a promotion, the prize money of winning a boxing match). Rather, the insurmountable challenge arises from internal tradeoffs that are impossible to convert into comparable units.

Consider the tensions that arise with physical and mental health. While perseverance is essential to success, when people persist in the pursuit of unattainable goals, they exhibit increasing levels of C-reactive protein, which is associated with generalized inflammation and increased risk of cardiovascular disease.[72] As such, the most adaptive response might be to disengage from the frustration of persevering—if only one could know either that the goal was truly out of reach or that success would come with continued, strenuous effort.

On the other hand, giving up puts our mental well-being at risk. The associated uncertainty that comes with change and the cost of abandoning part of one's identity generates stress and anxiety. Throwing in the towel can even entail a kind of existential crisis: "Resignation [from employment] is connected to disappointment in that every resignation marks a rupture, a quitting, the ending of something, that places someone Nowhere in respect to where they were before."[73]

Rationality is a valuable component of decision-making, but it is not the entirety of what it means to be human. It is surely inadvisable to allow emotions to overwhelm decision-making (e.g., quitting in anger during a heated argument with a supervisor or persevering in an abusive relationship because one's church condemns divorce)[74] or to summarily reject rationality in favor of nebulous intuition.[75] However, it is also impossible to give up on some sustained ventures without feeling disappointment in having failed to achieve a goal. In such cases, rather than suppressing and perhaps entrenching the situational depression of having quit an important pursuit, the healthy strategy is to recognize and regulate those feelings.[76]

Even in cases in which one is contemplating whether to quit or persevere and the situation is largely, if not entirely, prone to rational, quantitative analysis (e.g., comparing the salary at a current job to that of alternative employment), it is not clear that one ought to employ the methods of *Star Trek*'s Mr. Spock—even if such was possible. As Blaise Pascal advised three centuries before Gene Roddenberry created the purely logical Vulcan character, "There are two equally dangerous extremes—to shut reason out, and to let nothing else in."[77]

RATIONAL IRRATIONALITY: THE FULLY HUMAN QUIT

The application of cost-benefit analysis based on the expected value of quitting is a useful tool of human flourishing. But one does not build a house or a life using a single tool. The hammer of rationality is a necessary but not sufficient implement to making a good decision. We are also emotional beings, and the values of joy, disappointment, satisfaction, and anxiety are incommensurable with those of time, money, and status. It is wise to be attentive to various misperceptions, biases, and fallacies, but it is also smart to critically assess whether our decision truly reflects these erroneous ways of thinking.

This leads us to the next chapter, in which we explore another important feature of quitting—the role of free will. If we are forced to abandon a relationship, job, contest, faith, or practice, does this really constitute having quit? And just what is meant when a climber tells their partner that it's time to give up in these words: "We have no choice. There's nothing else we can do"?[78] Nothing? Really? We'll see about that...

6

The Role of Free Will
Coerced Quits Aren't Quite Quits

Imagine that you are in the downtown of a big city, heading to a lunch date, and, to your horror, you see a person falling from the top of a tall building. You might think to yourself, "What would cause someone to give up on life?" But can you assume that the person quit? What if they were pushed from the edge or told by some thug "either jump or your family will be killed." If either of these was the case, has the falling individual given up in any real sense?

Arriving at the restaurant, your dining companion lets you know that she won't be ordering any dish that contains red meat. You might think to yourself, "Well, that's rather admirable having made the decision to forgo animal flesh. I wonder what prompted her to become vegetarian?" Then you learn she was bitten by a Lone Star tick and has developed an unusual but well-documented allergy to red meat.[1] If she eats meat, her breathing will be labored, her pulse will plummet, and her throat will constrict. So, she hasn't so much chosen to quit carnivory as having been forced to do so.

Given your fondness for steaks, her condition makes the woman a mismatched romantic partner, but that's not an issue for you as you've given up having sex. Your fundamentalist minister preached a sermon last month on the certainty that premarital sex would assure eternal damnation. With your career aspirations, you don't intend to ever marry, so celibacy is the only way to avoid hellfire and brimstone. So, have you freely chosen not to have sex—or have you been psychologically coerced into chastity?

This imaginary case raises the important question of whether genuine quitting requires an act of free will. If you lack autonomy, does it make sense to say you've actually quit? An advocate of quitting noted that "sometimes, you make the choice to quit and sometimes the world makes that choice for you."[2] But "forced quitting" seems conceptually confused insofar as there is no agency, rather like the person pushed from the building.[3]

FREE WILL: PHILOSOPHERS NEVER QUIT ARGUING

Free will might appear to be a rather straightforward concept (but then, so did quitting when we started). If someone controls their own choices and actions, then they exercise free will. However, having the power to decide is not the same as being able to act on a decision. For example, you could choose to desert a military unit but be unable to do so for any number of reasons (e.g., you rashly expressed this desire and have been thrown in the brig).

As such, philosophers have shifted their analyses away from free will, given the difficulty of knowing the internal state of other people.[4] The more tractable issue is free action, or whether an individual behaves autonomously. In either case—will or action—the primary motivation for understanding the nature of an individual's intention or behavior is the matter of moral responsibility. In the context of our concerns, it doesn't make sense to hold a person blameworthy or praiseworthy for quitting if they could not have done otherwise.

Through causal determination, the physical sciences provide a potentially compelling way to raise doubts about whether we can act freely, no matter how it might feel to us. In brief, many physicists contend that if we could take into account all of the past states of the universe and add to

FIGURE 6.1. Statue of Liberty commemorating US independence, American democracy, and the liberation of the nation's slaves. Courtesy of Dominique James via Wikimedia Commons.

these the immutable laws of nature, the result would be a single, unique, and invariant future. Hence, there is no freedom.

Physicists have recently doubled down via quantum theory. According to this framework, the future is not strictly determined. Rather, it is the result of random processes such that we mistake probabilistic occurrence for free will. Intractably complex processes might be happening inside our brains, but we are no more at liberty to decide whether to leap from a high building than a stone is free to plummet to the earth when dropped. It is conceptually mistaken to hold a soldier accountable for being a deserter, just as it is nonsensical to blame the Sahara for being a desert.

Such a morally abject and existentially forlorn view of human existence has generated various rebuttals. The determinists' dismissal of free will is based on a metaphysical commitment to materialism. As such, one escape from the problem raised by physics is to accept mind-body dualism, such that free will can exist in the non-material former realm however the latter might be constrained.

Another approach was taken by American pragmatist William James, who was simply defiant: "My first act of free will shall be to believe in free will."[5] So there. The pragmatists saw little value in metaphysical debates given that they were empirically unresolvable. For them, the reality of free will was no more than a facile puzzle.

While much of the initial philosophical inquiry regarding free will was grounded in the matter of individual moral accountability, an extension of the ethical concern—sociopolitical accountability—has recently drawn attention. Political scientist Jennet Kirkpatrick has argued that individuals have the moral right to exit from social conditions that they find oppressive or immoral.[6] Nation-states that prevent citizens from leaving (quitting) are essentially prisons and violate Article 13.2 of the Universal Declaration of Human Rights.[7]

Foregrounding ethical considerations, given the apparent irresolvable metaphysics of free will, has likewise been adopted by some philosophers. That is, the starting point for their analysis is a commitment to moral autonomy.[8] We can be more confident that humans have ethical responsibilities than that they have ethereal capacities such as free will. This approach shifts the discourse and reconnects philosophy to the practical realms of human life.

In many aspects of life, we distinguish intentional acts from those that lack deliberation. Consider the legal domain. Insofar as intense emotions diminish a person's ability to act with rational intentions, we differentiate crimes of passion (e.g., second-degree murder) from those of premeditation (e.g., first-degree murder). In the psychological realm, suicidologists distinguish impulsive suicides from carefully planned suicides.[9] In the medical domain, hospice counselors see an important difference between individuals who perceive themselves as victims of unjust illnesses and lacking in control versus those who view themselves as empowered agents determining the balance of their remaining life.[10]

YOU WANT ME TO QUIT? MAKE ME!

People might sometimes quit without any pressure, but more often quitting happens under some amount of duress. So, whether one acts freely in terms of quitting is a matter of degree. The pressures that bear on a decision to quit can be subsumed under the concept of coercion. In short, coercion is the use or threat of force to cause an individual to act in a manner contrary to their own desires.

External constraints on our liberty to act as we wish take a variety of forms.[11] It's important to note that not every kind of coercion is ethically problematic. We act coercively when we put a violent criminal in prison, make a toddler hold hands when crossing a street, or force a CEO to adhere to environmental standards. However, we are justifiably concerned when force is used to make mature, moral, mentally competent individuals act against their will.

In understanding coercive force, we can adapt classifications of harm developed by organizations concerned with vulnerable individuals.[12] Although almost any form of harm has the potential to coerce an individual to quit, six of them are most highly relevant.

First, there is no doubt that slavery severely restricts an individual's ability to quit working. Indeed, scholars in the field of labor studies distinguish between waged labor and enslaved labor by whether one has the right to quit.[13] The waged laborer can quit, but the enslaved worker can, at best, escape. Hence, one of the major historical themes in Black studies is fugitivity.[14]

Next, domestic abuse is a form of harm that can make it difficult for a person to exit a dysfunctional relationship for fear of retribution. The abuser coerces the victim to endure by psychological manipulation, physical force, and economic pressure.[15]

Third, organizational abuse can manifest when an institution neglects the needs of vulnerable individuals, such as failing to provide adequate medical care in a nursing home. With regard to quitting, institutions can coerce individuals to remain in an organization, such as a church threatening an individual with eternal damnation should they defect.

Both domestic and organizational coercion shade into the fourth kind of harm: psychological or emotional. An individual who would otherwise choose to quit a relationship, job, religion, college, or contest can be pressured into persevering through humiliation and intimidation (e.g., a woman contemplating divorce might face harsh judgment by her minister or an athlete wanting to quit a competition could be cruelly mocked by a coach). But the opposite is also possible—one can be coerced into quitting, as when a boss harasses an employee until they resign or a person who belongs to a conservative political party is pressured to disassociate by liberal family members.

The fifth form of harm that is directly relevant is sexual and physical injury. As with psychological harm, a worker can be coerced into quitting by a sexually predatory employer or a soldier can be coerced into persevering by the threat of execution for deserting their post. Some forms of severe physical coercion are implicit in various ventures, such as the use of choking to force submission in martial arts matches.

Finally, an individual can be coerced by financial pressures. A student might be pressured to remain in college by parents who threaten to withdraw monetary support for tuition. Conversely, an individual could be coerced into breaking a marital engagement under the threat of being disinherited by a wealthy parent who does not approve of the fiancé.

―

As much as coercion might seem to be constraining, an argument can be made that a person is always free to act in any way they desire—the question is whether the individual is willing to suffer the consequences. Sure, there are undeniably coercive forces, but one can choose to persevere in a jujitsu match by refusing to submit and receiving a broken arm. For that matter, a believer can defy pressure to renounce their beliefs and become a martyr. Poverty, humiliation, pain, and death are all poten-

FIGURE 6.2. A frightened Viet Cong prisoner awaits coercive interrogation by the US military at Thuong Duc Camp. Courtesy of the National Archives via Wikimedia Commons.

tial consequences, but neoliberal rationality and philosophical metaphysics maintain that it is within every individual's power to defy external demands, assert their autonomy, and take responsibility for their decisions.[16] Comedian Louis CK made the ultimate argument about quitting and coercion when he generated uncomfortable laughs by telling an audience: "You don't have to do anything. You never *have* to do anything [pause] because you can kill yourself. If they send you a letter from Motor Vehicles, 'You have to come in...' No I don't, I'll kill myself. You can do that. You can do that once, but you can do it."[17]

Even if much less extreme neoliberal standards are applied, when Lieutenant Ehren Watada sought to quit military service during the Iraq War based on his belief that the United States Army was pursuing an unjust war of aggression, his explanation was untenable: "Although I have tried to resign out of protest, I am forced to participate in a war that is manifestly illegal."[18] He refused deployment, but he didn't simply walk away from the military. What he was really saying was that the costs of deserting were higher than he was willing to pay. In absolute terms, he was free to quit. However, this idealistic interpretation of free will is psychologically problematic.

Perhaps there are people who can quit anything, but most of us are constitutionally unable to act in particular ways. Even the metaphysical idealists would expect us to act rationally; if quitting specific endeavors would decimate our mental condition, irreparably damage our bodies, or otherwise constitute self-destruction, then doing so is unreasonable. The assertion that we are free to do whatever we desire is a claim that denies the fundamental nature and limits of what it means to be human.

THE THEORY MEETS THE REALITY OF QUITTING

Abstract frameworks with hypothetical cases can guide our thinking about the nature of quitting, but let's see how theories of free will/action and concepts of coercion play out with actual cases.

To begin, consider combat sports and a couple of classic quits in the boxing ring. Recall from chapter 3 the "No Mas Fight" and "The Thrilla in Manila," both of which ended with fighters quitting. Conventionally, we might assume that a boxer who quits is physically compelled to throw in the towel. However, in the case of Roberto Durán, it appears that the coercion was substantially psychological.[19] Sugar Ray Leonard was publicly humiliating him, and Durán called it quits to avoid further embarrassment.

In the Ali-Frazier match, the two men completed the fourteenth round with different perspectives.[20] Ali was ready to relent to the pain and exhaustion. Frazier was also badly injured, but he wanted to continue. However, his manager had seen fighters die in the ring, an experience that emotionally drove him to end the fight on Frazier's behalf. Minds and bodies were under tremendous duress in both corners.

In mixed martial arts, coerced submissions are built into the sport—at least in principle. However, some fighters make a case for the argument that one is never absolutely compelled to give up. For example, when Steve Cantwell caught Razak Al-Hussan in an arm bar, Cantwell began applying pressure, with the only options for his opponent being "tap or snap." Al-Hussan refused the former and accepted the latter.[21] At the highest levels of any sport, it is said that winning is 90 percent mental—and perhaps this also holds for whether an athlete can overcome their body's demand to quit.

Al-Hussan and other fighters have resisted external pressure to abandon their endeavors, but the most compelling cases in support of the human capacity to act freely despite brutal coercion might be found among religious martyrs. Under horrific physical duress, individuals have refused to renounce their faith. By sticking to their beliefs and defying the authorities, various Roman Catholic saints were crushed, flayed, grilled, and stoned.[22] Offering up one's suffering to God is evidently a psychological means of refusing to quit.[23] When Saint Cassian refused to make sacrifices to pagan gods, officials had his students (who had been "corrupted" by being taught about Christianity) repeatedly bash him with their tablets and pierce him with their iron styluses—an agonizingly slow way to die. In another religious context, according to the Pauline model of conversion, a flash of divine revelation compels one to abandon previous beliefs. Apparently, when God is a coercive agent, few humans can refuse to relent (even the Egyptian pharaoh eventually gave up after ten plagues).

While religious faith might allow one to resist coercion, at least in some cases moral principles are not sufficient. When one defies government authority, the result can be unbearable pressure.[24] Ann Wright, the deputy chief of mission for the United States Foreign Service, resisted her country's policy during the Iraq War until doing so meant choosing between quitting and dying: "It created such stress for me that I became a very unhealthy person, including symptoms of a heart attack. I had chest pains, pains in my arms, and so on. The medical officer said, 'we can't mess around with this,' and I was medically evacuated."[25] And so, she resigned from the United States Department of State and lived to tell the story.

As a retired United States Army colonel, Wright was surely aware of how the military perceives surrender and free will. War provides a compelling context for understanding the relationship between coercion and quitting. Members of the armed forces are held to a Code of Conduct in which all soldiers, aviators, sailors, and marines swear "I will never surrender of my own free will. If in command, I will never surrender the members of my command while they still have the means to resist."²⁶ This wording suggests that under extreme duress such as imminent death, an individual is no longer capable of free action and quitting is countenanced. In practical terms, a dead warrior is of no use to a military operation, while a prisoner of war can continue to resist the enemy. In philosophical and psychological terms, the Code of Conduct was written in expectation of conflicts between nations. However, it is seen as having the flexibility to guide a combatant's actions under a wide range of circumstances, including in conflicts with non-state militias that do not recognize the Geneva Convention's provisions regarding the humane treatment of prisoners.²⁷

Perhaps the most vivid cases of coercion during warfare arose within the Japanese military during World War II.²⁸ Take, for example, the battle for Okinawa. As this horrific struggle was approaching an inevitable victory by the United States, General Simon Buckner, the commander of the Tenth Army, sent a message to his counterpart, General Mitsuru Ushijima. The American general commended the courage and ferocity of his enemy's troops, noted their indefensible position, and called for them to surrender to stop the futile bloodshed. In reply, the Japanese general assured his adversary that every soldier under his command would fight to the death. Indeed, in General Ushijima's final order to his troops, he appealed to the coercive forces of military and cultural loyalty: "Every man in these fortifications will follow his superior officer's order to fight to the end and for the sake of the motherland."²⁹ Five days later, General Ushijima climbed a hill along with two officers, plunged the traditional dagger used in hari-kari into his abdomen, and was immediately beheaded by his sword-wielding comrade; his second-in-command then committed ritual suicide.[30] The coercive power of tradition dictated the manner of quitting.

Societally coerced quits needn't be as dramatic as ritualized suicide. Although mandatory retirement is generally prohibited in the United States, older individuals can be forced out of certain occupations (e.g., airline pilots and air traffic controllers). Other countries have a remarkable mixture of approaches to drive people into retirement. For example, in the Philippines, underground miners are required to retire at age sixty and professional racehorse jockeys at age fifty-five,[31] while in South Korea retirement is compulsory by age sixty in the private sector, and most companies lay off employees between ages fifty and fifty-five.[32] This practice is not legal in the United States, but studies have shown that more than half of workers over age fifty were pushed out of their jobs before they would have freely chosen to retire.[33]

Not unlike those in the aviation industry who can be forced into retirement because their jobs are judged to require exceptional mental acuity, professional athletes "age out" of their careers and are expected to quit when they are no longer performing at the highest level. Consider that Sasha Cohen won "only" a silver medal in figure skating at the 2006 Winter Olympics and was considered a has-been.[34]

Even those who continue to exhibit skills generally superior to those of younger competitors may be pressured by the media and fans to exit the sport. For example, Tom Brady was the oldest player in the NFL in 2022 at age forty-five (the average starting quarterback was twenty-eight).[35] Even so, he was the tenth best player out of sixty-eight starting quarterbacks.[36] His retirement in 2023 was evidently a case of social coercion.

Enormous pressure can be brought to bear by the public, particularly when a politician is involved. For example, Jaqui Smith quit as British Labour's home secretary in 2009 when the tabloids latched on to the story that she'd unwittingly billed the public for pay-per-view adult movies her husband had watched during their travels. The media feeding frenzy was unrelenting regarding this seemingly minor impropriety for which she was largely blameless, but the British public is prone to "periodic fits of morality in which privates lives of politicians are scrutinized."[37]

Moving from societal to individual and interpersonal pressures, psychological coercion can be intense and can function as a double-edged sword, capable of piercing deeply into an individual's will to either persevere or quit. Regarding the latter, an emeritus colleague told me of a faculty member in his department whose mental capacities had declined with age. Subtle hints as to his having become a liability were ineffective (academics being good at both passive aggression and ignoring social cues), so the department head went to the professor's house and delivered the message in unambiguous terms: "It's time for you to retire." There were tears, but the faculty member relented. The colleague who told me this story decided that he wanted to call it quits before anyone thought or said it was time for him to go. Now retired, he figures that he gave up his job but kept his dignity.

Conversely, worries about how one is perceived can compel individuals to persist in onerous endeavors.[38] For example, one might be a member of a religious community in which divorce is considered sinful such that interpersonal condemnation (let alone divine judgment) is psychologically debilitating. Divorce may also involve a kind of internal coercion. Take the case study of a woman whose identity was built around being a wife.[39] The stress of a dysfunctional marriage drove her to consider divorce, but abandoning her identity constituted a potentially devastating loss. For this woman, the psychological tug of war generated physiological misery, including angina, hypertension, headaches, indigestion, and menstrual irregularity.[40] This example of an American woman is magnified in documented cases of young women in Nepal who set themselves on fire—the ultimate, horrific quit—to avoid being coerced into arranged marriages that can entail rape and abuse.[41]

In what might seem to be an oxymoronic real-world case, it is also possible for an individual to freely choose to be coerced. Ultra-marathon runners enlist pacers for segments of a race to motivate the flagging athlete, using "tough love" just short of forcing a physically damaging performance.[42] And so, when someone is anticipating a difficult but valuable endeavor that would be tempting to quit, they might elect to put themselves in a position that makes perseverance more likely. Less dramatic than the case of long-distance running, one might pay a substantial fee to a gym and thereby impose a kind of financial coercion on themselves to exercise regularly.

Psychological coercion raises some interesting questions such as whether mental illness can prevent an individual from acting freely (e.g., is a person with obsessive-compulsive disorder free to quit checking that they've locked the door?). Perhaps the most obvious cases involve the coercive qualities of substance abuse. There is a sense in which we can understand the addictive drug as coercing the user, given that not all forms of coercion are imposed either intentionally or maliciously (e.g., the pressure to conform to social norms). Interestingly, the case of the addict involves not only an internal physiological demand for the substance, but successful quitting also involves an internal psychological commitment. That is, while pressures can be brought to bear on the addict by family and friends, the greatest likelihood of success is associated with individuals deciding that they are ready to change and voluntarily choosing to seek therapy.[43]

Surely one of the most compelling case histories with regard to suicide is that of Kay Jamison, who struggled with manic-depression and tried to end her misery at age twenty-eight—an event that launched her life's work and led to her becoming a professor of psychiatry at Johns Hopkins University School of Medicine.[44] Jamison notes that manic-depression, along with other forms of mental illness including schizophrenia and depression, is a predictor of suicide—particularly when combined with alcoholism.[45] At a physiological level, when serotonin is curtailed or its transmission impeded, studies of humans and other animals have shown an increase in aggressive, violent, and impulsive behaviors.[46] Given that suicidal attempts, such as Jamison's, are often impetuous (even in individuals with well-formulated plans the ultimate timing and decision to act are often rash), it appears that individuals are not acting freely. Jamison describes a lethal cascade of neurophysiology: Start with a genetic predisposition that lowers the threshold to suicide (likely through serotonergic vulnerability), then add a chronic or acute stress (e.g., mental illness or an emotional trauma), and "the likelihood of suicide may be unstoppably high."[47] In short, free will is subjugated to biological coercion.

The coercive power of psychological pain might allow us to understand many acts of quitting. Consider the possibility that one quits to preempt the feeling of failure or the distress of defeat. Quitting can be a tactic to avoid the dismal experience of checkmate, a third atomic bomb, an elbow being dislocated, a marriage's collapse, a pink slip, charges of campaign impropriety, or cirrhosis of the liver. When an endeavor is doomed, persistence merely increases the mental and perhaps physical misery.[48] If failure is inevitable or we have sound reasons for believing this is the case, then quitting empowers us to shift the "when" (not the "if") of an ending. Giving up rather than waiting for failure is both rationally and emotionally defensible when one is being humiliated, such as when one's spouse is cheating with a close friend.[49] By quitting, we retain an element of agency rather than allowing ourselves to be victims. Consider this account of a college student: "The class was populated with semi-professional dancers who swept the floor with me. I realized instantly that if this class were graded on a curve, I would fail. So I quit [and] didn't wait around, powerless, for someone to tell me I'd failed. I saw a chance to cut my losses and switch to a class where I would fare much better. I took control."[50]

As conceptually concise as it would be to understand quitting as an act of preemptive failure that allows the preservation of one's dignity and the reduction of one's suffering, this formulation fails to consider important counter-examples. Quitting can be more distressing than failing, given that the former entails taking action and the latter often happens through inaction—and we generally find it preferable to arrive at the same, unpleasant endpoint passively so that failure or defeat is not our fault.[51]

Let's entertain a few concrete cases in which failing might be psychologically preferable to quitting. For mountaineers, quitting is manifest as the act of turning back and failure is manifest as being rescued. A world-class climber has argued persuasively: "In truth, rescue has gotten easier, and that's good. But quitting, it seems, has gotten harder. Nowadays, rescue is cooler than retreat."[52] In short, there's more dignity, consolation, and social approval with failure.

Next, consider a rather different scenario in medicine. When doctors are attempting to resuscitate a patient, they often want to persist longer than a patient's loved ones allow.[53] For the physicians, quitting is emotionally fraught, but failure in the form of an irretrievably dead patient is evidently (and understandably) easier to accept.

Finally, when it comes to resigning from a job versus being fired, resignation can amount to a painful admission of one's shortcomings, while being fired can be explained away in various ways (e.g., the boss was a fool or the company was ruthless). Even when an employee quits, this act is typically inflected with a certain passivity in which one accepts the inevitable.[54] In this way, what might appear to be taking action (commission) is rendered as a kind of lassitude (omission) insofar as the individual is not acting freely but merely accepting events as they inevitably unfold.

THE COUNTERFACTUAL:
A PRACTICAL TEST OF FREE WILL QUITTING

If only... I'd left him before we had kids and he'd racked up credit card debt; I had quit smoking ten years ago; I hadn't sold my stocks when the market hit bottom; I had decided to pull our troops out of Afghanistan in the first year of my presidency. Regret is the feeling that arises when we ponder what philosophers call a counterfactual: I did X and a bad thing happened (which is factual), but if I hadn't done X (counterfactual), then the bad thing wouldn't have happened (e.g., if I'd had quit after one beer instead of six, I wouldn't have been arrested for driving under the influence). We can only rationally regret acting (or having to failed to act) if we could have done otherwise. Perhaps regret is guilt from which we learn something important.

And so, without a substantial element of free will, it makes no sense to feel regret. I can be sad that my elderly neighbor slipped on the ice and broke her hip, but regret would be sensible only if I could have chosen to take action that would have prevented her accident, such as shoveling her sidewalk instead of opting to watch a movie. Regret is a rationally grounded feeling that can serve to remind us of having made a poor decision.[55] This cognitive benefit might explain why people judge regret to be more beneficial that guilt, shame, or disappointment.[56]

Being humans, however, we are quite capable of having irrational emotions. We can feel elated after reading our horoscope or anxious on Friday the 13th. Along such lines, people who are born with handicaps (conditions about which they had no control) or who are disabled by an accident (an event for which they had no responsibility) may be further afflicted with a sense of shame, obligation—and regret—for being a burden on others.[57] I do not wish to deny their feelings, but I would strongly contend that there is no rational reason for a person with a disability to apologize for inconveniencing others based on a sense of contrition for a condition beyond their control.[58]

Those who advocate quitting as a general solution to our struggles take some implausible positions when it comes to regret. Contrary to the claims of these life coaches, regret is not necessarily irrational.[59] Further, there is no compelling argument for why we should avoid pondering "what if" when this reflection allows us to learn from past actions that were under our control.[60] In addition, some tactics to avoid regret are rather preposterous, such as the notion that "everything happens for a reason [because] the universe tends to have your back."[61] Such a happily vacuous teleology allows the individual to quit anything without second-guessing the decision.

Before we consider a few exemplar cases of regretful quitting, it's worth noting that the psychological literature on regret is a bit incoherent. Given the phenomena of omission bias and risk aversion, one would think that regret would be deepened if we have taken some action that yielded an adverse result.[62] While this is often the case, when people are asked about their greatest regrets, they focus on what they failed to do.[63] Perhaps we feel acute regret when we're actively responsible for some deleterious outcome, but our most abiding regrets arise from having passively missed opportunities.

When it comes to regret over romantic quits, we may feel remorse for having given up on a relationship, such as the fellow who reported "I realized that I didn't give the relationship a fair chance or fight hard enough."[64] Research has found that women more often than men focus on romantic regrets rather than other life domains.[65] And while breakups are more acutely disturbing for women, they are also more likely to emerge emotionally stronger and to completely recover, while men tend to never fully recover but simply stumble on to the next relationship.[66]

As for mountaineering (which might be a metaphor for love), quitting generates regret when a climber believes they freely made a poor decision to quit an expedition. A regrettable quit is one in which climbers are responsible for turning back due to interpersonal friction, poor planning, or some other factors that they could have, but didn't, manage. If a mountaineer subsequently returns and summits, "It doesn't erase the regret for the earlier failure."[67] Once again, pondering the counterfactual is not only rational but valuable when this mental reflection allows us to learn from past actions that were under our control.

Finally, an intense and abiding feeling of regret can arise from a sense of ethical failure. General Harold Johnson, army chief of staff in the Johnson administration, exemplifies how not quitting can be deeply affecting. After he realized that President Johnson was lying to the American people about the Vietnam War, the general told a colleague: "I should have taken off my stars. I should have resigned. It was the worst, the most immoral decision I've ever made."[68]

FREE WILL AND OTHER SPECIES: "HONEY, MAKE THE NEIGHBOR'S DOG QUIT BARKING"

When it comes to non-humans, do animal behaviorists have a model organism with which to study quitting? There are certainly many creatures capable of ending some behavioral sequence at a propitious time.[69] With my training in entomology, the reader might guess that I'd favor an insect example. Sensing (if not knowing or being cognitively aware) when to quit is a matter of life and death for mosquitoes. These insects have stretch receptors in their guts that signal the blood suckers to stop feeding—and if this neural pathway is blocked, the insect imbibes until it bursts.[70] In creatures more like us, bears use environmental cues to end their foraging and begin hibernation.[71] In my animal behavior course, I learned that when a canid, such as a wolf, signals submission by exposing its neck and belly to a dominant animal, the potentially lethal assault is instinctively terminated; the attacking wolf is rendered incapable of killing its opponent.[72] As with most things I learned forty years ago in biology, this is too simple an explanation, although the general phenomenon still holds.[73] Mosquito feeding, bear foraging, and wolf biting are all cases of animals terminating some activity, but these instances are thought by behaviorists to have a very strong neurophysiological compulsion, such that the creatures don't really <u>decide</u> to call it quits.

The flip side of being constitutionally unable to persist in some behavior is the inability to quit. Combine a strong sense of positive phototaxis (attraction to light) with having no evolutionary experience with invisible obstacles and you get a house fly that bangs unrelentingly against the window. Other, more complex animal movements may also be impossible to forgo, such as the migration of creatures ranging from dragonflies and monarch butterflies, to salmon and sea turtles, to arctic terns and sandhill cranes, to baleen whales and wildebeests.

For an animal to genuinely engage in quitting, it must, as with people, have been capable of doing otherwise. That is, the animal acts freely. But do non-humans have free will? The suggestion that task persistence is uniquely human and that most animals do not persevere at any particular endeavor for longer than twenty minutes would seem to be the view taken by scientists who have never spent hours listening to a neighbor's dog bark.[74] Of course, what constitutes a "task" is somewhat arbitrary on the part of the ethologist. A predator pursuing its prey would seem to constitute a single, coherent task. And according to animal behaviorists, both the prey and the predator are said to "choose" among various options that increase the probability of either successful evasion (prey) or capture (predator).[75]

Although my friends who are hunters seem to readily infer that their prey are making conscious decisions, perhaps the most compelling evidence of animals taking free action is found in intra-specific contests that resemble the combat sports of humans. These encounters between animals can be lethal, but they typically terminate when one contestant retreats in what seems to be a voluntary decision (e.g., blackbirds, bluebirds, chimpanzees, and lions fight over territory; baboons, elephant seals, gorillas, kangaroos, and pheasants fight over mates).[76] Particularly when animals engage in aggressive contests for social dominance, behaviorists do not shy away from referring to their subjects as choosing among various tactics.[77]

Returning to insects as potential exemplars of quitting, cricket fights between males conform to the "cumulative assessment model." Individuals persist in fighting until the sum of their opponent's actions reaches some threshold that is dynamically determined by the individual's previous experiences. That is, it takes more resistance by an opponent to cause a cricket to throw in the towel if the individual has a history of successful fights. The neurohormone that modulates cricket quitting is similar to biochemical substances associated with intra-specific battles in mammals, which suggests that "basic mechanisms of aggressive modulation may be conserved in phylogeny."[78] The scientists who conducted this research refer to the insect's "decision to flee"—an expression that suggests free will.

To strain what to some readers is already a thinly stretched argument for free will in other species, there is abundant evidence of severe, self-inflicted injuries and death in many zoo animals and other creatures experiencing acute stress from isolation, overcrowding, or confinement.[79] But whether rats, deer, dogs, lions, and even octopi inflict grievous damage to themselves with suicidal intent is highly debatable. This would require both free will and an understanding of their own mortality. In defending their colony, social insects often give up their lives, and while a few entomologists might contend that they are acting freely, probably no scientist would assert that they are aware of their imminent death.

If at least some animals have free will, as seems to be the case, we might wonder about the evolution of this capacity. It seems plausible that there is a significant survival advantage with regard to making decisions in highly variable conditions for which a fixed behavioral program would be unworkably complex. So, when did this capacity evolve? My inclination is to contend that free will (like quitting) comes in degrees. There is probably no moment in evolutionary history at which free will sprang into existence. I would propose that all organisms with central nervous systems likely have some ability to act freely in at least some contexts, particularly those species that have encountered novel and unpredictable challenges in their evolutionary past.

BEING LARGELY FREE TO MOSTLY QUIT

Perhaps every act of quitting (or for that matter virtually every action we take other than reflexive movements) has an element of coercion. The pressures of a job, expectations of a spouse, constraints of a contract, needs of a child, norms of a society, doctrines of a religion, rules of a contest, demands of an addiction, and judgments of a friend all function to push us toward or away from quitting. Furthermore, free will, to whatever degree we possess this capacity, complicates the form that quitting takes. We can choose actions along a continuum; we need not reduce our options to absolute terms. While we might decide to quit entirely and permanently, which makes for a conceptually simple framework, many quits are partial or temporary. But is it genuinely quitting when we practice giving up some habit, experiment with forgoing some pleasure, try out retiring from work, or sample living without some belief? These are questions for chapter 7.

7

Quasi-Quitting
Must We Give Up Completely?

"Jane dropped out of college this morning," said her roommate.
"Why would you say that?" replied a friend.
"Because she skipped calculus today."
"That's it? Heck, I heard Jane's changing her major from engineering to English."

This conversation illustrates the challenge of the partial or incomplete quit. If Jane skipped ten calculus classes, then it seems she has effectively quit that course. But even if Jane dropped calculus, she might not quit her current major. If she changes to English, however, we could say that she quit engineering. But she wouldn't have quit college, as her roommate claimed.

Some instances of quitting are unambiguous, such as a solider turning traitor, and some are permanent, such as a person dying by suicide. Less dramatic, tipping over one's king in chess is irreversible, and declaring a nation's surrender in wartime is definitive. But one can resign a chess game and remain in a tournament, and a nation's surrender can be conditional. So, it would appear that many kinds of quitting come in degrees of scope and duration (being partial and reversible).

Quitting exemplifies the sorites paradox (*sorities* is Greek for 'heap') proposed by Eubulides of Miletus in the third century BCE. Here's how it works. Take a pile of sand and remove one grain. You still have a pile. Continue removing single grains until just one is left. At what point was there no longer a pile? This problem gives rise to the continuum fallacy, which maintains that a concept is vacuous if we can't specify the precise conditions for inclusion in the notional category. However, some valid concepts are appropriately and necessarily vague, such as piles and quits.

We understandably seek clarity in our thinking, and sharp dichotomies provide this kind of cognitive satisfaction. But Aristotle, a contemporary of Eubulides, admonished in the *Nicomachean Ethics* (book 1, ch. 3 [1.3.4] / 1094b.24ff): "For it is the mark of an educated man to look for precision in each class of things just so far as the nature of the subject admits; it is evidently equally foolish to accept probable reasoning from a mathematician and to demand from a rhetorician scientific proofs." In other words, the nature of quitting does not permit the same sort of conceptual precision as physical density or electric charge.

To explore and, it is hoped, clarify what it is to quit, there are four considerations. Do we quit X when (1) we do less of X, (2) we temporarily stop doing X, (3) we do Y instead of X, and (4) we stop doing X but continue to think about X?

CUTTING BACK VERSUS CUTTING OUT: DOES DOING LESS COUNT AS QUITTING?

Our first form of partial quitting involves doing less but not stopping entirely. A prototypical case of such incomplete quits is the not-entirely-dry alcoholic, as considered in chapter 1. To briefly review, the conventional understanding of quitting an addiction entails that one completely forgoes the substance. Portrayals of alcoholism in popular media lead people to believe that should a single drink—even a few drops of the accursed liquor—pass over the individual's lips, then they are doomed to descend into a full-blown, unconstrained binge and return to Day 0 of abstinence. But such characterizations are fast becoming outdated.

As previously noted, "substance use disorder" (SUD) has come to replace "addiction," which lacks diagnostic criteria and evokes stigmatization.[1] Central to our conceptual concern with regard to partial quitting is the recognition that substance abuse counselors have developed a much more nuanced understanding of what it means to quit—a view that embraces the possibility of reducing, but not eliminating, the substance from a person's life. Indeed, *quitting* is not used as a term in clinical settings; *recovery* and *sobriety* are favored. This is not merely a euphemistic tactic. Counselors maintain that "quitting" connotes an absolute standard and sets up the individual for failure. The all-or-nothing framework combined with the commonness of relapse makes it difficult for a substance abuser to move past a regrettable event and try again, thereby generating a defeatist feedback in which they quit quitting.[2]

For many people with a SUD, the goal is to put an end to the harmful consequences of using a substance in deleterious amounts and frequencies. For some, this requires abstinence, as moderation is not viable (the condition typically portrayed in books and films). But for some alcoholics, for example, the goal might be to quit drinking in amounts that lead to adverse outcomes such as aggressive behavior. In such cases, a "partial quit" is conceptually plausible;[3] the individual might limit themselves to one beer a night (rather than a six-pack), so that there are no longer violent outbursts.

The case of SUD provides an important perspective on the question of whether quitting must be complete and total to warrant this approbation. The person who reduces drinking to the point that they no longer act aggressively toward others has quit becoming a violent individual (at least as a result of alcohol) without completely forgoing drink. In principle and practice, one can quit becoming inebriated while still drinking at a diminished level. What seems crucial to quitting is that *the individual reduces the intensity or frequency of some behavior to the point that there is a significant, qualitative change in the person's character or sense of self*. This change need not necessarily lead to a happier or more fulfilled individual; what makes for a "good quit" is a matter to be considered in section 3. For now, let's see how this altered sense of identity might work in various contexts.

People build their individualities around reliable patterns in life, such as imbibing a substance, performing a job, living with a partner, or practicing a religion. As such, quitting a drug, resigning a position, leaving a spouse, or renouncing one's faith can profoundly alter a person's identity.[4] Recall that Thomas Dumm proposed that terminating employment means giving up "one's life, one's being, one's soul."[5] Although this claim is rather hyperbolic, when quitting undermines an individual's sense of meaning as might be the case with some careers, the costs may be psychologically unacceptable.[6] But transformations of character need not require a complete termination of a self-defining endeavor.

Disengaging from some aspect of one's identity is possible with a diminishment of a particular behavior. Perhaps one decides to end a sexual relationship with another individual but continues a platonic friendship, or gives up on becoming a priest but continues to practice Catholicism, or reduces tobacco consumption from three packs a day to one cigar at Friday night poker games. All of these partial quits might well produce a profound, qualitative change in a person: "I am no longer his lover," "I am no longer pursuing a religious vocation," or "I am no longer dependent on nicotine."

In a classic scientific paper, Philip W. Anderson argued that in the physical sciences "more is different"[7]—that changes in quantity can give rise to changes in quality, a phenomenon noted by Karl Marx and nicely captured in this probably apocryphal exchange in the 1920s:

F. SCOTT FITZGERALD: "The rich are different from us."
ERNEST HEMINGWAY: "Yes, they have more money."

Without getting bogged down in the scientific and philosophical details, complexity theory explicitly recognizes the phenomenon of emergence, in which unexpected and novel properties appear even with gradual changes in control variables.[8] As with incremental additions (e.g., cyanobacteria gradually adding oxygen to the Earth's atmosphere until combustion became possible), partial eliminations can produce significant changes in the properties of complex systems, such as human beings and our societies (e.g., incrementally reducing a person's blood volume by a few milliliters an hour would produce a series of distinctive changes, and a gradual 25% reduction in material consumption would give rise to a dramatic alteration of how we live).[9]

I'm reminded of a psychology professor in whose lab I worked as an undergraduate. Dr. Turney was an animal behaviorist studying concept formation in birds and social dominance in mice. But he also understood humans—or at least children. Dr. Turney's son was extremely reluctant to give up his blanket at an age that would soon make the poor tyke the object of ridicule among his school-bound friends. The psychologist's approach was to begin by cutting the blanket in half, which did nothing to change the object's comforting quality. The next week, the blanket was again reduced by half, and the child continued to snuggle what was left. By the time this halving process had reduced the blanket to a few square inches, it was transformed into something entirely different and had lost the capacity to provide security. At this point, the boy quit his emotional attachment without trauma and discarded the scrap of material. Less was, most assuredly, different.

In physical terms, remove just a few ounces of uranium 235 from a thirty-three-pound pile and you transform the silvery-gray mound from being at critical mass for producing a nuclear detonation to being a relatively benign heap. Analogously, one might quit execrating a spouse's family and transform an explosive relationship into something tranquil while continuing to criticize the spouse's co-workers. Or one might remove a few beliefs about God (e.g., omnipotence, belligerence, or maleness) and dramatically alter the nature of one's faith without becoming an atheist.

There is a movement afoot to consciously produce qualitative change in one's life through a partial quitting of work.[10] Downshifting is the process in which one reduces the time devoted to work and reallocates those hours to more fulfilling endeavors such as family, friends, and self-development. As appealing as this strategy might seem, philosopher Neil Levy contends that these alternative activities provide only "ordinary meaning" while work is the sole source of "superlative meaning."[11]

In this regard, Levy offers a rather idealized conceptualization of work as not just "effortful engagement in difficult practices" but labor of the right kind and structure performed in the pursuit of genuinely worthwhile projects. In his view, typical downshifters are only half right in their semi-quitting insofar as they achieve greater personal fulfillment, but they fall short of promoting goods beyond themselves (which need not entail payment for one's labor). Self-indulgence may provide pleasure for the hedonist, but only work instantiates the human potential in terms of a life well lived. However, perhaps not everyone is seeking such higher-order meaning. Maybe shifting hours from working in the evenings to pursuing avocations or friendships produces a marked transformation into a markedly happier, essentially nicer, and significantly calmer person. If "more is different," then it could well be that <u>less</u> (work) could yield a very different individual.

Ironically, truly commendable downshifting is more like upgrading. An individual partially quits to devote time to endeavors that transcend oneself. In short, a virtuous downshifter quits spending so much time "working for the man" and more time working toward the "real goods" of moral, artistic, scientific, cultural, and other such realms.[12] Or as Robert Frost described "A Lone Striker" in the eponymous poem reflecting on working at a mill:

> The factory was very fine;
> He wished it all the modern speed.
> Yet, after all, 'twas not divine,
> That is to say, 'twas not a church.
> He never would assume that he'd
> Be any institution's need.[13]

To delve further into how incomplete quitting might evoke a significant qualitative change in the individual, imagine these conversations:

> "I quit watching television," said Rob.
>
> "But I saw you at a sports bar with your friends last Saturday," replied Tammy.
>
> "Yes, but the game was just playing in the background. Now, I spend my evenings reading to my kids rather than glued to the tube," answered Rob.

Maybe Rob didn't completely quit watching television such that he closes his eyes when encountering one or avoids places that have televisions. Rather, his claim is that he's dramatically shifted his priorities and reshaped his identity as a father.

> "I quit drinking caffeine," said Kate.
>
> "Didn't I see you at the diner this week with a cup of coffee?" asked Brad.
>
> "You did, but I was just being social. I'm a different person now that I don't feel a need for caffeine," replied Kate.

Kate's approach to caffeine resembles how many vegetarians I've encountered perceive carnivory. They don't buy or prepare meat for themselves or others. But when they are dinner guests, these mostly vegetarians are gracious in accepting what a host has prepared. It seems that they have cultivated a markedly different identity, even without absolutely forgoing meat.

One of the most famous partial quitters was Henry David Thoreau, who mostly left Concord to live in the woods. He didn't completely reject human society. On occasion, Thoreau strolled into town and dined with the Emersons. He wasn't a hermit at Walden Pond. But while there, he was sufficiently alone to develop a radically new sense of himself. Thoreau's exit from Concord was partial, but his resistance to the economic rules, cultural expectations, and unreflective norms of society led to a transformation of his identity—a striking change that those who disparage his incomplete departure cannot deny.[14] Thoreau's experiment lasted just two years, though, and this leads us to the next question about incomplete quitting.

GIVING UP, FOR NOW: DOES STOPPING FOR AWHILE COUNT AS QUITTING?

Having explored the possibility that quitting can be legitimately partial, let's turn to the matter of whether genuine quitting can be temporary. It seems reasonable to disqualify as quitting those instances in which one stops for a brief time with every intention of returning to the endeavor. Trivially, we would not say that a senior citizen has given up driving just because they've parked the car for a few days. More substantively, one of my teaching assistants withdrew from the university for a semester in the face of mounting pressures. This understandable suspension of enrollment didn't amount to dropping out, given the explicit desire to recommence her studies the next academic year. Likewise, an author who suspends writing a novel has not quit if he reallocates his time to caring for a spouse with a medical condition from which she is expected to recover in a few months, after which he intends to return to his literary project.

Competitive endeavors provide a variety of cases that inform an analysis of the temporal constraints on quitting. The team that calls a timeout has not quit the game. Likewise, when poker players fold, they leave the contest for a period of time, but the purpose of this ephemeral resignation is to remain in the game.[15] This is similar to mountaineers who turn back before reaching a summit due to hazardous conditions, thereby terminating the expedition and living to try another day— or not. If the climbers intend to use their experience to mount a subsequent assault on the peak, then it would seem mistaken to say they quit. But if they decide the summit is forever beyond their capabilities, then it is sensible to refer to their turning back as constituting a genuine quit.[16]

As a particularly challenging case, what should we make of athletes who retire only to return, sometimes repeatedly, to their sport?[17] Sugar Ray Leonard retired from boxing five times, fighting during the years

1977–1982 (then announcing his retirement, only to return a year later), 1983–1984 (then suffering his first knockdown in a professional bout and proclaiming retirement, which lasted two years), 1986–1987 (then issuing an unconvincing statement of retirement after beating Marvin Hagler), 1988–1991 (then declaring "tonight was my last fight" after being throttled by a younger opponent—a declaration that held for five-and-a-half years), and finally 1996–1997 (then saying "for sure, my career is definitely over for me in the ring").[18] Perhaps the on-and-off careers of some athletes are models for what's been called the millennial generation's "fluidity,"[19] although in the latter case this could be a euphemism for a lack of commitment to work or other such projects.

The phenomenon of ending and restarting endeavors requires perspicuous analysis. Rather than quitting necessarily being a distinct and permanent state (which is certainly possible, as in dying by suicide or ending resuscitation of a patient), it might often be a process of indeterminate length. As such, quitting is not what philosophers call a "success term" (e.g., "knowledge" is a success term that entails being right about something, while "belief" is not a success term insofar as it does not entail a particular accomplishment). I would contend that this account of temporary quitting is parallel to that of partial quitting in that the subjective state of the individual is crucial. But rather than having to produce some distinct, qualitative change in the individual for there to be a genuine quit in the former case, *a real-if-temporary quit must come with the explicit intention not to resume the endeavor*. If so, Sugar Ray Leonard quit after his lopsided defeat in 1991 but not in 1987 when he said of his retirement "I'll try, I'll give it a shot. But you guys know me."[20] So, let's see how this understanding of temporary quitting works in other contexts.

The analysis of a temporary stoppage being a real quit if the individual intends to sustain the condition is complicated by the ways people end relationships, for example. Many of us have experienced in our personal lives a kind of stuttering quit in the course of what psychologists call *goal disengagement*, in which we relinquish a project that is entwined

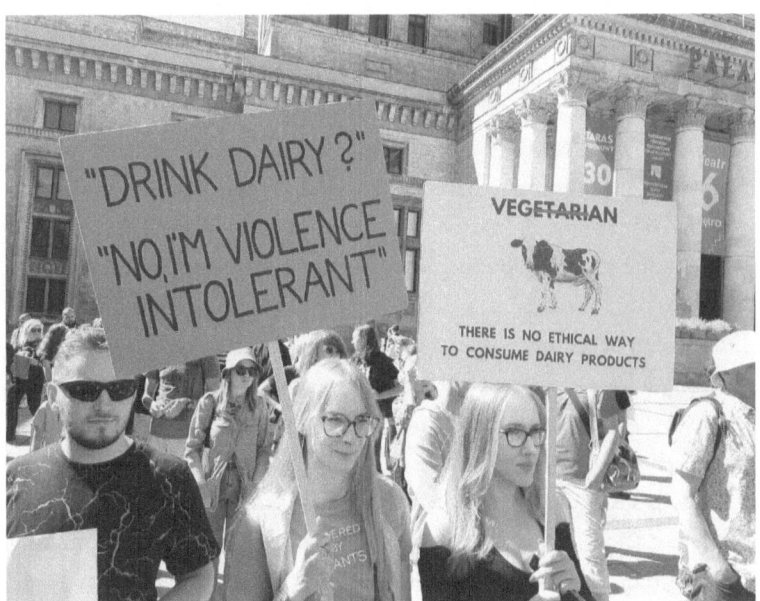

FIGURE 7.1. Vegan protestors at an Animal Liberation March in Warsaw condemning the consumption of milk, which most vegetarians permit. Courtesy of Tomasz Molina via Wikimedia Commons.

with our sense of identity in "a series of interrelated steps not a one-shot thing."[21] The presumptive goal of marriage is to sustain the bond "until death do us part." But marriages often end in the process of emotional detachment—a kind of goal disengagement—which comes in stages and degrees rather than a single definitive moment.[22] Trial separations do not constitute quits when they come with the intention of "working things out" and returning to the marriage rather than extending the separation into a divorce. However, these temporary estrangements often come with occasions that open old wounds and elicit grievances (e.g., when dropping off the kids, going to family events, and sharing assets). No wonder that 80 percent of marital separations (presumptively temporary quits) culminate in divorce (permanent quits, in the vast majority of cases). We might even interpret extramarital affairs as temporary quits that often pave the way to a permanent quit.[23] As for endings of other romantic relationships, these typically involve repeatedly (perhaps impulsively) breaking up and reuniting, along with growing ambivalence. The reality that genuine quitting of relationships can be a protracted, off-again-on-again process warrants extrapolation to other realms.

Quitting as an ongoing process applies to many contexts that involve repeated opportunities to persist—or renege. There is a very weak sense in which one might claim to have quit eating meat after skipping a slice of bacon one morning, but becoming a true vegetarian requires repeated occasions of renunciation. In a similar sense, one isn't genuinely celibate the day after forgoing a single opportunity for sexual intercourse. Likewise, an alcoholic might claim to have quit drinking if they skip their usual six-pack one evening, but sobriety demands an ongoing process of refusal.

Indeed, substance abuse provides a rich array of possibilities with respect to the temporality of quitting. To successfully quit smoking typically requires five to ten attempts, each a temporary or unenduring quit.[24] As for other drugs, some substance abusers quit cold turkey and without treatment, but for others recovery is a never-ending process.[25]

And so, while quitting can be an acute and lasting phenomenon, it can also involve a series of micro-quits in which the individual repeatedly ends and recommences the relevant behavior in the course of fostering the self-discipline that will sustain a permanent termination. We might think of quitting as a dimmer switch. Asking the exact point at which someone has quit is tantamount to demanding to know the precise moment at which the room is dark.

Becoming skilled at anything requires practice. To become virtuous, Aristotle advised making a habit of the virtues (along with the right motives).[26] In short, habit formation requires repetition. While we might think of consciously developing a good habit as a constructive tactic (e.g., flossing or exercising), quitting is often necessary to make room in our lives for more important things. There are no systematic studies of how much time is needed to entrench quitting, which surely varies as a matter of what is being forgone. However, we might reasonably guess that the parameters of quitting a habit are akin to forming a habit (although semantically convoluted, perhaps to quit chewing your nails could be understood as developing the habit of not chewing your nails). Research suggests that the process of establishing a new habit requires a period of about 3 months but ranges from 18 to 254 days.[27] And just as missing an opportunity to perform the desired behavior does not substantially impede habit formation, a series of temporary quits punctuated by occasional failures might well add up to an enduring and successful quit.

This notion of quitting in episodic bouts leads us to consider religious practices in which the faithful temporarily renounce some earthly desire. Mexican migrants to the US have brought with them the practice of *Juramentos*, pledges made to the Virgin of Guadalupe that commit the individual to refrain from drinking for a specified period of time.[28] More familiar, Lent and Ramadan are temporary quits (forty-six and twenty-nine or thirty days, respectively). Ramadan involves fasting from sunrise to sunset, but Muslims are also encouraged to forgo negative behaviors such as gossiping and swearing. For Christians, Lent provides more personalized renunciations, such giving up an individual's favorite food or drink, a bad habit, or some vice. Although people might well return to drinking soda or watching television, Lent can be understood as a "practice quit"—the opportunity to experience life without some material or psychological temptation. Temporary denial could lay the foundation for an ongoing practice, a possibility that substance abuse counselors can use as a culturally sensitive adjunct for treatment of Mexican and other Hispanic clients. In such cases, Lenten and *Juramentos* sacrifices would qualify as genuine quits insofar as they meet the criterion of intending—or at least being open to—a permanent change.

Perhaps we would become much more adept at quitting were there more structured opportunities in the secular world for trying out life without that which seems to impede our flourishing. "Dry January" is such a social experiment in which individuals renounce the consumption of alcohol for the month. Although the origins of this program may extend to the 1940s, the current initiative began with Alcohol Change UK.[29] A 2014 survey by the University of Sussex found that six months after Dry January, nearly three-quarters of participants reported fewer harmful drinking episodes and 4 percent were still not drinking.[30] In the former case, a temporary quit led to a partial quit—the fundamental question being the subjective perceptions and intentions of the individual.

Returning to the example of Thoreau at Walden Pond, he did not intend to make life in the woods a permanent condition. Although he didn't quit society by the temporal standard I've proposed here, Thoreau provided a compelling insight regarding the value of experimental forbearance: "A man is rich in proportion to the number of things he can afford to leave alone"[31]—or, I might suggest, the number of things he can afford to give up.

POTAYTO, POTAHTO: DOES SWITCHING BEHAVIORS COUNT AS QUITTING?

If you heard that someone had decided to move from a church aligned with the Southern Baptist Convention to a congregation affiliated with the Alliance of Baptists, you might not consider this a genuine quit. After all, aren't all Baptists pretty much the same? However, for that individual, the switch from a deeply conservative to a relatively progressive religious community could feel like a monumental change. And perhaps Tony Blair's leaving Anglicanism for Catholicism or the reverse by Pete Buttigieg might strike those outside these traditions as akin to trading Coke for Pepsi, but for these men the change might well have evoked anxiety, joy, or other powerful emotions.[32] Such psychological states are easier to imagine with a Catholic becoming a Scientologist (Katie Holmes), a Unitarian Universalist becoming a Muslim (Dave Chapelle), or a Christian becoming a Hindu (Julia Roberts), in which cases we might judge these conversions as constituting quitting.[33] Acquiring a new belief system entails relinquishing the older framework through cognitive, affective, and organizational disengagement.[34] Such separations can follow various trajectories, including heretically adopting a contrary religion or rejecting all religious beliefs, which would surely qualify as quitting.[35]

The question of whether switching from one behavior to another is a genuine quit is parallel to the earlier question of partial quits. In that previous case, the criterion was that diminishing the intensity or frequency transformed a person's character, making them a meaningfully different individual (not necessarily better or worse). I propose that *opting for version Y of some type of endeavor versus version X constitutes a quit if doing so is personally significant for that individual.* This subjective standard hinders or even precludes an observer from judging whether a change is sufficient to qualify as a quit.[36] While changing religious denominations is archetypal of such events, there are many other realms in which one can merely switch—or truly quit—versions of a practice.

Consider the case of a math major becoming either a statistics major or a dance major. The former switch might not seem to an observer as being a quit, although the latter almost surely would. But for the student, the change from the highly abstract, aesthetically compelling qualities of mathematics that are said to reveal universal truths to the very practical, nuts-and-bolts qualities of statistics that are perceived as tools for grubby experimentalists might well be psychologically and emotionally profound.

Next, think about the example of a smoker who switches to e-cigarettes. They've traded one type of smoking for another, so where's the quit? If the individual then starts wearing a nicotine patch, should we say the person has quit smoking or just swapped forms of nicotine delivery? Perhaps the answer lies in the individual's self-perception. Likewise, what should we make of someone who moves from using heroin to methadone—has the person quit in any meaningful, objective sense?[37] We might ask the more incisive question: How much of a change or substitution within some domain is necessary to constitute a true quit? And the answer ultimately depends on the effect to the individual making the change.

Perhaps for one student, the shift from majoring in math to majoring in statistics is a seamless move, but for another student the change might come with hours of angst over abandoning the rarified dream of discovering a core feature of the universe and accepting the crass reality of crunching data. Likewise, an acquaintance who hears that a couple has given up on trying to have a baby and opted for adoption might suppose that there is little difference insofar as they become parents either way, but the couple might experience great emotional turmoil over how a baby comes into their lives.

With respect to relationships, about three-quarters of people who divorce subsequently remarry, so they have quit on a particular partner but not on the idea of marriage.[38] What's key for our purposes is that one divorcée might see the breakup as merely the pragmatic termination of a bad decision after a hasty wedding in Las Vegas, while another might feel utterly heartbroken despite the impetuous courtship and nuptials. Complacency or despondency—the emotional stakes could differ tremendously.

As for employment, the subjectivity of how it feels to substitute one job for another is crucial to whether doing so constitutes quitting.[39] When I left the science of entomology in the College of Agriculture to become a professor of natural sciences and humanities with a spilt appointment between the departments of philosophy and creative writing in the College of Arts and Sciences, the change was emotionally charged for me. I liked being a scholar, but I had grown tired of the intellectual constraints and the grants-and-publication treadmill in science. And so, I quit a particular discipline, a change many people might understandably have interpreted as no big deal given that I remained in academia.[40] My case illustrates the core principle and challenge with regard to whether switching is a true quit—subjectivity is both crucial to the prospective quitter and largely inaccessible to others.

Changes in political life can also have this sort of externally indeterminable quality. An activist or resister might choose to leave a country, which would seem to be an unambiguous quit, but the individual could maintain political attachments, foster solidarity back home, and engage in continued disruptions through various channels such as social media so the person doesn't feel as if they'd left their homeland.[41] Conversely, an individual could change political parties while remaining in their commu-

FIGURE 7.2. Black Lives Matter protest in Times Square, New York City, two weeks after the murder of George Floyd on May 25, 2020. Courtesy of Anthony Quintano via Wikimedia Commons.

nity but experience great emotional distress.⁴² Likewise, a patriotic soldier who surrenders or retreats might feel devastated by having quit the fight, while another might see these actions as having merely opted for other, less direct tactics in a continuing fight against the enemy.⁴³

Individuals also can exchange a strong for a weak commitment or vice versa.⁴⁴ Returning to religious practices, one could undergo so-called deconversion in rejecting highly demanding beliefs of a tradition, such as abstinence from drinking or dancing, or by abandoning belief in an omnipotent God for a version in which humans collaborate with the divine in the ongoing creation of the world. Conversely, in what's termed an "oppositional exit," a person could adopt a more strident belief system, such as a mainline Presbyterian joining a fundamentalist, hyper-Calvinistic church.

In a parallel case with regard to rejecting weak social views for strong commitments, many activists have disavowed non-racism as insipid and embraced anti-racism.⁴⁵ From the outside, the change might seem merely semantic with no substantive effect on the individual. However, the former version is a defensive claim, while the latter formulation puts an individual on the offensive in terms of contesting racism. We might think of the difference as akin to an atheist quietly and privately refusing to say "under God" when reciting the Pledge of Allegiance versus passionately and publicly opposing public prayer before sporting events and legislative gatherings.

The distinction between partial and substitution quits can become blurred, as with cases of political resignations. As noted earlier, most British cabinet ministers are also members of parliament, so they remain in the House of Commons after resigning a ministerial post.[46] As such, when a minister resigns, this could be understood as either a partial quit (the individual left an appointment in the executive branch but stayed in the political system) or a substitution quit (the individual switched from being a minister to being a member of parliament). For our purposes, ministerial resignations would qualify as genuine quits if the individual perceives this diminishment of power as personally significant.[47]

The intense feelings of an individual switching from one behavior or practice to another, even when such a change may not appear significant to others, leads us to the final consideration of incomplete quitting: Does one ever fully leave behind a meaningful aspect of life, or do such departures resonate indefinitely such that quitting is a never-ending psychological process?

ENDING AND REMEMBERING: MUST WE FORGET IN ORDER TO QUIT?

We might think that once a quit is completed, we're done. While there is a sense in which the end of a war, marriage, or boxing match is absolute in objective, physical terms, all of these endings might well linger indefinitely in psychosocial terms. The Vietnam War is an archetypal case of a quit that persists in memory and continues to shape our national identity and frame our contemporary experiences. This conflict lasted from 1963 to 1973 for the United States (arguably longer, depending on how one dates the entry and exit from the conflict), but the cultural memory of the futile struggle persists.

In 1990, President George H. W. Bush addressed the American people's concerns about military intervention in the Middle East: "Let me assure you, should military action be required, this will not be another Vietnam."[48] As a reporter wrote at the time, "Vietnam hangs in the collective subconscious like a bad dream, a psychic wound that leaves the patient forever neurotic."[49] Bush's assurances notwithstanding, US troops were battling in Iraq for the next twenty years.

I maintain that when it comes to decisions that substantially alter our individual or collective identity, *terminating an action or process that constitutes a complete quit in overt empirical terms may persist indefinitely as an ongoing process in which we perseverate about the decision.* In this regard, consider that many people refer to their divorces for decades after their marriages legally ended. In an ironic sense, their former partner remains their "ex" until death do them part—an exemplification of a never-ending ending. And despite his claims to the contrary, it certainly appears that Roberto Durán never quit replaying the fight against Sugar Ray Leonard (recall the infamous "No Mas" ending), as boxing journalists have argued that Durán continued to take on opponents for another twenty years to prove himself.[50]

What factors are in play when it comes to whether an objective ending persists as a subjective experience? At least three elements contribute to this incompleteness. First, an individual might repeatedly return to a significant time in their life to reflect on the ways an event shaped—and continues to form—their identity. The recurrent memory of quitting informs relevantly similar occasions. The pain of a difficult divorce might be recalled when an individual considers whether to deepen a relationship that seems to be leading toward marriage—either becoming averse to commitment or being drawn into a defiance that the next marriage will fail. The disappointment, even humiliation, of having publicly quit a contest can pervade a person's psyche, whether in a combat sport (e.g., Robert Durán), an Olympic event (e.g., Simone Biles), or a chess match (e.g., the infamous blunder of Jaime Latasa Santos in which he resigned from a winning position).[51] And, of course, "another Vietnam" is America's way of revisiting that terrible war and its ignominious ending to inform the advisability of entering new military conflicts.

Second, the cognitive core of persistence is our capacity to regret past actions, as discussed in chapter 6. To review, agency is essential to experiencing regret—genuine quitting is substantially voluntary, not strongly coerced. Otherwise, we might feel sadness or grief, but there's no reason for self-reproach. Recall that this formulation is a bit too simple, as one might be fired from a job (an ending without choice) but regret having chosen to act in ways that resulted in the dismissal. In this case, one doesn't regret the firing per se.

The human ability to second-guess a decision is intrinsic to our mental architecture. Psychologists have developed "decision justification theory" in which regret can arise from an individual's comparative evaluation of outcomes (e.g., after reviewing the game, the chess player who foolishly resigned could readily see that he was one move away from winning) and from a person blaming themselves for a poor choice (e.g., the spouse who engaged in a frivolous and poorly concealed affair that led to divorce). As such, regretful contemplation of quitting may provide a touchstone for future—and, it is hoped, better—decisions.[52]

Interestingly, the deepest regrets are those arising from what we failed to do, as evidenced by the so-called Zeigarnik effect in which the mind clings to uncompleted tasks.[53] We might perceive ostensibly completed quits as having created uncompleted tasks, such that we continue to perseverate over the counterfactual of a successful marriage, contest, or war. Moreover, whether we choose action or inaction, decision justification theory suggests that greater regret comes with decisions that are inconsistent with our own standards of behavior and intentions. In this context, at least some quitting generates a sense that the foundation of our identity is undergoing reformation.

Third, quitting itself might be a long-term, even unending process, to which one returns on a regular basis (ironically, quitting then becomes a matter of perseverance). When one has quit some behavior that was presumably rewarding earlier in life, an individual could be chronically tempted to quit their quitting and return to the earlier pattern. A smoker might experience cravings for a month and a drinker for years.[54] Vegetarians desire meat for a matter of hours or years based on anecdotal reports, and celibates might need to fend off sexual desires for an entire lifetime.[55] One may need to re-quit daily (or even more frequently) for months or years, depending on what is being abandoned.

As such, even when an individual has objectively stopped some behavior, the quitting may be subjectively ongoing. Some psychologists advise people to give up completely and unreservedly when quitting proves to be necessary, but letting go entirely might be an implausible standard given the nature of our memories, the value of reflection, and the allure of imagining what might have been.[56]

The bottom line is that when we quit something that contributes substantially to our individual or collective identity, we can expect that we will not readily forget the transformation. In some cases, it is not too strong to say we are haunted by the ghost of regret. Despite the linguistic softening in which a baby is "placed" rather than "given up" for adoption,[57] many birth mothers experience remorse for years.[58] But even when we are proud of having quit, and perhaps particularly in such cases, we have reason to revisit the decision. There is much to recommend recollecting the times in which quitting allowed us to flourish so as to summon the wherewithal to repeat such self-affirming acts. With some frequency, individuals come into my Unitarian Universalist congregation—a religious community that is, or at least aspires to be, radically welcoming—having quit another religion that inflicted some sort of trauma (e.g., teaching that the individual's homosexuality was evil or that their mental health struggles were divine punishment). Even so, there is often a sense of loss, particularly when a person's family is deeply rooted in such a faith tradition. There appears to be a complex mixture of regret and relief, but the experience of quitting becomes itself a vital part of the person's identity—and hence, something that understandably, even laudably, persists.

This condition of an enduring consciousness of having quit might be understood as liminality—a term originally used by anthropologists to refer to the middle stage in a rite of passage in which an individual is at a threshold, between the pre-ritual status and what follows.[59] This purgatorial sense of anxious incompleteness has been broadened to include times of cultural change in which there is a feeling of fluid dissolution.[60] With regard to quitting, it might be the case that an individual who continually recalls life before renouncing a religion, leaving a spouse, abandoning a career, giving up during a race, or submitting to an opponent is living in between what once was and what is yet to be.

FINAL THOUGHTS, MORE OR LESS

This analysis of partial and incomplete quitting might be understood as an intriguing philosophical exercise that problematizes what originally seemed like a rather straightforward concept. However, most important concepts in our lives lack sharp boundaries; they are continuous rather than discrete. One might imagine oneself as a liberal, educated, honest, straight, old, white man who never quits, but all of these qualities come in degrees. The complexification of quitting is more than an intellectual puzzle—it is vital to our leading meaningful lives.

If we don't understand what it is to quit (or lie, cheat, or steal), we might well believe that winners never quit or good people never lie, cheat, or steal. Without a conceptual grasp of quitting, we might quit flippantly, as if it had no substantive role in shaping the course of our life or identity—or we might constantly avoid doing so in the belief that quitting is invariably a kind of moral degeneracy that undermines our character. We'll get to the matter of what makes for a "good quit" in due course, but rushing to this normative analysis would be like asking what makes for justifiable deception before having a clear sense of lying (e.g., are partial truths lies; is exaggeration lying; must lying be intentional; are "white lies" really lies). Given the pervasiveness and importance of quitting, it behooves us to understand what constitutes a genuine quit.

Quitting is layered and nuanced, as exemplified by the following scenario. A prisoner tells his attorneys to quit seeking a stay of execution and thereby consciously begins the process of dying. On the way to the gas chamber he is a "dead man walking." His imminent death bears similarities to a hospice patient; both are seemingly resigned to their mortality. But what if he struggles against the restraints at the time of his execution—was his resignation incomplete? From the outside, we can think of his death as sharply delineated by the pronouncement of the attending physician. However, what about the nurse who started the IV for the lethal injection and wonders if doing so was a partial killing, even if she didn't inject the deadly drugs. We can imagine that as a result of his final ending, she unendingly ponders her role, quits the profession, and years later continues to think about what might have been had she stayed in medicine.

Micro-quits, dimmer switch quits, critical mass quits, practice quits, haunting quits, and liminal quitting—the concept is complicated but not intractable. In chapter 8, I'll pull together these diverse threads and develop a working definition of quitting.

8

Defining Quitting
Assembling the Puzzle Pieces

The final task of this section is to pull together the various elements of quitting and formulate a working definition of this varied and complex concept. To this end, I'll begin by briefly exploring the nature of definitions and then elucidate the meaning of quitting in a systematic manner, along with considering the role of imprecision.

QUITTING: BY DEFINITION ...

There are three principal approaches to defining a concept. First, one can provide an exhaustive list of things that qualify. For example, it might be possible to define "ball" by enumerating all such objects: baseball, basketball, bowling ball, football, soccer ball, tennis ball, and so on. For most concepts, such a list would be unwieldy, so one might opt for the second approach.

Next, one could "legislate" what constitutes a ball: a round object that is thrown or struck during a sporting competition. Such a decree is authoritative and leaves no room for arguing whether there are balls other than in sports (e.g., yarn balls, hamster balls, and snowballs).

However, we often seek a more expansive, even if contestable, account, which leads us to the third approach.

Finally, an "essential definition" specifies the necessary and sufficient conditions that must be met. Such a definition should not exclude widely accepted cases (e.g., specifying that a ball is spherical omits footballs; specifying sporting contests excludes ball bearings). Further, an essential definition should not include anomalous cases (e.g., specifying that a ball is a piece of sports equipment with a circular cross-section includes footballs but also includes baseball bats). So, we might propose that a ball is a roundish object typically used in games. Having included the equivocal term *roundish* allows for footballs and rugby balls, but does "typically used in games" open the door to atypical cases such as planets and testicles? We'll later consider more deeply whether vagueness can be necessary, even desirable.

Although definitions provide analytical and rhetorical clarity, we can use words quite effectively without explicit definitions. For example, we understand one another when saying "please give me a glass of water" or "add some water to the fishbowl" without having a precise elucidation of this substance. One might contend that water is H_2O, but what we take to be water includes hydrogen (H^+) and hydroxyl (OH^-) ions, along with isotopes of hydrogen (deuterium and tritium) and oxygen (^{16}O, ^{17}O, and ^{18}O).[1]

We also use many descriptive terms in everyday language without clarifying borderline cases, saying such things as "Bob is bald" (even if he has some wisps of hair on his head), "Leslie is tall" (even if she is only 5'7"), or "raspberries are sweet" (even though they are tart and contain less than 3% sugar).

QUIT: VERB (TRANSITIVE, INTRANSITIVE)

In the pursuit of the clearest possible understanding of what we mean by "quitting," one might suggest that the pains we've taken so far to explore the core and boundaries of the concept could have been avoided by simply turning to a dictionary. So, let's consider what a sampling of these sources has to offer. According to the *Collins*, *MacMillan*, *Merriam-Webster*, and *Oxford English* (OED) dictionaries, quitting includes the acts of abandoning, departing, desisting, leaving, relinquishing, renouncing, resigning, separating, and withdrawing.[2]

The modern uses of "quitting" share a very general sensibility across these dictionaries: stopping or ceasing. The OED includes "to cease to engage in an action or activity," while according to *Collins*, "If you quit an activity or quit doing something, you stop doing it." *MacMillan*'s definition is "to stop doing something." Such definitions encompass any and all endings including trivial stoppages (e.g., we quit driving when stopped at a red light). However, they accord with the colloquial usage found in various self-help books about quitting, such as the contention that "quitting is merely the choice to stop something that you have started."[3]

While there are similarities among the dictionary definitions, there are also important differences that make it difficult to synthesize a coherent understanding of quitting from these standard sources. For example, *Merriam-Webster* emphasizes the act of giving up rather than stopping. And according to *Collins*, "If you quit, or quit your job, you choose to leave it." This element of free will is absent from the other dictionaries and would seem to be a potentially vital consideration.

MacMillan includes a definition that to quit is "to leave a job or school permanently." No other source specifies the duration, let alone the permanence, of a quit. Again, this element is important insofar as it means that should one drop out of college and then re-enroll years later, the individual didn't quit. Indeed, quitting is presumably held in abeyance for the lifetime of the individual, pending the possibility of returning to a job or school (or presumably a relationship or chemical dependency).

Finally, *Merriam-Webster* considers that admitting defeat constitutes quitting, which covers such actions as surrender by a soldier and resignation by a chess player. This possibility is not found in the other dictionaries, although perhaps admitting defeat is a way of giving up per *Merriam-Webster*'s version.

In addition to conceptual inconsistencies, the dictionary definitions have a number of other shortcomings. The primary tactic the dictionaries use is to list a number of near-synonyms in an apparent effort to cover a wide range of meanings. For example, the OED defines quit as "to abandon, relinquish, or renounce" and "to leave, resign, or withdraw from (a job, occupation, institution, etc.)." But these equivalencies don't capture the nuances of terms such as abdicate, concede, forgo, refrain, or surrender. In addition, they do not allude to contemporary euphemisms such as pivot or disengagement.

More problematic are the cases excluded by the dictionary definitions. Recall that defining a ball as spherical left out footballs. As for quitting, none of the dictionaries address the possibility of partial or temporary quits. Rather, they imply complete and enduring cessation. They exclude cases such as going from smoking a pack of cigarettes per day to a single cigar at the monthly poker game (or potentially even a single cigarette on one's deathbed) or giving up drinking for "Dry January" to test whether one might wish to forgo alcohol on a continuing basis. In addition, the standard definitions do not take into account the subjective experience of the individual but indicate that quitting can be observed with the cessation of an overt activity. So, what if one abandons their belief in God or stops resenting a sibling's success without any observable evidence?

Remember, too, that desirable definitions are not overly inclusive. Defining a ball as any round object that engages people's interest would include astronomical objects and bacterial cells. As for quitting, the dictionary definitions include stoppages that wouldn't normally be considered as quits. These sources say nothing about whether ceasing is a normal or expected endpoint of an endeavor. As such, graduating from college would be quitting insofar as one stops attending classes, and retiring at age sixty-five would be quitting insofar as one stops working. In addition, most of the definitions do not consider coercion, so leaving a business partnership at gunpoint would qualify as quitting.

WE WON'T QUIT UNTIL WE HAVE A DEFINITION

Our task is now to construct a definition that includes the many manifestations of quitting (section 1) but excludes events that are far outside the bounds of reason. In so doing, the result will synthesize what we've come to learn about this profoundly important and pervasive aspect of human existence (section 2).

Let's begin with a simple formulation: *Quitting is the task of terminating one's commitment to a state or process.*

For something to constitute being a task, the one who quits must engage in some kind of action. Now, there is debate as to whether thinking is a mental action, with some arguing that "thinking" is a verb and hence grammatically an action, that thought is inseparably entangled with action, and that if thinking is merely entertaining a proposition, then it's not an action.[4] Without getting too far into the philosophical weeds, let's take it that insofar as quitting involves making a decision or changing one's mind and not simply pondering possibilities, it is an action regardless of whether it generates an overt, bodily event.

Another valuable aspect of defining quitting as a task is that this allows quitting to be a continuing process (e.g., the alcoholic who is tempted every day but refuses to drink) as well as a temporally discrete event (e.g., a soldier surrendering to the enemy). The inclusion of both states and processes in the definition allows the termination of addictions and marriages, which might be characterized as states, as well as the cessation of processes such as wars, careers, dietary practices, and chess matches. Indeed, it's not necessary to decide if something is a state or a process (e.g., whether being a Catholic constitutes a belief state or a set of practices such as attending Mass, confessing sins, and taking communion).

There is, however, a significant shortcoming with this definition that was also attributed to standard dictionary definitions. That is, my simple definition is overly inclusive in that reaching the normal or expected endpoint of an endeavor would qualify as having quit. Graduating and retiring would be quitting, as would an author ceasing to write a novel upon submitting the manuscript to the publisher or a boxer stopping a fight after fifteen rounds (although they may continue their commitment to the practice of writing and boxing, respectively). We wouldn't want to say that a widow engaged in quitting because she terminated her commitment to a marriage upon the death of her spouse. One might even argue that all life processes have expected or typical endings.

And so, let's refine the definition: Quitting is the task of terminating one's commitment to a *typically ongoing* state or process.

With this further specification, we can exclude those endings such as graduation and retirement after the normal duration of education and work. However, this provision allows us to say that the individual who leaves employment and lives in a beach shack at age forty has quit the workforce. Likewise, the student who leaves college to live with his uncle in the aforementioned shack after a year of study can be said to have quit higher education.

However, there may still be edge cases. First, consider a person who falls asleep at the end of the day. Typically, we stay awake for about sixteen hours, so we wouldn't say that individual has quit trying to stay awake if they went to bed at midnight. But what if they give in to sleep at 7:00 p.m.? Perhaps it's typical for that individual. So, it might be necessary to individualize, at least to some extent, what is expected. Next, consider the person who stops dating someone after three or four meetings. What is a typical duration of a potentially romantic engagement? Refusing a second date wouldn't seem to be quitting given that there isn't really a commitment, but ending the association after the tenth date would seem to be quitting, particularly if the individuals have agreed to an exclusive relationship and neither normally breaks up after so many dates.

Setting aside the necessary imprecision in the definition (i.e., we wouldn't want to try to specify the exact duration that typifies every human state or process for each individual), another problem arises. At this point, we would take it to be quitting if the early sleeper had been unable to stay awake after a grueling day at work or the romancer had been told to "break up or die" by a jilted lover who discovered the budding relationship.

In light of this concern, the definition must be further amended: Quitting is the task of *voluntarily* terminating one's commitment to a typically ongoing state or process.

This additional word is essential to exclude terminations that are either unintentional (e.g., the worker who is unable to stave off sleep) or, more crucial, coerced (e.g., the romantic partner who ends a relationship upon threat of death). Of course, "voluntarily" entails a significant but not complete freedom of action. As explored in chapter 6, the element of free will is a conceptually sticky matter, such that some would contend that all actions involve an element of social, economic, political, or biological pressure, while others would maintain that we are always free to act in accord with our will—and to face the consequences of doing so. Notwithstanding this contention, given most people's psychological capacities, the definition of quitting excludes instances of extreme coercion.

As with the last refinement, one can readily imagine edge cases with respect to acting freely. Suppose the hypothetical jilted lover simply said "you had better break up or I'll bash you," or "if you don't break up, I'll key your car," or "if you don't break up, I'll say mean things about you on social media," or "if you don't break up, I'll cry." The first threat seems to undermine a fully voluntary termination of the relationship depending on your skills in self-defense, while the last threat would appear to leave voluntarism largely intact depending on your degree of empathy. Again, the additional element in the definition could be relativized to individual cases, but listing all reasonably conceivable instances would be implausible (e.g., one acts voluntarily in terminating a romantic relationship if the individual is threatened with assault but outweighs the assailant by at least twenty-five pounds and has substantially greater skills and experience in physical altercations).

And so, let's turn our attention to another problem with the evolving definition. What about trivial cases such the individual who abandons reading a tedious book or turns off a boring movie? Our present definition would include as quitting such easy decisions, as when someone decides to no longer shave or stops wearing socks with sandals.

At this point, our definition needs to be further refined to exclude trifling possibilities: Quitting is the task of voluntarily terminating one's commitment to a typically ongoing state or process *of considerable meaning to the individual.*

The added constraint of "considerable meaning" excludes stopping insignificant activities and makes evident that quitting entails substantial difficulty and resistance to change.[5] Furthermore, "meaning" might be cashed out in terms of a person's sense of identity, integrity, or life goals (e.g., one might derive meaning from a particular career or religion), but it could also be understood as a state or process of bodily or neurophysiological significance (e.g., an addiction or anxiety). The provision of "to the individual" relativizes quitting to each agent. And so, the same termination of an endeavor for one person might meet the conditions of quitting because that person derived significant meaning from the venture (e.g., the person's selfhood was vested in being Catholic) while not being a genuine quit for another person who took the same venture to be of nominal importance (e.g., the person's Catholicism was merely an unreflective, familial habit).

The definition is getting a bit long, but there is another important matter with regard to providing a plausible description of this behavior. As presently stated, one might infer that quitting is, or could be, a coldly analytical task like computing the costs and benefits of alternative actions using a spreadsheet. A person encountering the definition and knowing the cultural value of rationality could readily imagine quitting to be a dispassionate calculation of expected value after which an objective decision is made.

Conversely, there is nothing to suggest that quitting might just as well be an emotionally driven task, perhaps fueled entirely by rage or misery. This behavior could well be an exemplar of unreflective spontaneity—a kind of psychic reflex that circumvents cognition. And given our propensity for irrationality, it would not be difficult to imagine that some people quit almost anything with no more thought than they give to cringing in fear or striking in anger.

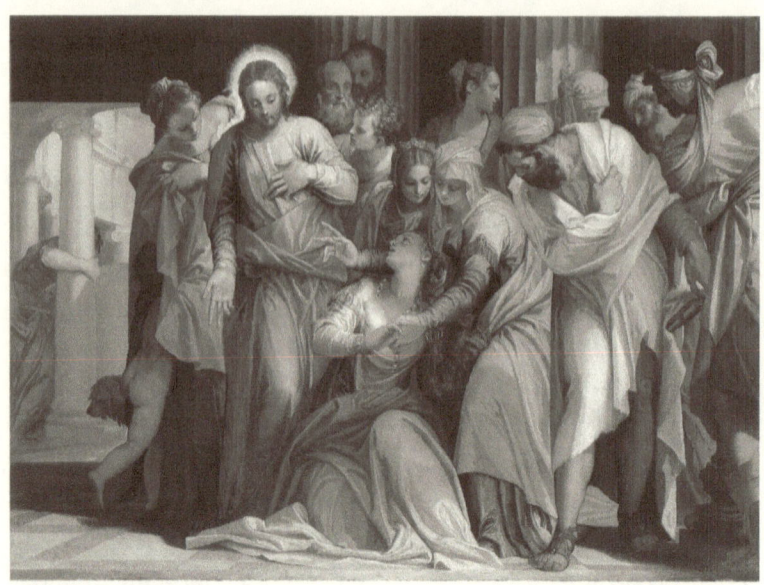

FIGURE 8.1. *The Conversion of Mary Magdalene* (from a life of sexual sin) by Paolo Veronese, circa 1549. Courtesy of the National Gallery in London via Wikimedia Commons.

However, since we are psychologically complicated beings, it's important to consider that quitting has elements of both thought and feeling.

───

To make clear the nature of quitting, further elucidation is needed: Quitting is the task of *integrating rational and emotional considerations* in voluntarily terminating one's commitment to a typically ongoing state or process of considerable meaning to the individual.

By adding the provisions of rationality and emotionality, the definition is descriptively accurate with regard to the human condition (as explored in chapter 5). And with the further condition of integration, quitting becomes an act that entails both of these aspects of our lives, without specifying either that their synthesis is tilted to one or the other realm or that the synthesis is well-balanced—only that elements of thought and feeling are present and somehow blended for better or worse. There is no recipe or formula for how one combines these fundamental aspects of life in the course of quitting. Rather, the definition recognizes that people do not end meaningful ventures without some emotional element or do so without some critical thought.

We're almost there, but there is a final pair of related questions that a definition of quitting must address: How long must the termination last, and how complete must it be? As it stands, one might believe that a person has quit eating meat if they proclaim themselves to be vegetarian one night and forgo bacon for breakfast the next morning. Conversely, one might equally well assume that a person has not quit gambling if they desist for fifty years and then buy a single lottery ticket on a lark. Likewise, one could contend that a person has quit habitually cursing if they avoid all expletives that are prohibited by the Federal Communications Commission, while others might argue that a person hasn't given up cursing if they continue to utter "goldarn" or "geez."

—

The final definition now takes the complete and exhaustive form intended to include diverse instances and exclude dubious cases: Quitting is the task of integrating rational and emotional considerations in voluntarily terminating one's commitment to a typically ongoing state or process of considerable meaning to the individual *for a time or degree sufficient to produce a marked subjective change.*

The added conditions avoid the intractable problem of objectively specifying the duration and completeness of a termination that constitutes quitting. As investigated in chapter 7, perhaps the only (or at least the best) approach to deciding if an act constitutes a genuine quit is to relativize the effect to the individual in subjective terms. The necessary duration, therefore, is that length of time needed to produce a distinct shift in the agent's sense of self. One individual forgoing sex for a month might substantially alter the person's identity (perhaps they never went more than a week without intercourse), while another individual's new commitment to celibacy might not produce any marked change after a month (maybe they often went many weeks without intercourse). Likewise, the (in)completeness of renouncing a state or process is relativized to its effects on reshaping the individual, such that reducing the time spent on social media from six hours a day to one hour might dramatically transform one individual's perspective on the world, while it might only slightly perturb another individual without producing any significant change.

As now formulated, the definition has a few limitations. The primary concern of this project has been to understand quitting in terms of the individual. Hence, there are three potential objections.

First, the context of action and the focus of change are not concerned with people other than the agent. It is conceivable that a rather easily dismissed termination of commitment with little effect on a person might not qualify as a genuine quit, but the impact to others could be substantial.

For example, imagine that a person feels only a weak devotion to his spouse and children, the marriage having merely fulfilled social expectations and the kids difficult for him to find lovable given his own childhood and psychological status. In contrast, his wife is deeply devoted to marriage and family in light of her religious beliefs. And so, he announces that he's leaving the family and heads out the door, never to be seen again. From his perspective, he hasn't quit because he was never really committed, and leaving didn't result in any substantial change in his self-image. From his wife's perspective, his departure was spiritually and emotionally devastating and utterly changed her identity as a dutiful wife.

So, one might consider the definition deficient in that it fails to explicitly take into account the effects on others. However, this is not a purely solipsistic framework. The well-being of others is part of one's own meaning. Relationships are of considerable importance to emotionally healthy individuals, and ending various commitments (e.g., quitting a career, substance, or religion) will often affect family and friends who are vital to an individual's core identity. That said, to include the perceptions of others that are not woven into one's sense of self is highly problematic, as this would make quitting a function of how anyone, in any association with the agent at any time, perceived the action.

A second concern with the individualization of the definition is that it seems to exclude group quits and collective actions. This could be solved by striking references to the individual with language such as: Quitting is the task of integrating rational and emotional considerations in voluntarily terminating commitment to a typically ongoing state or process of considerable meaning for a time or degree sufficient to produce a marked subjective change. However, allowing the possibility of communal agency and subjectivity creates some rather sticky problems. What does it mean for an entire group to act voluntarily, and is this abrogated if one of the members was coerced to agree with the others? Does a group have the sort of emergent agency that gives rise to commitments and meanings other than those felt by its members? Can groups have a shared subjectivity, or is this merely the sum of individual feelings and impressions? For example, can a corporation, town, or society quit sexism if there is still one misogynistic person in the group? Can a nation quit slavery if some citizens continue to remember and be shaped by this past condition? Ultimately, a definition that allows for collective quits creates an avalanche of metaphysical issues that are beyond the scope of this book but about which there is good reason to have serious philosophical reservations.

Third, one could object to the individualization of quitting on the basis that this perspective is culturally biased insofar as Western societies exalt the individual over the group. However, a reply to this objection would be that the definition allows for cultural differences in terms of what commitments warrant "considerable meaning," and all humans are capable of experiencing a "marked subjective change." We can imagine a culture in which a young adult leaving their parents' home would be monumentally impactful and constitute an unambiguous quit, while doing so in another cultural context would be considered a completely expected and typical departure without their having any sense of quitting a familial relationship.

WITTS AND QUITS: THE NECESSITY OF VAGUENESS

Perhaps the greatest concern with my synthetic definition of quitting is the entirely fair objection that many of the terms are imprecise. Just what is meant by "typical," "considerable," and "marked"? These are vague notions in that there is no bright line separating what is typical from what is atypical, considerable from inconsiderable, or marked from subtle. This seems a bit like defining a rhinoceros as a rather big, generally gray, nearly hairless, mostly solitary animal. Such would be an unsatisfactory definition of a rhino, as these creatures have some sharply distinguishing characteristics (e.g., having one horn and a prehensile upper lip), as well as the proffered characteristics having underlying continua (e.g., size and solitariness). Quitting, however, is fundamentally a continuous concept with features that come as matters of degree.

Our inability to specify necessary and sufficient conditions for a concept may actually be a general feature of language. Austrian philosopher Ludwig Wittgenstein famously argued that the plurality of meanings we find in language is comparable to the varied manifestations of phenomena.[6] In *Philosophical Investigations*, Wittgenstein considers the multifarious instances of what we collectively call "games," such as card games, board games, ball games, and party games. As we move in no particular order from poker to chess to cricket to tag to charades to musical chairs, certain similarities crop up (e.g., poker and chess require cognitive prowess; poker and cricket involve elements of deception; cricket and tag entail foot speed) while others disappear (charades can have any number of players while cricket cannot; tag is a children's competition while poker is played by adults; musical chairs has simple rules but chess does not). In §66 of *Philosophical Investigations*, Wittgenstein describes the result of our comparing games as "a complicated network of similarities overlapping and criss-crossing."

The tangle of similarities we find among divorce, resignation, submission, conversion, surrender, and suicide with regard to quitting is what Wittgenstein called a "family resemblance" (§67)—a term used earlier by Friedrich Wilhelm Joseph von Schelling and Arthur Schopenhauer. Members of a family might share hair texture, eye color, nose length, body height, and emotional temperament, but a particular individual might lack any of these features and still resemble their relatives in other ways.

FIGURE 8.2. Portrait of Nicholas II of Russia and his family, exemplifying the physical characteristics of the Romanov lineage. Courtesy of Boasson and Eggler via Wikimedia Commons.

Based on Wittgenstein's elucidation of family resemblances (§§66–9), we can construct a model that is a bit more explicit than his verbiage. Imagine having four items (1–4), each with three features (among possibilities A–F). And so, item 1 has features A,B,C; 2 has B,C,D; 3 has C,D,E; and 4 has D,E,F. Each item in the series shares two features with the next item, but by the time we get to the fourth item, it has nothing in common with the first. Clearly, there is no necessary or sufficient feature for this collection. To make the example more vivid, we have soccer ball (round, hollow, kicked), basketball (round, hollow, thrown), baseball (round, thrown, leather), football (oblong, thrown, leather) such that the soccer ball and football have nothing in common based on these chosen features. And so it would go with Richard Nixon's resignation,

Henry VIII's annulment, Eddie Slovik's desertion, and Robin Williams's suicide. All of these quits have overlapping features of resemblance. Finding the almost necessary and generally sufficient conditions for a definition requires features that are vague but not vacuous, such that quitting is a family of related instances.

A final consequence of this conceptual framework is that there are prototypical and marginal cases. A beach ball is an exemplary case of being a ball, while a glass eye is an edge case. Likewise, turning in one's letter of resignation is a prototypical case of quitting, while "quiet quitting" is an iffy case. While we can sensibly speak of states and processes without sharp delineations (e.g., baldness), there will be inevitable, but not conceptually fatal, disagreement about whether various cases are valid examples (e.g., do "quiet quitting," "cyberloafing," and "bare minimum Monday" constitute quitting).[7]

FROM DESCRIPTION TO PRESCRIPTION: THE REALLY HARD TASK

Having developed a necessarily imprecise but reasonably substantive definition of quitting, it would seem we have arrived at a set of parameters that have a complexity commensurate with that of the concept we seek to understand. Although we may be vexed by vagueness and frustrated that some cases are clearer than others, we should recall Aristotle's admonition "to look for precision in each class of things just so far as the nature of the subject admits."

And so, it's time to quit quibbling and turn our attention to an endeavor that is as important and difficult as figuring out what constitutes quitting. That task is the work of resolving, to the extent possible, what makes a <u>good</u> quit. There is nothing in our definition that suggests whether a particular quit is wise or foolish, courageous or cowardly, just or unfair, temperate or extreme. Actions are value-neutral—there can be normatively good and bad protesting, touching, speaking, laughing, praying, and teaching.

In philosophical terms, we now turn from the metaphysics of quitting (what it is) to the ethics of quitting (what makes is justified).

SECTION 3
Practical Guidance

Quitting is like sex. Both are taboo subjects, society has generated a profusion of euphemisms, everyone does them in one way or another, they are important elements of life, and we want to be good at them. Plenty of books written by variously qualified people provide advice—if not rigorous philosophical perspectives—about quitting and persevering, and even more sources offer hints, tips, and recommendations regarding physical intimacy.

Rather than rush into a how-to exposition, it would seem that a sex therapist would want to first consider all of the manifestations of sensual pleasure that are legion in the human species. For the therapist, various published sources provide a taxonomy of forms, functions, positions, and partners. And for the reader interested in the varied versions of quitting, I offer section 1 of this book.

Next, the counselor (or client or reader) might benefit from a conceptual analysis to understand just what is meant when someone says they want to improve their performance. What are the physiological, psychological, sociological, and philosophical foundations of bona fide sex—or quitting. As in section 2 of this book with regard to quitting, one might gain valuable insight from crafting a definition of sex that is neither too inclusive (e.g., every pleasant, tactile experience) nor exclusive (e.g., only intromission).

This leads me to section 3, the payoff in which I try to figure out what constitutes <u>good</u> quitting. As with sex, there are various theories to consider. Perhaps good quitting and good sex are all about the results, regardless of the intentions. Or maybe these practices are about acting in accord with one's duties or another's rights, such that having the best of intentions is all that matters regardless of whether there is a satisfying outcome.

As we'll see, there's a third option in which good quitting (and perhaps sex) is really a matter of cultivating one's character—of being the kind of person we aspire to be. Such an individual develops a kind of practical wisdom that is both intellectual and experiential. Doing "it" right (whether quitting, copulating, writing, reading, parenting, exercising, or most anything of importance) means doing something in the right amount, for the right reasons, at the right time, in the right way. This is what emerges when we instantiate the virtues to realize the human potential. Beyond this, there are no formulas or rules that will assure we are good quitters or lovers.

However, even when we have considered a situation and made an entirely sound decision to quit (or to enact sensuality in some manner), there is one final matter. We might *know that* this is the thing to do but not *know how* to operationalize our ambition. So, the final consideration in this section develops some heuristics for quitting well, with the understanding that "book learning" is useful, but practice makes perfect.

9

Quality Quitting
Cultivating Character

We now turn to the challenge of what constitutes a *good* quit. To begin, we need to know the object of the verb.[1] All things being equal, to quit stealing or smoking is good, and to quit caring for one's children or being faithful to one's spouse is bad. As such, quitting is morally ambiguous, and its goodness or badness depends critically on the context.

The philosophical realm of normativity is concerned with what we ought to do in a given situation. The richest source of inquiry in this regard comes from the field of applied ethics. What constitutes justifiable quitting might extend beyond moral analysis and involve aesthetic and cultural values (e.g., sending a beautifully crafted poem to inform a minister that one is leaving a religious community or conducting a ritual suicide to sustain honor in one's society), but moral frameworks have the advantage of being both highly developed and relevant to understanding if quitting is the right thing to do and being potentially (or at least ideally) universalizable.

Some people would say that a good quit (or other action) is whatever an individual decides it to be. Such relativism with regard to quitting works no better than it does in terms of ethics. Some quits are better than others, no matter what the individual thinks. To quit a job by spray-painting obscenities on the CEO's car is a bad way to resign. To torture one's cheating partner on a medieval rack is a bad way to break up.

And so, let's consider the "Big Three" ethical systems as a starting point: consequentialism, deontology, and virtue.

COMMON SENSE:
A GOOD QUIT PRODUCES GOOD RESULTS

Many people would contend that an action is right if it produces a desirable outcome. This basis for normative judgment is called, sensibly enough, consequentialism. So, if lying to a malevolent authority saves dozens of innocent lives, then surely one ought to be deceptive. And if quitting a boxing match keeps one from suffering a traumatic brain injury, then by all means quit. Anecdotes abound regarding quits in the business sector that generated good outcomes for individuals who moved on to lucrative careers.[2]

Consequentialism is taken one step further by utilitarianism. According to this ethical framework, an action is right if it generates the greatest good for the greatest number. The surrender of the Japanese in World War II saved millions of lives, offsetting a loss of cultural pride and national identity. Conversely, and at a less dramatic scale, it has been argued that government employees are not obligated to quit and face unemployment when their agency is pursuing harmful policies if the worker doesn't have the power to alter the course of events by resigning and "going public" with their concerns.[3]

As intuitively appealing as utilitarianism might be, this normative basis for quitting has some major problems. The first difficulty comes with understanding the nature of the good. What is it that we seek to maximize through our actions, including quitting?

Classical utilitarians such as late eighteenth-century philosopher Jeremy Bentham maintained that we ought to maximize human happiness, which can be understood as bodily pleasure (positive utility) or the absence of pain (negative utility). Through a kind of hedonic calculus,

FIGURE 9.1. John Stuart Mill, famed British philosopher who held that we ought to produce the greatest aggregate happiness. Courtesy of the London School of Economics Library via Wikimedia Commons.

we can determine whether to quit. The martial artist whose elbow is about to be dislocated by an opponent need only figure how much pain will likely ensue versus the probability of escaping from the arm bar, turning the tables, winning the prize money, and enjoying the pleasures of decadent living. An alternative classical formulation of the good was advocated by John Stuart Mill. He argued for so-called higher pleasures, such as freedom, friendship, and beauty—famously contending that it was better to be a dissatisfied human than a satisfied pig. He would have us quit watching mixed martial arts matches on television and start reading Shakespeare.

Other formulations of the good have since been developed. Preference utilitarianism maintains that whatever an individual desires is good (e.g., if you prefer to quit eating meat, then that is good for you, but if I prefer to quit eating grains while consuming lots of meat, then that is good for me). A conceptual cousin of preference utilitarianism is ideal utilitarianism in which the good is whatever makes life worth living—a standard for quitting that presumably excludes only suicide. These approaches echo the shortcomings and open-endedness of expected value, which "can be measured in health, well-being, happiness, time, self-fulfillment, satisfaction in relationships, or anything else that affects you."[4] With this version of consequentialism, it seems that a vacuous relativism, even solipsism, is just around the corner.

No matter which formulation of the good one chooses, we encounter the problem of apples and oranges. Incommensurability was considered in the context of cost-benefit analysis, an approach that aligns with utilitarianism. The "greatest good" suggests a quantifiable standard of measurement. Suppose we choose something as simple as pleasure and attempt to employ Bentham's hedonic calculus. He believed it was theoretically possible to add up the multifactorial elements of pleasure and pain. Maybe this works in theory, but how does the highly paid but bored employee determine whether the upsides of wealth (good food, drink, entertainment, and other luxuries) offset the drudgery of the job? And this presumes that only the worker's pleasure matters and not that of others who might be affected by a decision to quit.

Another problem with consequentialism is the inherent difficulty of temporal uncertainty. To determine if a quit was justified, one must look backward in time; to assess whether a pending quit will be sound, one must project forward in time.

As for retrospection, we encountered the challenge that was presented with respect to counterfactual reasoning. We know what transpired following a quit, but we can't know what would have occurred had we persevered. If a student changed from being an engineering major to a dance major, they know if they feel happy and enchant audiences (hence, a good quit by utilitarian standards), but what if they had stayed in engineering (maybe the student would've graduated, discovered a design flaw in a bridge, warned the builders, and saved dozens of lives) or decided to major in physics, political science, or poetry (remember that utilitarianism requires not just more good but the greatest good)? Those who criticize political leaders who chose not to resign in protest over the Vietnam War and the Iraq War speculate that had they done so, thousands of lives would have been saved.[5] But here's an honest appraisal by renowned utilitarian ethicist Peter Singer of Colin Powell's decision to remain as secretary of state: "Powell could have had a very significant impact if he had resigned and said he couldn't support this war. Maybe the nation would not have gone into the war; I don't know."[6] Exactly. Nobody knows whether the greatest good for the greatest number was achieved.

This leads to a related problem: rationalization. Consider the advice given by an advocate of quitting who guides the reader through a convoluted justification for resigning from a job:

> Is it fair to your company for you to stay when you're performing at less than your best [an implausibly high standard]? . . . By having someone in a position where he or she doesn't fully want to be [few people are absolutely devoted to their work], the company is missing out on having another employee who may dedicate much more effort to the job [or perhaps the new hire is even less committed] . . . Therefore if quitting your job will make you a more pleasant member of society, then perhaps it's immoral *not* to quit [the implication being that amiability is a vital social good].[7]

Studies have shown that a decade after divorce, three-quarters of women say their life is better than it was earlier, but might this simply be post hoc rationalization given that they can't know what the quality of their lives would have been had they persevered?[8] Of course, it's not as if we are completely unable to make reasonable inferences about what was likely to have happened (e.g., staying with an abusive spouse is almost surely going to lead to further suffering), but the certainty that we ascribe to alternative outcomes is often low and infused with a desire to justify our decision. This leads us to the temporal flipside of the consequentialist problem.

Prospective results are what the advocates of expected value use to assess the advisability of quitting. This approach is not without justification insofar as the short-term consequences of an action are often reasonably predictable, based on relevantly similar cases. Other people have quit jobs, relationships, battles, and religions, and it behooves us to learn from their experiences.[9] But here's the rub: Our lives are ultimately unique, with situationally incomparable features.

The problem is a bit like the doctor who advises that you quit smoking based on studies showing that this behavior dramatically reduces life expectancy for the average individual. This is great advice unless you're George Burns, who smoked 300,000 cigars in his 100 years of life.[10] Conversely, the student who appeals to their academic adviser that dropping out is a viable strategy because Bill Gates and Mark Zuckerberg quit Harvard and became fabulously wealthy might be told "yes, but you're no Bill Gates" (the flaw of appealing to exceptional cases is vividly illustrated here, as the stories of Zuckerberg and Gates are also used as evidence to support the value of perseverance.)[11] Averages don't assure consequences, but cherry-picked anecdotes are an even worse approach to predicting the results of a decision.[12]

While we can't know everything about the consequences of quitting, we can know something and predict, to some degree, the likely results of our decision.[13] One might well argue that insofar as people may be harmed by our quitting, we are ethically obligated to make reasonable, temporal inferences.[14] This seems plausible, but we must also recognize that the reliability of our predictions declines rapidly with time. I was a happier fourteen-year-old after quitting piano lessons, but am I a happier sixty-five-year-old for having given up? As I periodically struggle to recover those musical skills and derive pleasure from my feeble achievements, I have to seriously doubt whether my long-term happiness was maximized by not becoming far more proficient at the keyboard.

One solution to the retrospective and prospective problems of consequentialism is to double down on the temporal perspective. Some would have us focus exclusively on the future, always looking forward to making the best of our decision to quit.[15] All that matters is what we do with the opportunity created by our having abandoned some venture. As a friend told me, "We make a surrender or resignation good by what we do with the freedom that comes with leaving the struggle behind." This approach captures the first half of Søren Kierkegaard's famous admonition: Life must be lived forward. However, such a purely future-oriented perspective fails to take into account the second half of Kierkegaard's salient observation: Life must be understood backward.[16] We can only get better at quitting if we recall and learn from our experiences.

The final problem for a consequentialist analysis of quitting is parallel to the problem of moral luck in which some (un)desirable result comes from an action that would otherwise appear to be ethically (in)defensible. Imagine that a rich mountaineer pays their way onto a climbing team despite being ill-prepared for the venture. This individual is soon frightened by the journey before any real risk to competent climbers develops. The coward insists on turning back; when the team refuses, the individual cuts their climbing ropes and forces them to quit the expedition. As they begin their descent, an avalanche sweeps through the area where they would have been had they continued. For the consequentialist, this would be a good quit because it resulted in saving everyone from harm.

In contrast, imagine that a chronically abused worker waits until the company's work schedule can be adapted to accommodate one fewer employee and calmly informs their cruel supervisor of a decision to leave the company. The boss is outraged, sets fire to the workers' lounge to show them the price of disloyalty, and the flames kill a dozen people. For the consequentialist, this would be a bad quit given the results.

The consequentialist might try to save the theory through what's called "rule utilitarianism," which is a way to avoid the problem of moral (un)luck. This approach involves developing general principles such as "don't quit a job via a letter to the editor" or "don't quit a relationship through a text." But sometimes a public declaration of one's resignation exposes unjust labor practices that might only be changed with social pressure, and sometimes a person could be at dire risk if they break up with a partner in person. General rules are generally useful, but the devil (or angel) is in the details of each situation.

DO YOUR DUTY: A GOOD QUIT REQUIRES THE RIGHT REASON

Henry David Thoreau left Concord's cultivated society to live at Walden Pond. For him, the exit was what mattered, not any political consequences.[17] When Thoreau wrote "it is not a man's duty to devote himself to the eradication of any, even the most enormous wrong . . . but it is his duty, at least, to wash his hands of it,"[18] he captured the essence of deontology—acting in accord with duty, whatever consequences ensue.

Perhaps we psychosocially favor outcomes as a measure of goodness because we can observe the results of another person's actions (e.g., a friend left their dysfunctional marriage and was much happier and healthier). Our intentions are private—and we know people can lie about their reasons (e.g., that friend says they quit because their spouse was abusive, but the actual motivation was they were afraid of being caught in their own infidelity).[19] For the deontologist, quitting is the right thing to do not because it yields particular results but because it is done in accord with duty. By using this framework, we can avoid the multifarious problems of consequentialism. A good outcome, whatever that means, doesn't matter.

Duties are the flipside of the normative coin from rights. If I have a right to resign my position, then my employer has a duty to allow me to quit. This example illustrates the libertarian (or negative) duty insofar as the boss is obligated to not interfere with my exit from the workplace. My supervisor needn't help me carry my personal items out of the building or do anything to facilitate my leaving. They just can't interfere with my freedom to quit. Likewise, a minister could be said to have a duty to allow congregants to quit the church. However, libertarian duties can get complicated through coercion. Would the minister be wrong to tell their flock: "You should know that leaving the faith is tantamount to entering the fires of hell. But I won't stand in the way. You're at liberty to choose eternal damnation"?

Now imagine a friend who declares they've given up eating meat. When you ask for their reason, the reply is: "Animals have rights. Livestock live in constant pain—and that's just wrong." In this case, the vegetarian is asserting that people have an egalitarian (or positive) duty not to cause suffering. We are obligated to quit carnivory insofar as our meat eating contributes to the violation of another being's rights. Similarly, a soldier has a duty not to desert. Doing so might put others in imminent peril, but that's merely a consequence. The deontological reason is that the soldier has taken an oath to obey orders. Desertion involves a soldier's breaking a promise, and we have a duty to tell the truth (more on that in a bit).

Not every good act arises from a strict duty, however. The deontologist recognizes supererogatory duties in which people engage in heroism, such as quitting one's life in order to save others. Falling on a grenade to shield your comrades is praiseworthy, but failing to sacrifice yourself in this manner is not blameworthy.

In addition, there are imperfect duties that have practical limitations. For example, we might have a duty to quit buying foods whose production contributes to suffering, but we have lots of choices about how to structure our eating habits—and all foods produce some harm to some sentient being. So, a deontologist couldn't look into our grocery cart, pull out an industrially grown tomato, and condemn us because we failed to buy from a farmer's market that's twenty miles away and open one day a week.

Finally, there are duties arising from natural rights, such as the right not to be enslaved. As to whether we then have only a negative duty to not own slaves or a positive duty to facilitate the escape of slaves, many people would contend the latter. Other duties arise from special rights that are conferred through a specific agreement. For example, the rules of mixed martial arts provide a competitor with the right to signal submission and obligate the opponent to cease, while such an option is not explicit in the midst of a bar fight. Rather provocatively, it has been argued that we do not have the right to quit some social endeavors when we have taken advantage of the benefits of an institution through a tacit agreement.[20]

—

All of this is fine if we accept that people ought to act in accord with duties that entail respect for rights. But where do these duties and rights come from? Most simply, rights arise because humans are intentional, self-aware beings so that for life to have meaning, we must be allowed freedom to pursue ventures of our choosing. But, of course, philosophers provide more erudite accounts.

Famous eighteenth-century German philosopher Immanuel Kant provided the first cogent rationale for the origin of duties.[21] He based his argument on rationality being a universal, distinguishing feature of humans and from there developed a categorical (meaning unconditional) imperative. The most conceptually accessible version of his conclusion is the "Formula of Humanity," which requires that we always treat people as ends in themselves and never simply as a means to our ends. For example, it is always irrational, and hence wrong, to lie (or to break promises, as in the aforementioned case of the deserting soldier) because doing so contributes to the erosion of trust and contributes to everyone disbelieving anything that someone says. And this would negate the distinction between speaking the truth and lying, which would logically contradict the nature and meaning of lying (or promising).[22] So, we have a duty to quit lying.

Twentieth-century philosopher William David Ross provided a less convoluted foundation for duties.[23] His derivation was based on intrinsic or core human goods. Imagine there are two worlds that are identical in all ways, except in one there is virtue, pleasure, and knowledge while the other has none of these features. Which would you prefer? Presumably, the former. From this thought experiment, Ross argued that there arise seven prima facie duties: beneficence, gratitude, non-maleficence, reparation, fidelity, justice, and self-improvement. It's easy to see how these duties might pertain to quitting. Self-improvement would obligate us to quit smoking. Non-maleficence would require us to quit a job that entails putting people into debt they cannot afford. And fidelity would necessitate that we end an extramarital affair.

Normativity based on deontological principles has two serious shortcomings. First, the advantage of avoiding the messiness of consequentialism comes at a cost. If results aren't relevant to our decision to quit, then acting in accord with duty can yield terrible outcomes about which we are morally indifferent. Kant's uncompromising duty to always tell the truth gives rise to the "Nazi at the door" problem in which you are hiding a Jewish family in your attic, the Gestapo knocks on your door, and the officer asks "are there any Jews in this house?" If you tell the truth, they will be slaughtered, but as a good deontologist you reveal their presence.

It's not difficult to imagine cases in which acting in accord with one of Ross's prima facie duties would yield dismal consequences. For example, self-improvement might demand that you take night classes, and beneficence could require you to volunteer at the soup kitchen on weekends. But the results of fulfilling these duties are that you ignore home maintenance, including changing the batteries in the smoke detectors and cleaning the lint trap in the dryer (you can see where this is heading).

One solution to such scenarios offered by some deontologists is that terrible results can override duties (e.g., you don't have a duty to quit your job as a shill for the credit card company if doing so would bankrupt your family and leave your sick child without medical care). Setting aside the question of just how awful the results need to be to trump a duty, this solution is just sneaking consequentialism in the back door—and then we're right back to that theory's difficulties.

The other major problem with deontology is that of how to resolve conflicting duties.[24] In 2010, the Wyoming state legislature adopted "Cowboy Ethics" into state law.[25] This philosophically naive and largely symbolic gesture exemplified the problem of rule-based systems, requiring individuals to both "always finish what you start" and "do what has to be done"—with no means of deciding what to do when quitting needs to happen (e.g., leaving an abusive marriage). The same problem arises with much more intellectually sophisticated deontological systems. How would Ross have us decide whether to favor fidelity or non-maleficence in a dysfunctional marriage in which the children are being emotionally harmed? Critics of American politics contend that a serious problem is that government employees must pit loyalty against speaking publicly or simply resigning in opposition to a harmful policy.[26] It's been argued simplistically that a soldier who finds a combat mission to be unjust has a duty to desert and voice their concerns,[27] as if there was no other duty such as fidelity or perhaps gratitude (let alone potentially terrible consequences) to consider.

Ross's solutions in cases of conflicting duties are twofold. He maintains that there will be an intuitively more compelling duty but admits that we might not be able to identify which has greater priority, so the practical value of this claim is dubious. Alternatively, we are justified in ranking our duties by strength of relationship (e.g., family before friends and fellow citizens before foreigners). But how does this apply to whether one should quit a marriage (do biological children trump adopted children, where does a spouse stand in this sequence, and do grandparents count)? Finally, political scientists have contended that a public official's first duty is to their conscience, next to the process of democracy, and then to their political superiors.[28] But this is of little value as the first priority does all of the normative work, and this duty to one's conscience would seem to pertain to everyone and reduce decisions to a kind of individual relativism.

CULTIVATE THE VIRTUES:
THE GOOD QUIT TAKES CARE OF ITSELF

A good quit is, simply put, what a virtuous person does—at least according to the standards of ancient Greek philosophers, upon which a great deal of modern normativity is built. Many, arguably most, of our moral, aesthetic, and cultural values can be linked to the teachings of Socrates, Plato, and Aristotle. Their contention was that good acts arise from good character. There's no further analysis to be made. As such, virtue ethics is grounded in the agent rather than in rules, as is the case with utilitarianism and deontology.

FIGURE 9.2. A detail of the central portion of *The School of Athens* (1509) by Italian Renaissance artist Raphael. Courtesy of Raffaello Sanzio via Wikimedia Commons.

This is why being called a "quitter" is such a harsh judgment—it connotes a character flaw. The quitter (remember, this epithet does not apply to one who has chosen to quit only a particular endeavor) has a chronic inability to persevere, a disposition to give up easily, a weakness to accept challenge.[29] In the context of virtue ethics, being a (serial) quitter is a moral failing. Again, this does not mean that all instances of quitting are deplorable.

The key to becoming a person who quits (or does anything) well is to cultivate the traits or dispositions that are found among those whose lives instantiate the human potential. And this is no small task in the modern world. There is a widespread belief that the United States is facing a crisis of character.[30] Although too simplistic, there's a core of truth in describing US society as having embraced hedonism in the 1960s, pursued narcissism in the 1970s, endorsed materialism in the 1980s, lapsed into apathy in the 1990s, and then climbed aboard the roller coaster of anxiety in the 2000s.

Western culture has been criticized as too individualistic, but there's a normative upside to basing virtue on internality. If our lives are driven by external factors, then human conduct reduces to mere stimulus-response as we are coaxed or coerced to act.[31] A virtuous quit cannot be a matter of giving up to pursue a carrot or avoid a stick. However, the Greeks also recognized that we live in community—and the virtues are both self-generated and other-directed. In the dialogue *Crito*, Socrates refuses to quit Athens and avoid his execution because to do so would have been acting in his narrow self-interest, harming those left behind by undermining the social order.[32]

This is all well and good in the abstract, but the principled rubber meets the practical road when we specify which character traits constitute the virtues. What are these qualities that, if one possesses them, assure that quitting will be done well? Various times and cultures have generated quite a list (the italicized virtues are those proposed by Aristotle in *The Nicomachean Ethics*), including ambition, awe, charity, chastity, cleanliness, *courage*, dignity, diligence, dutifulness, faith, forgiveness, *fortitude*, friendliness, frugality, *generosity*, gladness, gravity, honesty, hope, humility, humor, industriousness, *justice*, kindness, love, *magnificence*, *magnanimity*, manliness, mercy, order, patience, piety, pity, *prudence*, resolve, respectability, selflessness, silence, sincerity, *temperance*, tenacity, tranquility, truthfulness, wholesomeness and *wisdom*. This foundational work in Western philosophy provided two important perspectives—both relevant to quitting.[33]

First, Aristotle developed the Doctrine of the Mean, the idea that virtues lie between deficiencies and excesses of character traits. For example, courage is flanked by cowardice (a deficiency of resolve in the face of danger) and brashness (an excess of daring when threatened). Courage is having the appropriate confidence in fearful situations. As such, we can think of a good quit as lying between a gutless escape from adversity and an obstinate persistence amid travails.[34]

Second, Aristotle relativized the virtues to the individual's capacities. What might be courageous for a trained soldier in battle would be foolish bravado for a regular citizen. But it's also possible for a military leader to exhibit "toxic positivity" and persist in battle to a foolish extreme.[35] Less dramatic, we can appreciate how resigning from a well-compensated but not entirely satisfying career at age sixty might be foolhardy, while doing so at age thirty might be courageous.[36] Likewise, submission by an experienced fighter caught in a distressing position might be cowardly, while an inexperienced fighter refusing to give up in the same situation might constitute courage.

Although Aristotle came up with nine virtues, they can arguably be distilled to Plato's four cardinal virtues.[37] The first of these is courage, which is variously understood as conviction, mettle, and daring. In terms of quitting, courage would be characterized by an individual resigning from a high-paying, prestigious position in an evil corporation. Such a person must confront fear (e.g., of losing income), uncertainty (e.g., of finding other employment), and intimidation (e.g., by enraged superiors).

Next is wisdom, which is sometimes equated with prudence or the ability to discern an appropriate course of action. If a college student has decided to break up with a romantic partner, doing so in a three-word text ("I'm dropping you") during the psychological stress and emotional vulnerability of finals week would be clearly unwise—and perhaps rather cowardly.

Justice is the third of the cardinal virtues, which we might interpret to be fairness or righteousness. Contrary to accounts of purportedly justifiable quitting that are entirely self-interested,[38] this is an explicitly other-regarding virtue that requires knowledge of what is deserved by all who are affected—and quitting almost invariably impacts others.[39] The high school football coach who tells the officials that his team is forfeiting at halftime when the score is 68–0 and his players are likely to be seriously injured is making a fair and honorable decision on behalf of his team.

The final virtue is moderation, which can be understood as temperance, self-control, or discretion, with particular application to restraining one's physical appetites. Reducing our excessive eating, drinking, sex, social media, video games, and other corporeal pleasures to the extent that our character is qualitatively changed to more fully realize the human potential would be virtuous. Hence, this character trait pertains to partial quitting (see chapter 7). Interestingly, even striving, which is sometimes taken to be an unconditionally admirable quality, is a vice in excess; persistence promotes flourishing only when applied judiciously.[40]

It's apparent that the cardinal virtues overlap, and this interdependence allowed Aristotle to unify them—at least for our purposes with regard to quitting—under the concept of *phronesis*.[41] This is a kind of intelligence that can be acquired partly through teaching but also requires life experience—or the integration of book smarts and street smarts. The term most often used for *phronesis* is *practical wisdom*. Indeed, wisdom subsumes the classic virtues insofar as courage is wise action in dangerous situations, justice is wise action in interpersonal relations, and moderation is wise action in the context of pleasure.

Phronesis is concerned with the particular features of a situation. One can learn general principles, but successfully applying them in the real world requires having accumulated firsthand knowledge. As such, there is great value not only in achievement but also in struggle and failure, as the latter experiences provide vital lessons.[42] The value of integrating intellectual knowledge and practical experience is exemplified in universities, where classroom learning is combined with laboratory, workshop, performance, and internship elements. Likewise, in the trades, the development of an individual from apprentice to journeyman to master reflects a path toward *phronesis* (not a term typically applied to carpenters, electricians, or plumbers but surely an appropriate way of understanding the cultivation of excellence in a profession).

In terms of practical wisdom, a good quit is one that constitutes the right amount, for the right reasons, at the right time, in the right way. This is a large order, but such a synthetic understanding of what it means to take wise action is why Socrates considered wisdom to be the master virtue and Aristotle held that *phronesis* is both necessary and sufficient for being virtuous.

The virtue-based approach to normativity does not necessarily produce different decisions than either utilitarianism or deontology in that we might think of acting with practical wisdom as a duty, which is likely to generate good consequences. However, one does not pursue virtue out of dutiful aspirations or to generate favorable results. Rather, cultivating virtue is how we strive toward the highest human good—a life well lived. And such a life includes quitting.

I do not mean to suggest that quitting is itself a virtue. Doing so would be what philosophers call a category error, which is to say that quitting is not the kind of thing that constitutes a virtue.[43] Rather, it is an action (like parenting, working, or fighting) that can be undertaken virtuously—or not. A hospice counselor spoke of dying in these terms, saying that it can be done with generosity, discipline, patience, and wisdom.[44] In this context, a good quit culminates with being at peace or, we might say, ending well.

Of course, virtue theory is not without its critics, and there are five commonly raised objections. First is the imprecision of a normative system being based on the character of agents. But this feature is what allows us to avoid the irresolvable conflicts of rule-based systems such as consequentialism and deontology. Next, a seemingly unlimited number of traits have been proposed as virtues. However, these various qualities are plausibly complementary, not conflicting, when understood and practiced properly and proportionately. Third is a concern for the lack of consensus regarding what constitutes virtue in a pluralistic society. Not that such agreement is essential (we don't want to lapse into cultural relativism), but most, if not all, of the virtues are recognized in some manner across diverse groups, and what varies is usually not the philosophical principles but their operationalization. Fourth, it has been asserted that the cultivation of the virtues is self-centered, putting the individual as the locus of value. However, it is clear that many of the virtues (e.g., charity, generosity, justice, mercy, and selflessness) are explicitly other-regarding. Finally, there is an objection that the ability to develop the virtues is strongly dependent on external factors, such as education and family, so the approach is not egalitarian. While not everyone has the same opportunity to cultivate the virtues, this doesn't preclude each person from doing what is in their power to pursue human flourishing, even if being a sage is out of reach for almost all of us.

A GOOD QUIT: ASSEMBLING THE PIECES OF *PHRONESIS*

Good quits reflect and foster the constitutive virtues of *phronesis*: courage, wisdom, justice, and moderation. Furthermore, a situation might also provide an opportunity to cultivate some of the "leftover" virtues. In this regard, dignity, integrity, and respectability are often relevant with regard to aligning a quit with one's nature insofar as the virtues are relativized to each person's capabilities. Ultimately, these threads of virtuous living are woven into a good life that instantiates the human potential (which surely entails good quitting), that allows deep happiness (rather than shallow mirth), and that enables us to flourish and thrive (albeit with no assurance of psychological ease or physical pleasure).

Researchers have explored extensively what constitutes adaptive or "good" persistence.[45] The focus on this behavior may reflect the general sense that persevering is an admirable quality. But, of course, potentially foolish persistence can only be countered with wise quitting, and much less work has been devoted to when one ought to throw in the towel. That is our task using *phronesis* as the framework. So, in chapter 10 we'll consider why, what, and when to quit, and in chapter 11 we'll ponder how to quit. But a warning: Given that virtue theory is not a matter of deriving rules for living, that virtue is relativized to each individual's capabilities, and that practical wisdom means acting appropriately based on life experience (along with teachable principles) pertaining to highly diverse situations, there will be no simplistic formula, pocket guide, or decision tree. There will, however, be a great deal to think about.

10

The Trifecta of Quitting
Why, What, and When?

When it comes to a good quit, three questions arise: Why quit (is there sound justification)? What to quit (is the right thing abandoned in the right amount)? When to quit (is it neither too soon nor too late)? These questions are not always independent. For example, if one stays too long (when) in a dysfunctional romantic relationship (why) such that a child becomes part of the equation, completely severing ties with a partner may be untenable (what).

The standards of virtue pertain to this trio of questions. Most succinctly, a good quit requires *phronesis*. The two elements of practical wisdom—keen analysis and cultivated intuition—are exemplified by a professional poker player who's considering whether to fold.[1] First, the individual must have "book smarts" (i.e., able to calculate the odds of winning a hand). Second, it is crucial to have the "street smarts" that come with experience. Craig Varnell described such a scenario: "Say a seventy-year-old man is playing tight while I have queens and he raises me. Analytically, you should never fold [in these circumstances], but he's not played a hand in hours. Based on the whole game, I fold. Even if he was bluffing, it was a good quit. You can't be a robot. A good player is a profiler."[2]

In exploring the "why, what, and when" of quitting, I'll reflect on what students in my honors course on quitting shared of their experiences. In addition, it will be helpful to have some consistent cases to consider across the trio of questions. Here are five exemplars reflecting a range of situations based on my experiences.

First was the decision of whether to quit my career as a scientist. Although conducting entomological studies for fifteen years had been rewarding, this endeavor was increasingly insufficient to fulfill my cognitive, emotional, and creative needs. I had grown weary of the grant-chasing, publication-generating treadmill of research. But I was good at science and this was all I had until . . .

Until next came my desire to become a published writer of creative nonfiction, using my experiences as an ecologist to explore questions of environmental ethics, aesthetics, and spirituality.[3] However, dozens of rejections by various editors early in this endeavor led me to wonder whether I should give up on becoming a writer.

Third, I developed a daily habit of drinking eight (or more) cups of coffee. This intake of caffeine produced heart palpitations, triggering a latent anxiety disorder that sometimes became debilitating. Whether or not caffeine is technically addictive,[4] it sure felt that way when I was trying to quit.

Fourth, I'd been a practicing Catholic until I went to college and became a lapsed Catholic. After I graduated and married, there was little doubt that this religion no longer resonated with my beliefs and largely failed to meet my needs. However, quitting the church felt like a big step—at least without a viable alternative.

Finally, after my father died and my mother was sliding steadily into dementia, my weekly phone calls (and occasional in-person visits when I returned to my hometown) began to steadily diminish in frequency and duration as she became less aware and I became more distressed by her condition. But can a son quit on his mother?

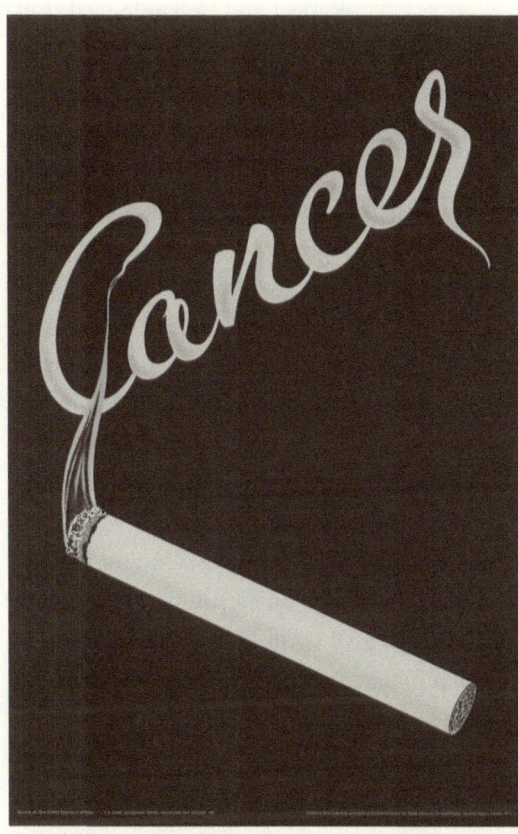

FIGURE 10.1. A 1958 poster created for World No Tobacco Day to encourage twenty-four-hour abstinence and long-term quitting. Courtesy of New Zealand Archives via Wikimedia Commons.

WHY: GOOD QUITS NEED GOOD REASONS

When asked to reflect on their lives, the question the students in my course most consistently thought they'd gotten right was why they had quit—whether having given up on a relationship, job, addiction, course of study, sports endeavor, musical instrument, or religious practice. Based on this small but thoughtful sample, it appears that we often have good reasons for quitting. A wide range of cases can be distilled into three plausible rationales for giving up: the hardship of persevering, the likelihood of imminent failure, and the promise of an alternative venture.

Hardships can entail serious risk to physical and psychological well-being. With regard to corporeal danger, the most unambiguous cases arise in the course of military surrenders when death is imminent. However, there are parallels in the martial arts and mountaineering.

Mixed martial artists are often put in positions in which dislocated joints and broken bones are virtually certain if the fighter refuses to submit. Such cases can serve as vivid examples of bad perseverance (versus good quitting), as recounted by world title holder Michael Bisping: "Josh Hayne's face was red with blood . . . he had no quit in him . . . I poured on the punishment but Josh still wouldn't signal surrender. I let him get up and decked him again. This wasn't defiance, this was denial. It was now the referee I was appealing to. I was unrelenting and, with forty-seven seconds left, [the referee] finally rescued my opponent from his own courage."[5]

Mark Jenkins, a world-class climber who summited Mount Everest, complicates the "why" of a good quit based on hardships. He contends that while it might be advisable to give up if the hazardous situation results from poor attitude, planning, or teamwork, the good reason for turning back does not obviate bad causes.

Physical damage can merge into psychological and emotional harm, given the intimate connection between mind and body.[6] The trauma can be vivid when it comes to life-saving medical interventions. The decision of when to cease resuscitation is enormously complex, particularly when it involves a child. Such a determination takes into account the patient's physical condition and mental capacities if they are eventually revived (given that "time is brain"), as well as parents' values, which are manifest through intense emotions.[7] This leads us to the next danger that can provide a justification for quitting.

The parent and physician agonizing over a decision to quit life support are confronting their sense of self—their identities as caregivers. Likewise, others who ponder whether to terminate a venture may wrestle with whether doing so undermines their sense of being a spouse, lover, worker, boss, soldier, teacher, cop, humanitarian, Christian, and so on.

An individual's cherished role can conflict with their moral integrity, dignity, and character when deciding to quit an endeavor.

In this context, good reasons for quitting take various forms. In academia, the intense competition for resources can become so grueling that it undermines an individual's dignity.[8] And in public life, it has been argued that there has to be a line that an official refuses to cross.[9] There are countless examples of professional resignations that have been tendered to avoid intolerable damage to an individual's career and reputation. The most explicit such efforts to minimize harm are evident in British politics, where ministers engulfed by controversy can avoid continuing public criticism by resigning their cabinet-level positions and returning to Parliament—even when their positions turn out to be correct.[10]

In a broader sense, a poor quit has been characterized as "inconsistent with your own standards of behavior and intentions," which is to say, one's identity.[11] A reciprocal way of understanding this overarching principle was proposed by a military historian at West Point who maintained that "it is good to desert a bad cause" (such as draft dodgers' virtual desertion during the Vietnam War, particularly those who had the integrity to accept the consequences of their decision, such as Muhammed Ali).[12]

The military context also provides an overarching principle for differentiating good and bad reasons for quitting. A prospective cadet who gives up during "Beast Barracks"—the grueling initiation into the United States Military Academy—is viewed as weak in character, but those who transfer at the end of their freshman year, after they've demonstrated the capacity to endure hardship, are seen as making a discerning, even wise, decision that the military does not align with their identity.[13] This distinction between a petulant excuse versus a legitimate rationale leads us to the second justification for quitting: the likelihood of imminent failure.

The Serenity Prayer captures the quality of *phronesis* when it comes to facing insurmountable challenges and imminent failure: "God, grant me the serenity to accept the things I cannot change, the courage to change the things I can, and the wisdom to know the difference."[14] Surely, it is foolish to persevere in an endeavor, both if achievement is unattainable (recognizing that the future is uncertain)[15] *and* if success is understood in terms of reaching a particular, overt result (one could refuse to quit a struggle that cannot be won as a way of cultivating the virtue of courage, humility, or loyalty).

An individual might have undertaken a project, such as pursuing a degree in ecology, with a reasonable but necessarily incomplete understanding of what will be required. With time, they might discover aspects of the venture that make it functionally impossible to achieve (e.g., a student failed to grasp the amount of higher mathematics used in ecology versus their capability in this realm).[16] In such futile endeavors, quitting is a sound decision.

In other cases, one might have comprehended the nature of the endeavor, but insurmountable adversity emerges, such as examples offered by my diverse consultants: a medical team caring for a chronically ill patient realizes they are merely prolonging death;[17] the British government grasps that it is facing an unwinnable war in the American Revolution;[18] an individual who has lived for decades with unrelenting misery due to untreatable depression contemplates suicide;[19] and an elderly hospice patient diagnosed with aggressive, terminal cancer quits chemotherapy and its brutal side effects.[20] Individuals with practical wisdom discern if there is an unbridgeable gap between one's abilities and goals; they don't imagine a light at the end of the tunnel when there is not a glimmer of hope.[21]

We turn now to our third and final rationale for why one ought to quit: the promise of an alternative path. Rather than abandon a doomed endeavor (a negative motivation), an individual might justifiably decide to abandon a pursuit that could be successful to reallocate time and energy to a project that is substantially more likely to allow the person to thrive (a positive motivation).[22] Indeed, it has been argued that when parents contemplate their child wanting to quit a sports team—thereby evoking the challenge of balancing individual desires with the commitment made to others (i.e., Ross's conflicting duties of self-improvement and fidelity)—the key is whether quitting is accompanied by engagement with a new, character-building goal.[23]

The classification of quitting explicated in management science includes the category of "comparison quitters."[24] These individuals engage in rational analysis of their position without emotional negativity toward their employer. They resign because they have good reason to believe another job has significantly greater potential to provide what they need to flourish. In seeking work that allows them to cultivate the virtues, their quitting manifests practical wisdom.

So, how do I fare in my own five case studies by the standard of *phronesis* in answering "why quit?" As for my decision to leave scientific research for the arts and humanities, there was no imminent professional danger. However, I had lost the fire in my belly for chasing grants and publishing papers, so there was an impending sense of failure—or at least the anticipation of being unable to thrive as a professor of entomology. Most important, this abandonment was justified by the pursuit of projects that were better aligned with my maturing scholarly identity, as well as the perceived (and realized) opportunity for personal flourishing.

With the departure from scientific research, I committed to becoming a published author of creative nonfiction. To this end, I invested a sabbatical leave in writing a set of essays integrating my experiences of the six-legged world with ethical and spiritual insights. I submitted them to various publications and decided not to second-guess my venture until I received 100 rejections—a writer's equivalent of a mountaineer's "turnaround time"[25]—at which point I would conclude there was an unbridgeable gap between my abilities and my goals. To my relief, an acceptance from a major publication in environmental literature arrived before I reached my threshold.

Third, when I was almost constantly drinking coffee during the workday, consuming at least eight times the recommended daily dose of caffeine,[26] I could feel my heart racing in the afternoon. This sensation made me anxious, which made my pulse increase in an awful, positive feedback loop. You might well wonder why I kept drinking so much coffee. I didn't associate coffee, palpitations, and anxiety for some time (scientists can be dense despite our love of causal explanations). When the connection was finally made, I dramatically reduced my caffeine consumption. Whether or not there was truly medical danger, it felt that way—and this provided a sound reason for all-but-quitting.

Fourth, I drifted from Catholicism but didn't fully part ways until I married after graduating from college. My wife (a less than theologically avid Presbyterian) and I sought a religious community that accorded with our emerging adult identities. We didn't feel animus toward the religions of our youth but believed we were moving toward something better. Seeking to improve our lives, we tried out various churches and finally resonated with a Unitarian Universalist congregation, remaining in this denomination ever since.

Finally, my weekly phone calls to my mother declined in duration and frequency as her dementia worsened until I finally quit calling. I sensed that she liked hearing my voice, but she couldn't remember that I'd called almost immediately after hanging up. My excuse for giving up was that the logistics of getting a nurse to bring and hold the phone for her had become an ordeal for caregivers; the real reason was my own discomfort and heartache. Emotional cowardice can be disguised with allusions to one's psychological welfare. I had no virtuous reason for quitting.

WHAT: QUITTING THE BATHWATER AND KEEPING THE BABY

While my students were generally confident that they had good reasons for quitting, they were less sure about whether they'd quit the right thing or the right amount. Sometimes they managed to partially forgo some endeavor, which allowed them to flourish. For example, one student was juggling multiple sports in high school and decided to quit playing baseball. He reallocated his time to basketball and soccer but continued to enjoy playing catch with friends and following his favorite major league team.

FIGURE 10.2. Still image from the 1927 film *A Reno Divorce*—a story of marriage, divorce, and reconciliation. Courtesy of University of Washington via Wikimedia Commons.

Another student who had been pursuing music with a dream of performing professionally realized that he wasn't going to make it in that hyper-competitive field, so he shifted his energy to playing guitar as a fulfilling form of leisure—a dramatic change in his self-image but one that provided a creative outlet during his pursuit of a degree in business.

Yet another individual finished his first year at West Point—a very prestigious and demanding appointment that would have clearly shaped his identity—but decided that this path did not align with his ideals. However, he did not quit higher education, transferring to the University of Wyoming to continue his studies.

These examples illustrate quitting the right thing, in the right amount, but when it came to relationships, there was a general sense among my students that they lacked practical wisdom by often partially quitting rather than giving up entirely. The common mistake was trying to be "just friends" after a quasi-breakup. These young people could recount badly handled romantic quits, even to the point of still being unwilling to pursue another relationship in some cases. I suspect that a permanent exit from romance is very unlikely for any of them, although a complete but temporary abandonment of romantic pursuits might allow individuals the opportunity to reflect on what led to intense and acute unhappiness.

Given our commitments to meaningful endeavors, choosing exactly what to quit can be a significant challenge.[27] *Phronesis* in this context entails the discernment to "quit the right thing, and only the right thing, which requires figuring out the specific area that isn't serving you."[28] One might be miserable at work and hastily conclude that resigning is a smart course of action. However, it could be the case that the displeasure is not with the job per se but rather with hypercritical co-workers or a demanding supervisor. If so, then resolving conflict through mediation or perhaps transferring to another unit within the firm would be potentially far savvier tactics, allowing the individual to accrue continuing seniority, enjoy a healthier work setting, and thrive without the stress of seeking employment in another company where the conditions may well be equally or even more onerous (particularly given that 85% of employees feel dissatisfied due to social isolation, poor management, and pervasive disrespect).[29]

—

Considering my own set of quits, I can't claim they are exemplars of *phronesis* when it comes to having given up the right things, in the right amounts. Perhaps my best quit was ending my career as a scientist to create the opportunity for fulfilling work in philosophy and creative writing—a matter of giving up one professorial identity but persevering within academia. As for my goal of becoming a published writer of nonfiction, had I reached my preset limit of rejections during my initial foray, I most likely would have quit excessively, even petulantly—abandoning the entire literary venture to focus exclusively on academic publishing in the realms of environmental ethics and philosophy of science. Next, my partial abandonment of coffee drinking largely avoided the short-term misery of caffeine withdrawal, but in retrospect it was an opportunity (still available, I hasten to admit) for me to fully quit and find perhaps even greater pleasure in the wonderful variety of herbal teas that are available. With regard to my apostasy, I would have almost surely denounced all religion—an excessive quit—had it not been for my new wife's positive social experiences in her previous religious community. Instead we converted and have thrived in our Unitarian Universalist Fellowship. Finally, I definitely quit too much when I stopped communicating with my mother. Phone calls were an emotional struggle, but there's no good reason why I couldn't have sent picture postcards. She still enjoyed images, and caretakers could have read the messages at their convenience.

SOONER OR LATER: TIMING IS (ALMOST) EVERYTHING WHEN QUITTING

The element of a good quit that was most challenging for my students—and perhaps many people—was deciding when to throw in the towel—whether the context was a college major, romantic relationship, friendship, job, journey, contest, or avocation. Most often the failure was in waiting too long, although it is surely possible to give up too quickly. And I must say that my Gen Z students seemed to have much greater capacity for critical self-reflection than did a TED Talk–featured prototypical millennial who excelled at post hoc rationalization.[30]

Why is it so difficult to get the timing of a quit just right—neither too early nor too late? As Kenny Rogers sings in "The Gambler," knowing when to hold 'em and when to fold 'em is the key to winning in poker (the lyrics of which, as a friend complains, provide no actionable advice). We might take poker as a metaphor for life insofar as we are constrained by rules, dealt cards by chance, and must decide how to play our hands when outcomes are, at best, probabilistic. Even unabashed advocates of quitting recognize that "no single measure or how-to formula can possibly address the question of the right time to quit. There are simply too many variables in any situation."[31] In other words, the cultivation of *phronesis* is crucial to the well-timed quit.

Analysis of workplace resignations has revealed three very different strategies employees use to decide when to quit.[32] So-called preplanned quitters time their exits for some specific moment in the future—for example, "I'll quit this job in two years, when I'll have saved enough to take that dream trip to Europe." There's not much a manager can do to prevent such departures, but the second strategy is contingent and therefore amenable to mitigation. "Conditional quitters" also plan to resign, although not upon some predetermined passage of time but when a particular event occurs—for example, "I'll quit this job if I get another offer that pays at least 50 percent more," or "I'll resign if my supervisor mocks me again in front of the staff."

Both of these strategies can instantiate *phronesis*, assuming that the conditions are developed rationally based on reasonable expectations arising from professional experience. This criterion is crucial, as it's entirely possible to have unreasonable time lines or triggers (e.g., "I'll quit on my birthday if my co-workers fail to bring a cake, thereby proving their disdain for my feelings"). While these two strategies are potentially justifiable, the third category that pertains to the timing of quitting has very little to recommend it in terms of practical wisdom.

Conditional quitting can, in an extreme form, manifest in "impulsive quitting." In this case, an individual quits not according to any temporal plan but in a moment of pique, perhaps due to some perceived offense or betrayal. Such quitting is impetuous, lacking either significant job dissatisfaction or detailed deliberation.[33] This spontaneity is inimical to contemplative wisdom but can manifest in young people who are both able to live cost-free with their parents and unable to commit to a project.

When it came to the timing of a virtuous quit, students in my course exhibited an intriguing trend with respect to gender. Well before we'd explored ethical frameworks, including the nature of virtue, the students wrote critiques of Hiroo Onoda, the Japanese officer who refused to surrender until nearly thirty years after the end of World War II. All six female students judged that he had persevered too long, while five of the six male students argued that his behavior, although futile, was defensible in epitomizing dutifulness.

In subsequently exploring what made for a good quit, we interpreted that the men had unconditionally valued qualities associated with honor and courage, while the women perceived that any virtue—even loyalty or selflessness—taken to an extreme becomes a vice through Aristotle's Doctrine of the Mean. In the course of discussion, the guys had to admit that Onoda had pushed beyond what constituted admirable devotion. And so, how can we avoid the dual pitfalls of quitting too late (e.g., Second Lieutenant Onoda) or too soon (e.g., France's capitulation to Germany)?[34]

—

Avoiding a premature quit means having developed the ability to persevere through difficult periods while moving toward a reasonably achievable goal (whether it's a tangible outcome or an intangible character trait). In the British Parliament, quitting early and often when a politician doesn't get their way on policy matters can become a disingenuous strategy.[35] For Clare Short, who served the British government in various capacities, this political equivalent of crying "wolf" was ultimately a source of derision among legislators.[36] Quitting too readily as a calculated tactic is surely the exception; most people give up prematurely due to a lack of grit or guts (e.g., a wealthy backer who staked Craig Varnell dropped the poker player when he was down $30,000—and in the next tournament Varnell won half a million dollars.)[37]

The capacity to delay gratification and thereby avoid rash quitting is an acquired skill. This ability increases with education and age,[38] as one's life experiences reveal that constantly giving up when the going gets tough fails to yield happiness. Such self-discipline pertains to relationships (e.g., not breaking up after the first argument), investments (e.g., not divesting at the first downturn), and virtually all other substantive human endeavors.[39] That said, it's probably never too early to quit substance abuse,[40] as addiction can become increasingly entrenched with time.[41]

The hazard of persevering too long fuels the cottage industry of "quit advocates" who coach their followers to more expeditiously exit jobs and relationships. But we ought to be cautious when it comes to accepting a heuristic that good quits happen sooner rather than later. For example, it is asserted, without evidence, that most managers hang on to employees too long, such that the right time to fire someone is the first time doing so crosses one's mind[42]—a rather extreme bit of advice that lacks empirical justification and would seem likely to thrust one into the realm of "too soon" (impulsive firing being no more advisable than impulsive quitting). However, even those who have less business-minded perspectives maintain that people tend to unjustifiably endure an eroding quality of life, whether this pertains to mortality[43] or romance.[44] And when it comes to euthanizing a pet, we often allow the animal to suffer too long for selfish reasons.[45]

Many of the fallacies associated with decision-making (e.g., the sunk cost fallacy, loss aversion, and escalating commitment) lead us to tolerate greater unhappiness than would seem to accord with practical wisdom. The tendency to persist too long might also arise from a vice that was well-known to Aristotle—vanity, which is an excess of pride. When it comes to the martial arts, sensei Angerhofer teaches that ego on the part of a novice drives the competitor to foolishly persist and suffer physical and emotional injury. On the part of an advanced fighter, conceit can result in imposing their will on less able students, resulting in a bad quit by the beginner from which nothing is learned.[46]

It is difficult to accept that old fighters, soldiers, and scholars eventually lose their edge. This might be particularly problematic for those who once performed at a high level or possessed great power.[47] As former mixed martial arts champion Michael Bisping put it, "I'd raged against the reality for so long but, now that I'm in my forties, I find it easy to accept that my time has come and gone."[48] This sense of having lost one's relevance explains, at least in substantial part, the high rate of suicide among older white men who perceive themselves as having become burdens, no longer useful to family and community.[49]

So it is that waiting too long may be a matter of ego as an individual refuses to admit that they are past their prime and perseveres in the irrational belief that even greater success is yet possible. Such undignified persistence might be offset by an understanding that although a person is no longer performing at their peak as a teacher, actor, athlete, researcher, fire fighter, minister, physician, laborer, or lover, it is possible to morph into the role of mentor to individuals with less experience—if only society valued the practical wisdom of those who have learned a great deal through trials and tribulations. Often, a timely quit means losing pride but retaining dignity. And when done well, it is possible to lose one long-cultivated identity while gaining another.

As with my students, getting the timing right when it comes to quitting has been a personal challenge. By this criterion, I have few good quits, although I like to think I'm cultivating practical wisdom that will better serve me in the coming years.

To begin, I probably persisted too long in my scientific career as I waited for new opportunities to arise rather than making them happen. I spent considerable time casting about in search of alternative paths (including applying to very different positions in other universities and even exploring the ministry). On the other hand, perhaps I quit too soon. With patience and creativity I might well have found another line of scientific research that would have been fulfilling while allowing me to step back from the stress of constantly pursuing grants and contracts (a significant, if not the only, source of my dissatisfaction).

Next, although I set a "turnaround time" for my foray into creative nonfiction, I might have persevered in some way even after 100 rejections. Turning back on an expedition is a definitive quit to avoid peril, but a wannabe writer can camp on a mountain of rejection slips and continue to make timid forays toward the peak—hence the risk of quitting too late. On the other hand, I wrote quite a few poems some years ago with the idea of adding this genre to my repertoire, and I gave up on this venture despite having a couple of poems published in very obscure places. Perhaps I quit too soon, before I paid the price of admission into this literary realm—or maybe I just didn't have the gumption to devote the 10,000 (likely more) hours to succeed.[50]

My third quit was probably my best in terms of timing. Okay, I was indefensibly obtuse in making the connection between my coffee consumption and my discomfort with anxiety and palpitations. However, once I realized the cause and effect between too much caffeine and too many heartbeats, it didn't take long to dramatically cut back.

Had I (partially) quit any faster, I would have brought on the headaches, irritability, and fatigue associated with withdrawal, and quitting any slower would just have been procrastination, which is not to be confused with the virtue of patience.

Fourth, breaking up with Catholicism was very much akin to dragging out the quitting of a romantic relationship. I limped along without having to work through the emotional difficulties by maintaining a long-distance relationship with the church—spending time with her whenever I was back home from college on holidays to keep my parents happy (they liked her very much). This "too late" estrangement didn't have a serious downside in terms of psychological cost, as it's possible to simply live in denial for years without confronting what isn't working. But there was an erosion of my character, insofar as I lacked the courage to declare to myself and my family that I was parting ways—that the relationship was a sham. Not until I'd cheated on Catholicism with other religions and fallen for Unitarian Universalism did I explicitly break up.

Finally, I quit on the relationship with my mother, or at least communicating with her, too soon. Her cognitive abilities were in decline, but she was still capable of moments of recognition and joy when I stopped calling her. There was no wisdom in the decision, which was never entirely explicit (another bit of cowardice), to effectively terminate our increasingly one-sided "conversations." My only excuse was a lack of experience in such matters. *Phronesis* requires practice.

WHY, WHAT, AND WHEN TO QUIT: A SUMMARY OF SMARTS

In two, very disparate endeavors, there is a striking convergence as to what constitutes a good quit according to those who have achieved distinction in their fields over the course of decades. When I asked physicians who specialized in pediatric critical care how they developed expertise with respect to quitting a medical intervention, their answer was that doctors should begin with lots of coursework on basic and advanced life support; then participate in simulated codes (e.g., a four-year-old rescued from a family pond with a given set of vital signs); next observe and participate in actual codes, which include intensive debriefing sessions; and eventually become a team leader who knows what every person is doing while simultaneously assessing the emotional and moral context of each unique case. With continued study and experience (book learning and street smarts), a doctor comes to know when it's the right time to quit resuscitation through having cultivated practical wisdom encompassing courage, discernment, fairness, and self-control.[51]

And when I asked the highly respected sensei how his martial arts students became skillful in quitting, he replied that novices have the greatest tendency to be injured, as they've not grasped either escape or submission. In his dojo, the development of practical wisdom comes through "scaffolding," in which one learns a complex task by a mentor's initially providing plenty of systematic instruction (book learning), which is gradually withdrawn as the student grasps a concept through personal experience (street smarts). Ultimately, there is no substitute for practice or, as the sensei put it, "tap out early and often." There are teachable heuristics, but they will never allow a fighter to realize their full potential given the myriad ways they can be put into a dire situation that requires courage, discernment, fairness, and self-control.[52]

So it is that the centrality of *phronesis* ironically dooms, to an important extent, this section of the book on how to engage in a good quit. Nothing that I can write will replace the arduous firsthand lessons of the reader in mastering the art of quitting—whether in the realm of leaving a relationship, resigning a job, renouncing a religion, abandoning a belief, or rejecting an identity. However, there is value in book learning, a necessary but not sufficient element of practical wisdom. Excellence depends on thinking as well as doing. So, we'll forge ahead with the final and ultimate challenge of how to quit well. For even if an individual has a fully justifiable reason, a good sense of proportionality, and a mastery of timing, one still has to enact the decision. And the best quit in principle can be sabotaged by a bad method in practice.

11

How to Quit
Virtuosity and Virtue

After pondering the elements of why, what, and when to quit, a person might come to the well-reasoned and emotionally compelling conclusion that they ought to quit—a relationship, job, profession, religion, diet, habit, contest, investment, treatment, or any other endeavor. A philosopher would say this individual knows <u>that</u> they should quit. Generally speaking (let's not go too far into the philosophical weeds), "knowledge-that" pertains to propositions such as "I know that heroin is an addictive substance." We can sometimes extend the conventional formulation of a factual statement to a normative assertion. A person might have good reasons to say "I know that I should quit using heroin." Such a justified belief might be understood as conditional knowledge that can be fleshed out as "I know that I should quit using heroin if I want to flourish in my career and relationships."

But intellectual knowledge is distinct from practical knowledge.[1] For our purposes, one might know <u>that</u> quitting some project or condition is the right thing to do in terms of virtuous living; however, it does not follow that one knows <u>how</u> to go about doing so.[2] As such, philosophers distinguish know-that from know-how. A person suffering from a compulsive disorder might know <u>that</u> they ought to stop repetitively washing their hands but not know <u>how</u> to stop this behavior. While the hand washer might have no idea about how to quit, there can also be such an abundance of ways to quit a venture that one is unsure of how to proceed. For example, one might end a relationship by ghosting the other person, sending a text, writing a letter, leaving a voice mail, conversing in person, or presumably using any one of fifty ways to leave a lover (according to Paul Simon's 1975 hit song).[3] However, what concerns us is not merely executing a departure but enacting a quit that is consistent with our thriving. In pursuing a meaningful life, what we seek is how to quit with courage, wisdom, justice, and moderation—we aspire to *phronesis*.

Ending substance abuse, the most intensively studied form of quitting, exemplifies the difficulty of how-to. Consider smoking, which the surgeon general has warned us about for almost sixty years. It's easy to know rationally that one ought to give up cigarettes, but it's wickedly difficult to know how to do so. While researchers crank out more than one peer-reviewed journal article a week on cessation methods, they struggle to recommend an unambiguously best approach.[4]

The justifiably vaunted Mayo Clinic simply lists ten tips that one might try to reduce tobacco cravings.[5] Another prestigious research institution published "What's the Best Way to Quit Smoking," which promised an answer, but the article unhelpfully suggests that a smoker might try various medications alone or in combination, along with counseling. The highly qualified writer (a Harvard Medical School professor and physician at Massachusetts General Hospital) further proposes that going cold turkey might be worth a shot, given that this approach has a higher success rate than gradual strategies.[6]

Fifty years ago, my parents didn't have nicotine gum or patches, so they quit cold turkey, which was miserable for them—and for us kids who had to weather their withdrawal. Today, we have a variety of nicotine replacement therapies to treat smokers, the most recent being varenicline or Chantix, which is functionally the methadone of nicotine addicts. If you're still wondering about the best tactic, my search of the Amazon website using "how to quit smoking" produced dozens of books offering methods that are purportedly easy, quick, permanent, and natural while tapping into the help of God, psychedelic mushrooms, coloring books, and alkaline foods.

Giving up drugs or anything else substantive in our lives is individualized, complicated, and irreducible to a "How-to Guide." However we might derive some principles for good quits that accord with practical wisdom.

TACTFUL QUITTING: CALM, COOL, AND COLLECTED

Among the most extensively documented quits are those of politicians. Based on an abundance of cases, political scientists have developed a classification of strategies describing exit from public office,[7] and this framework includes options that also pertain to non-political realms. First, one can persevere in their role and resist covertly (e.g., the so-called quiet quit in a workplace). Next, an individual can leave surreptitiously (e.g., stop going to a church without any pronouncements). Third, one can hold on as long as possible and then navigate the gray area between leaving in discreet silence versus by public declaration (e.g., an unhappy lover breaks up with an alcoholic partner and shares the rationale with only family and friends). Finally, a person can leave in public protest to alert others of a situation (e.g., announce on social media that one is becoming vegetarian and post images of animal confinement facilities).

Setting aside covert resistance, which seems like an unsustainable approach that would eventually exhaust one's emotional well-being or undermine one's integrity, let's begin with the second strategy—quitting discretely. This how-to aligns with the advice of a self-proclaimed "quitting evangelist," who recommends that one should quit kindly and gently so as to burn the fewest bridges.[8] This would seem to be a plausible baseline with practical and principled upsides, as making enemies is not generally advisable. In the fields of law, business, and government, the norm is to exit with quiet dignity and eschew a public display of dissent.[9]

The custom of the "proper quit" can be an affectation of the elite, as those in the upper class are twice as likely to resign quietly as are those from other classes.[10] However, tact may also constitute practical wisdom, as in the case of United States Attorney General Elliot Richardson, who could not countenance President Richard M. Nixon's order to fire the special prosecutor during the Watergate investigation.[11] The White House sensed that the nation was in great peril and a public protest by Richardson could divide the country or seriously weaken the office of the presidency, so Richardson left without fanfare.

There might also be personally pragmatic reasons for not burning bridges by publicly reprimanding and inflaming one's superiors. For example, John Denham, a minister of state at the home office, stayed within the bounds of accepted discourse in British politics when he discretely resigned over Tony Blair's decision to commit troops to the Iraq War. His political acumen was rewarded by Gordon Brown, who replaced Blair as prime minister and named Denham to a new cabinet post.[12] As a rule, politicians who choose less confrontational exits experience fewer personal and financial repercussions,[13] and the same likely holds in all human interactions and professional contexts, from chess and boxing matches to jobs and social clubs.

Showing respect for others and humility in oneself often constitutes *phronesis*, particularly when the responsibility for an untenable situation is shared, as in many—arguably most—romantic relationships. All parties are much more likely to reflect on and learn from a quit—whether husband or wife, employee or boss, minister or parishioner, victor or vanquished—when the exit is civil and nobody is solely faulted. Public shaming (and even private blaming) almost invariably evokes defensiveness, which forecloses an opportunity to learn.

―

Of course, discrete quitting runs the hazard of creating the impression that nothing is wrong in a government, business, or relationship when others might benefit from knowing of a serious problem.[14] As such, the fourth strategy—walking the tightrope between private and public quitting—can be implemented. One can carefully and thoughtfully communicate the reason for quitting to those who would gain from that knowledge. A fine example of this hybrid strategy is the resignation of William Jennings Bryan, the United States secretary of state under President Woodrow Wilson.[15] Bryan was a pacifist and told the president that he'd resign if Wilson took a hard line after the Germans sank the *Lusitania*. When Wilson rejected conciliation, Bryan quit, saying he had to follow his conscience, whatever the cost to his political career. While he publicly opposed war in front of huge crowds, Bryan remained privately cordial with Wilson. When the United States entered World War I, Bryan quit his antiwar agitating and urged all Americans to stand behind their president.[16]

In terms of navigating the logistical details of a private or hybrid quit, one should be keenly aware that leaving a personal or professional relationship may provoke anger and even violence. As such, practical wisdom entails that one be circumspect with regard to the "where" of quitting. Indeed, relationship therapists advise that individuals consider past behavior of a romantic partner and break up in a manner and place that takes into account personal safety.[17] Given the emotional stakes of other relationships, the same advice would apply to informing a business partner or supervisor.

TUMULTUOUS QUITTING:
OUTSPOKEN, OUTSMARTING OUTRAGE

Let's now consider the remaining "how-to"—the public quit. While *phronesis* would seem to most often manifest with tactful quitting, which does not put others on the defensive (and perhaps in the mode of retribution) or throw gasoline on the fire of interpersonal conflict, a highly visible ending has three defensible goals: avoiding harm, explaining oneself, and creating change.

As for the matter of harm to oneself and others, there are times in which it is sensible, even virtuous, to draw attention to a dire situation. In terms of protecting oneself, being open about a rationally justified quit can guard against insidious efforts to sabotage one's reputation by whoever is upset by the decision—sometimes the best defense is a good offense. Beyond personal concerns, conspicuous quitting by a whistleblower can warn others of imminent harm or call attention to ongoing injustice.[18] Most of us would affirm the moral courage of an engineer who publicly resigns and notifies the press because a bridge has a flawed design, a factory worker who walks off the job and calls attention to unhealthy practices in a food processing facility, an abused woman who breaks up with her partner and uses social media to warn others of domestic violence, or an adolescent parishioner who quits his church and informs the membership of the minister's sexually inappropriate contact.

The challenge for public-protest resignations—at least in politics and, by extension, in most other contexts—is to assure others that the action is genuine and free of ulterior motives. Virtuous behavior ought to be grounded in the intrinsic worthiness of cultivating one's character, not in the benefits of accruing accolades. We are rightly dubious of individuals who quit conspicuously to advance their self-interest by distancing themselves from problematic situations. Real-world instances include President Donald Trump's insiders who resigned after the January 6 insurrection and United States State Department workers who resigned flamboyantly during the Iraq War.[19] Rats that leave a sinking ship to wash their paws of a badly captained voyage are no more admirable than this terribly mixed metaphor. We are also justifiably suspicious of those who resign theatrically while asserting their moral purity, such as individuals who virtue-signal by quitting organizations that are less than perfectly woke in their policies and language.[20] Finally, we judge harshly those who quit as a vindictive tactic to harm the reputation of others.[21]

There is much to be said for the second goal of a public quit—the opportunity to share with others the rationale for one's decision. Among Aristotle's virtues is the proper pursuit of being respected or honored (as the mean between being conceited or pusillanimous).[22] Giving an account of one's actions is consistent with cultivating warranted esteem. Unsurprisingly, one of the best procedural frameworks for this element of quitting comes from the realm of politics.

FIGURE 11.1. The 650-member House of Commons is the United Kingdom's lower house of Parliament. Courtesy of the UK government via Wikimedia Commons.

The standard protest resignation from the British government culminates with the individual giving a statement in Parliament, during which they explain their reasons for quitting. In a typically gracious maneuver, the individual states an intention to support the government in all matters other than the one that precipitated the resignation (unless the official is also changing parties).[23] This formal opportunity to explain oneself is a means of going on the record with regard to a repugnant government policy and establishes a basis for others to later reflect on the thoughtfulness of the resigner. In rare instances, a cabinet member intensifies their moral outrage by eschewing decorum, bypassing Parliament, and going directly to the press.[24]

When a person quits an organization, relationship, or other endeavor, we might reasonably expect that family, friends, colleagues, and others are likely to interpret the decision as evidence of weak character—an incapacity to persevere through difficulty. As such, sharing the rationale with the people who are aware of the quit but not its reasons can be a valuable means of sustaining, even enhancing, one's respectability. An individual exhibits admirable courage, wisdom, and justice if they quit a job because the employer was insidiously profiting from the deception of vulnerable people, ends a relationship because the partner was secretly exploiting students for sexual favors, or forgoes chemotherapy because the otherwise private misery of the treatment made it impossible to savor time with family.

In explaining the basis for one's quitting to others, there may be tradeoffs between honesty and dignity. A climber might be too scared to continue but tell her partners that she's turning back because of injury or sickness. A politician might be anticipating charges of sexual impropriety but announce that he's quitting to "spend more time with family." Or an aging scientist might realize that she's unable to keep up with the newest methods but assert to the institution's board of directors a desire to move into administration. Do such falsities lack virtue? The answer is, of course, contingent and complex. If deception is intended to avoid harm to others (e.g., the family of the disgraced politician), then dishonesty might be justified. And if the lie provides others with a means of avoiding rash foolhardiness in the face of danger (e.g., the climber's fear could be appropriate for the conditions and the others might be in the grip of a sunk cost fallacy), then it might be virtuous. But, of course, the climber might simply be cowardly, the politician disgraced, and the scientist dishonorable. The devilish vice (or angelic virtue) lies in the details and turns on whether the deception makes the individual a better person while taking into account the well-being of others.

—

The final and most idealistic, but not entirely unrealistic, purpose of a public quit is to catalyze change—whether in an institution, community, or individual. Turning once again to the well-documented realm of politics, a study of US history concluded that "the success of a public-protest resignation is not solely the distance it causes the President to retreat but also the opportunity to elevate democratic discourse."[25] And in the UK, the "most aggressive of resignations" by a pair of long-serving chancellors were credited with bringing down Margaret Thatcher.[26]

Likewise, conspicuously quitting a company, university, or church for well-justified reasons can help move the organization toward practices that promote the flourishing of those who remain behind. However, "going public" with one's complaints can be a highly fraught strategy in that the individual can easily appear to be merely vengeful and querulous rather than genuinely concerned about the organization and its members. The challenge is even greater when it comes to intimate relationships, in which case even well-meaning critiques are more likely to evoke defensive entrenchment than honest reflection and growth. In a sense, divorce records, which include the grounds for the dissolution of a marriage, are a de facto public quitting. Although it is possible, there is surely reason to doubt whether public records or social media often stimulate change in philanderers, abusers, or scoundrels.

HOW (NOT) TO QUIT: INEPT EXITS

While we can make progress at quitting by observing those who have become skillful, we can also hone our practice by considering inept quits. Even those who advocate for more frequent quitting recognize indefensible forms, described as "threatening quit" (e.g., a lover uses emotional coercion to force a partner into some change), "disappearing act" (e.g., an employee simply stops coming to work and leaves the perplexed supervisor scrambling to find a replacement), "big bang" (e.g., a tennis player curses the line judge, flings his racquet, storms off the court, and refuses to return because close calls didn't go his way), and "stealth quit" (e.g., a church board member encourages the others to persevere during a difficult time while preparing to announce her resignation).[27]

Most of what we might consider to be badly performed exits exhibit a failure of character with regard to one or more of the cardinal virtues that constitute *phronesis*. Such shortcomings can be manifest at both large and small scales. As to the former, the US exit from Afghanistan in 2020 was a tragic bungling that exhibited a deplorable lack of courage (hunkering down inside the airport perimeter and leaving US citizens to find their own way out), wisdom (effectively turning the country over to the Taliban), justice (failing to protect Afghan allies who had risked their lives to assist the US military), and moderation (scrambling to withdraw troops in just five months and leaving behind billions of dollars of military hardware).[28]

One of the most spectacularly inept quits at the scale of the individual was that of John Stonehouse, a member of the British Parliament who held various ministerial positions beginning in 1957.[29] Having established a number of companies whose financial failings he attempted to cover up with creative accounting, in November 1974, Stonehouse decided to escape government investigations of his financial misdeeds along with a failing marriage. He traveled to Florida and faked his death by creating the appearance that he'd gone swimming and drowned in the ocean. This might have provided an operationally successful, if morally atrocious, lesson in "how to" quit one's business and personal relations, except one must remain hidden to pull it off. Stonehouse, however, soon reappeared without much guile in Australia, where he hoped to set up a new life with his mistress. Once discovered, he was arrested and sent back to the UK. In explaining his bizarre conduct to Parliament, Stonehouse appealed to having experienced a mental breakdown because his political ideals had been chronically frustrated (not because he was engaged in financial crimes and infidelity). Incredibly, the Labour Party did not expel him because its parliamentary majority was razor thin. Two years after his disappearing act, Stonehouse was convicted of fraud, theft, and forgery—and only then did he resign from the Privy Council (advisers to the British sovereign), becoming one of only three people to do so in the twentieth century.

So it was that Stonehouse managed to exhibit cowardice, foolishness, inequity, and licentiousness in the course of quitting badly. While this case seems obvious, what might have once seemed a poorly performed quit may become appropriate, even judicious, at a different time—and practical wisdom requires that one attend to changing social conditions.

—

When I began my work as a university professor in 1986, my aging colleagues considered it to be professional, even honorable, for one to announce an intention to retire well in advance and then quit to make room for younger faculty with new ideas and greater energy. Today, senior professors often hang on to their declining careers for many years. Moreover, when they finally retire, they frequently don't let the administration know in time to begin an expeditious search. Thirty years ago in the sciences, seeing young faculty quit one institution to upgrade their status at another was relatively rare, while today it is expected that they will be "on the market" continuously, seeking a better position elsewhere—and leaving their department in the lurch. Not to sound like a curmudgeonly geezer, but these contemporary exits seem like bad quits insofar as they disregard the academic community. And therein lies the explanation for why such exits are not indecorous.

Universities—like many other organizations—have shifted from a conceptual framework of a community based on reciprocity, respect, courtesy, and loyalty to quasi-corporations founded on self-interest and financial productivity. The appearance of accountability and efficiency is vital (ironically, the best way to increase one's salary is to obtain a letter of offer from another institution—a strategy that is profoundly inefficient as faculty game the interview system and waste considerable organizational resources in the process). My university, like many others, has adopted the corporate metaphor and uses the language of the standard "C-suite," with chief executive, financial, and information officers. In an organizational structure dominated by transactional calculations rather than human relationships (faculty and staff are now "human resources"), most every decision is made in terms of solipsistic gains and losses. Entrepreneurialism, in which one takes fiscal risks in the hope of personal advancement or profit, has replaced communalism.

As such, quitting is merely a move in this game (nothing personal, you understand), so the only badly done quit is one that fails to advantage the individual. Junior faculty have no institutional fidelity, and senior faculty have no assurance that retirement will create a new opportunity for a younger scholar (salary funds often are reallocated to non-academic uses). When it comes to the how-to of leaving, universities and other workplaces have become "frivolous games" in the philosophical terminology of Eddy M. Zemach and thereby lack abiding or solemn duties.[30]

QUINTESSENTIAL QUITTING: PRACTICE MAKES PERFECT

In a sense, Aristotle's insight was that the cultivation of virtue resembled the development of other human skills. Just as becoming a virtuosic musician requires long, difficult hours of practice, becoming a virtuous person demands that an individual repeatedly and diligently align their actions with the Doctrine of the Mean until doing so becomes second nature or a "settled disposition."[31] And so, becoming adept at applying *phronesis* to the task of quitting means that we must employ the same fundamental method for achieving excellence in any endeavor: We must practice.[32]

As such, the question becomes: How do people—particularly young people—gain opportunities to accumulate the experiences of quitting that would contribute to developing practical wisdom in this regard? Oldsters are fond of decrying the poor judgment of youth, but what can we expect in a society that largely protects children and adolescents from gaining experiences that are essential to their lifelong cultivation of practical wisdom?

—

The most explicit opportunity for learning how to quit takes the form of cultural rituals. With regard to developing the virtues, "The rituals that cultivate strengths can be thought of as simulations: trial runs that allow children and adolescents to display and develop a valued characteristic in a safe (as-if) context in which guidance is explicit."[33] Outside of religious practices such as Lent and Ramadan, we provide few such chances in our society. There is the tradition of the New Year's resolution, but this often takes the form of beginning some laudable endeavor with little chance of continuation (e.g., "I'll go to the gym three times a week"). But perhaps we should take a page from a friend of mine who adapted this ritual to decide what he'd forgo for the coming year, with one important caveat. At the end of December, he was free to decide whether his life was better for having renounced some habit, indulgence, or vice. Maybe this would make a particularly fine ritual to perform on the first and last day of each month (a year being quite a commitment).

FIGURE 11.2. A boy plays the piano, as diligent practice is the best way to improve one's skills in music and life. Courtesy of woodley wonderworks via Wikimedia Commons.

Ending personal and professional relationships is difficult to do well. As for romantic exits, perhaps "puppy love" among children and romantic crushes among adolescents provide some opportunities for developing practical wisdom in this realm. Adults certainly struggle with how to break up well, and a shortage of practice might be to blame—at least in part. Given that the average American has about five sexual partners in a lifetime,[34] there are relatively few chances to get better at leaving (not that I'm advocating promiscuity as a means of practicing breakups). With regard to employment exits, a typical American holds and quits more than a dozen jobs in their lifetime,[35] which provides substantially more opportunities to hone practical wisdom. Perhaps this is a good reason to encourage young people to take part-time jobs. After all, "responsibility" in the workplace means not only learning to arrive on time and give an honest day's work but also to quit judiciously.

Quitting a contest or a team may be one of the most available opportunities for young people to develop and apply *phronesis*. The entanglement of ego and emotion in the course of a chess game, a judo match, or a football season provides a rich context for practicing resignation, submission, or parting. A high school poker team might provide particularly good, if highly unconventional, chances to develop a range of relevant skills. Interestingly, given the potential of sports to provide literal and metaphorical playing fields in simulating real-life decisions, a significant upside of Title IX (which required balanced opportunities for females in school athletics) might have been in creating opportunities for young women to practice quitting and apply these experiences to other aspects of their unfolding lives.

Perhaps the paucity of structured opportunities to practice quitting partially explains young people's proclivity for experimenting with respect to diets, including many renunciations that are harmless or beneficial. Part of becoming a vegan or vegetarian as an adolescent may be motivated by health or moral concerns, but there is also likely to be an element of contrarianism as individuals shape their identities. In any case, giving up meat, energy drinks, or processed sugar provides an opportunity to experience abstention and learn how to best share the decision with others.

Unfortunately, many young people also have the chance to practice forgoing substance abuse (e.g., nicotine vaping is self-reported in 12% of eighth graders, 20% of tenth graders, and 27% of twelfth graders).[36] In addition to substance use disorders, addiction to video/internet gaming has been found in about 8 percent of youth between ages eight and eighteen,[37] and social media dependency is particularly problematic in children.[38] In an increasingly technologized world, cultivating the ability to quit (at least partially) among our youth is becoming a vital skill for their lifelong flourishing.

As for the ultimate quit, suicide is the second-leading cause of death among people ages fifteen to twenty-four in the US. Nearly 20 percent of high school students report having had serious thoughts of suicide, and 9 percent have made an attempt to take their lives.[39] With regard to "how-to," it is important to understand that people choose a method with which they are practiced, familiar, and comfortable (e.g., males use guns, females take poisons)—and it is important to know that if this favored means is unavailable (e.g., guns and drugs are secured in the home), the individual doesn't typically resort to a next-best choice.[40] Again, practical wisdom among mental health professionals requires not only formal training but also real-world experience.

—

Our contemporary efforts to protect children and adolescents from stress, struggle, and failure result in few relatively safe opportunities to practice the art of quitting insofar as quitting is inevitably a difficult decision to make and enact given that whatever we are forgoing provides some amount of pleasure or meaning. As such, many young people don't have abundant chances to practice (and botch) quitting until they leave home to pursue college, vocational education, or work.

Given the challenge of quitting, there is surely a place for skilled counselors (versus unqualified self-help advisers) to work with young adults with respect to whether and how to exit various endeavors. Taking a page from research on ending substance use disorders, efforts are most likely to be successful when there is both internal motivation and therapeutic assistance.[41]

Ultimately the individual, whether a teenager, thirty-something, or septuagenarian, must do the quitting. No amount of "book smarts" accumulated through reading, videos, or support will replace the "street smarts" that come with performing the action. One must step up to the plate. But learning to hit a baseball—or to quit a boxing match, romantic relationship, professional career, or chemotherapy regimen—is surely facilitated by a skilled coach or a wise mentor.

SAGACIOUS SURCEASE AND ERUDITE ENDING (NEVER QUIT BUILDING YOUR VOCABULARY)

I'll admit to being something of a skeptic when it comes to the value of therapy (probably a bias of my upbringing in which personal problems were not discussed and seeking help was not even considered). However, two of the therapists I interviewed for this book provided moving, honest, and profound insights with regard to how one quits phronetically, although neither used this philosophical term.

Dr. Robin Barry, a relationship therapist whose work focuses on family caregiving in the Department of Family Medicine at the University of Toledo Medical Center, shared stories of her application of practical wisdom to quitting. When she resigned from the University of Wyoming (where I came to know her), she recounted poor administrative decisions in her resignation letter in an effort to help those remaining at the institution, and when she divorced her husband, she told him in advance rather than serving papers on him out of the blue. Without going into detail, let's just say that neither of these tactics yielded the desired results. But with regard to cultivating her character, they were fruitful: "Quit in a way that is consistent with the person you want to be—in a way that will make you proud in retrospect."[42]

As for how-to quit, the spiritual director at the Hospice of Laramie, Dr. Lou Farley, spoke of the "style of dying." He contrasted those who exhibit a pervasive gratefulness and "glow with the joy of a life well-lived" with those who are praying to die while they "forget the present and make nothing of the moment." He considers a good ending to be one in which "the process of dying affords the individual and cared-for others the seed of generosity, discipline, patience, and wisdom"—qualities that surely accord with *phronesis*.[43]

CONCLUSION

A Few Last Words Before I Quit

Teaching and quitting have a great deal in common (and perhaps learning shares many qualities with persevering, but that's another issue altogether). Quitting is woven into our lives through relationships, jobs, contests, habits, beliefs, and identities. And as with quitting, teaching takes place in a staggering range of contexts—whenever our words are heard or our actions are observed by others who learn from us. Such diversity means that one cannot apply the same reasons and methods in teaching a dog to sit, a kindergartener to use scissors, a teenager to drive, a college student to speak German, a politician to understand climate change, or a pitcher to throw a curve ball.

This is not to say that there are no overarching principles that pertain to teaching, but it is to say that practical wisdom is ultimately the best way for one to apply theory and practice to particular instances—as with quitting. Some rules of thumb can serve as good starting points for teaching (e.g., don't attempt to instruct a pupil who has no interest in learning, and do teach in a way that motivates your students). And so, in this final section I'll try to extract a few heuristics with regard to quitting as a kind of principled foundation on which one can pursue practical wisdom.

Perhaps the most valuable guideline for teaching that I've learned in my thirty-nine years as a professor is that one should strive to comfort the afflicted and afflict the comfortable—to reassure the self-doubting student that they can learn and to challenge the self-assured student that they don't know everything. Discerning when to pat a back or kick a butt is the art, indeed the *phronesis*, of teaching.[1] I hope that this book, distilled into this conclusion, will reflect a teacherly artfulness for my readers.

THE ESSENCE OF ENDING: PHRONETIC APHORISMS

Given the complexity of quitting in terms of its forms, reasons, and methods, trying to condense the essential features of this profoundly important element of life into a few rules will inevitably oversimplify some features. However, quitting and its inverse, persevering, have provided rich soil for producing aphorisms going back to the fifth century BCE with Confucius offering "it does not matter how slowly you go as long as you do not stop"[2] and Gautama Buddha teaching that "men give up one thing to take up another, but in spite of numerous changes they do not find peace. They are no better than monkeys who let go of one bough to take hold of another, only to let it go again."[3] In the twentieth century, we have Babe Ruth averring that "all ballplayers should quit when it starts to feel as if all the baselines run uphill"[4] and Vince Lombardi famously asserting "quitters never win and winners never quit."[5] But because I don't find that the dozens of sayings available on the internet and elsewhere adequately convey the core ideas of my project, I will take the risk of adding to the storehouse of potential enlightenment. My contribution consists of five aphorisms while harboring no illusions of their capacity to become timeless pearls of wisdom.

HAMMERS AND SPREADSHEETS ARE USEFUL TOOLS FOR ARTLESS TASKS, BUT DECIDING TO QUIT IS MORE LIKE MAKING LOVE THAN DRIVING NAILS OR CALCULATING COST-BENEFIT RATIOS. By this, I mean to remind the reader that while justifiable quitting does not eschew cost-benefit analysis, as there is surely a place for this kind of quantitative reasoning, there is no way to craft a value-free spreadsheet. What one deems to be important constitutes the columns and what one finds negligible warrants exclusion (e.g., should one include a partner's irritating habits, culinary skills, or foot odor when deciding whether to end a relationship). Furthermore, recall that the intractable problem of an analytic approach is that we cannot convert all of our values to a common unit (e.g., how much does a short commute count versus an aggravating supervisor). As such, the art of quitting, or love making, or parenting, or teaching lies in developing the practical wisdom of grasping the (ir)relevance of many physical, psychological, and philosophical elements. And the most important of these pertains to the development of one's genuine flourishing, which leads us to the next aphorism.

A SKILLFUL SCULPTOR KNOWS WHEN TO STOP CHISELING, JUST AS A WISE PERSON UNDERSTANDS HOW TO QUIT IN THE COURSE OF SHAPING A LIFE. So it is that quitting is inescapably vital to the lifelong project of cultivating one's character such that the kind of person one aspires to be is central to if, why, when, what, and how one ends any important venture. Of course, it is often difficult, even painful, to disengage from the pursuit of some goal that shapes one's identity.[6] Conversely, being willing to glibly abandon the old and take on a new persona is a vacuous way of living. The challenge is to flourish at the so-called edge of chaos—that space of a dynamic system lying between desultory disorder and resolute rigidity.[7] We might think of quitting as a tool that one picks up and puts down in the process of crafting a life. As philosopher Robert E. Goodin put it: "What is the most appropriate mix of striving and settling, within any one life, or indeed within a society as a whole? That is hard to say, and quite probably for the very good reason that there is almost certainly no general, determinate answer."[8]

Likewise, artist-educator Clara Lieu notes that "knowing just when to declare a work of art finished [i.e., when to quit] is an eternal struggle for many artists."[9] The solution she offers is a set of teachable heuristics from a wise mentor, combined with encouraging her students to experiment and experience for themselves—a compelling formulation of *phronesis*.

QUITTING MAY BE FINISHED IN TERMS OF AN OVERT BODILY ENDING, BUT IT OFTEN PERSEVERES IN ONE'S MIND AND HEART FOR A LIFETIME. That is, quitting anything important is likely to be an enduring process, the external resolution of which might be achieved but the internal finality of which may never be reached. For many difficult decisions, such as ending a marriage, career, religion, or addiction, we want to put the past behind us and achieve that consummate state of "closure"—as if we were a butterfly metamorphosing into a new, nectar-sipping life, devoid of the harsh memories of the time spent chewing on bitter leaves. But such a fanciful ideal is contrary to cultivating a good life insofar as practical wisdom entails that we remember and learn from our quits. We get better at living and fulfilling our potential both by recalling those quits that were poorly justified and executed so we don't repeat our mistakes and by recollecting those quits that were principled and virtuosic so we can replicate our masterstrokes. As such, quitting is a perennial process, not a fleeting event or static condition. We should take some measured and merited pride in our scars as well as our successes when it comes to quitting (Aristotle considered warranted pride in our accomplishments, if not our injuries, to be a "crown of the virtues").[10]

SHOULD YOU QUIT A SPOUSE, JOB, RELIGION, CONTEST, HABIT, OR IDENTITY? DECIDE WHO ARE YOU AND WHO YOU ASPIRE TO BE. Quitting is profoundly situational and deeply personal. Remember that the virtues are individualized to one's capabilities. For one person, leaving their religion might be emotionally effortless and cognitively undemanding (perhaps they have only a weak association with a denomination through their family's merely habitual attendance of church services), while for another individual conversion could be intellectually arduous, psychologically traumatic, and socially fraught. My sense is that in contemporary American society, when faced with difficulty, we too readily quit difficult endeavors that warrant the labor of persistence (e.g., marriages and jobs) and we too uncritically persist in ventures that justify abandonment (e.g., end-of-life medical interventions and military conflicts). But these generalizations are rife with important exceptions and contingencies, given the diversity of contexts (e.g., the abused spouse and the presence of peacekeeping troops). The person who wonders whether they ought to quit is confronted by descriptive (who are you) and aspirational (who do you hope to be) questions. The answer to these questions requires that one knows—or at least reflects deeply regarding—their abilities, limitations, and potentials. This demand leads to our final aphorism.

THE HARDEST PRECEPT OF ALL: THE COURAGE TO JUDGE

In contemporary society, quitting is steadily becoming acceptable, but judging is increasingly objectionable. We ask rhetorically and accusatorily "who are you to judge." The answer might be that you are a moral individual seeking to improve yourself and foster a more just world, which requires that you have the guts to decide what is better and worse. But perhaps that's a bit too quick. These days, people distinguish among assessing (in which one considers all of the relevant factors in a situation), evaluating (in which one draws neutral conclusions from an assessment), and judging (in which one expresses a value-laden decision based on an evaluation). The first two of these are deemed to be permissible, but the last step is anathema to a society that seeks unconditional tolerance of all people and perspectives. However, I'll propose a last aphorism in defiance of this well-intended but naive cultural view.

IF MAKING JUDGMENTS IS TOO HARD, THEN QUIT. QUIT TRYING TO CULTIVATE GENUINE FRIENDSHIP OR FOSTER AUTHENTIC CHARACTER. Perhaps this is a bit harsh, but unless we're willing to honestly reflect on, and then praise or condemn, our actions and those of others, we are endorsing a kind of insipid relativism or

FIGURE 12.1. Adolf Eichmann is sentenced to death by three judges at the conclusion of the Nazi's war crimes trial. Courtesy of National Photo Collection of Israel via Wikimedia Commons.

admitting that we are reluctant to bear the burdens of learning from our actions and sharing honestly with friends. If we refuse to contemplate the reasons for and enactment of quitting, then we are giving up on cultivating practical wisdom. These labors are the work of constructing one's character in pursuit of what the Greeks called *eudaimonia*, an abiding state of genuine well-being. Such a condition is not one of hedonistic satisfaction but the realization of our potential. In modern life, philosophers might refer to this as "authenticity"—a term developed by the existentialists who insist that it is up to us to make sense of and give meaning to our existence.[11] These thinkers are critical of our tendency to conform to social norms, as doing so is simply making excuses for our behavior rather than acknowledging our freedom. It is our task to create ourselves and take responsibility for our decisions, including whether to quit.

In delving further into making judgments, let's begin with the most socially taboo critique: Is another person's quitting justified? The key to making such a determination is our capacity for empathy, or the ability to understand, however incompletely, the thoughts and feelings of another person. This form of shared experience fosters connection, while sympathy creates separation by merely feeling sorry for another person.[12] Of course, empathy will be inexact given that our capacity to imagine someone else's physical and mental state is necessarily an extrapolation of our own experiences.

When your son throws down his baseball glove and storms off the field because he's dropped another pop fly in practice, you can "get" his frustration and judge both his reasons and the form of quitting to be unacceptable while your practical wisdom shapes just how you can most compassionately and effectively engage the child. Likewise, given that I'm married to the same woman after forty-three years and she's supported my non-linear career path from the sciences to the humanities and arts, I can empathize with my friend who's decided to divorce her husband based on his refusal to affirm her desire to change careers, which requires moving to another city, and I can conclude that she's justified in leaving. As a good parent or friend, one not only assesses and evaluates but summons the courage to judge and provide people one cares about with what one believes to be constructive feedback, whether it reproves or endorses their quitting. Finding the right mentor is a challenge, as evidenced by the conflicting recommendations of a self-help author who both lauds and disparages parental feedback—and ironically dismisses advice from self-help books.[13]

An absolutely essential element of empathetically judging others is being keenly aware that one might well be mistaken. We must have a sense of epistemic humility and a willingness to amend our opinion as we come to know more about the other person. Perhaps your son tells you that the other kids are mercilessly mocking him for his lack of baseball skills and the coach is unwilling to curtail this cruelty. And so, his quitting now seems quite justifiable. Or maybe I discover that my friend is in a manic phase because she's stopped taking her medication, and this new job is no more than a fantasy about joining Cirque du Soleil despite her having no dance or gymnastic training. If so, her divorce now appears to be extremely ill-conceived.

Daniel Kahneman won the 2002 Nobel Prize in Economics for his work challenging the assumption of human rationality in economic models. This famed behavioral economist was asked "the secret to good quitting." His answer: "What everybody needs is the friend who really loves them but does not care much about hurt feelings in the moment."[14] Perhaps we all need an intimate, tough-love confidante with this great-hearted disposition. While the interviewer interpreted Kahneman's answer to mean that we need someone to provide the unpleasant truth that we are on a path we need to abandon,[15] it is just as vital to hear that our plan to quit appears inauthentic (in modern philosophical terms) and reflects a shortage of courage, wisdom, justice, or moderation (in ancient philosophical terms). We need to hear that persevering is sometimes foolhardy, but we also need to be told when quitting undermines our character.

The somewhat more socially acceptable task is to stand in judgment of oneself. For those who are—or believe themselves to be—their own harshest critics, lots of popular psychology sources advise against this internal dialogue.[16] However, I came across one source that recommended that people accept their inner critic, learn from their mistakes, engage in constructive self-reproval, and critique their work (not their self-worth)—all of which struck me as sound advice for those seeking to cultivate *phronesis*.[17] It undoubtedly feels better to engage in self-affirmation, forget about past mistakes, practice self-compassion, and eschew regret. And there's much to be said for celebrating one's successes, including when a quit is well-conceived and implemented. But figuring out what went wrong is also vital to improvement. A US military leader must probe painstakingly into what can be learned from the wars in Iraq and Afghanistan,[18] just as a martial arts sensei insists that students analyze how they came to be in a position that required submission to an opponent.[19]

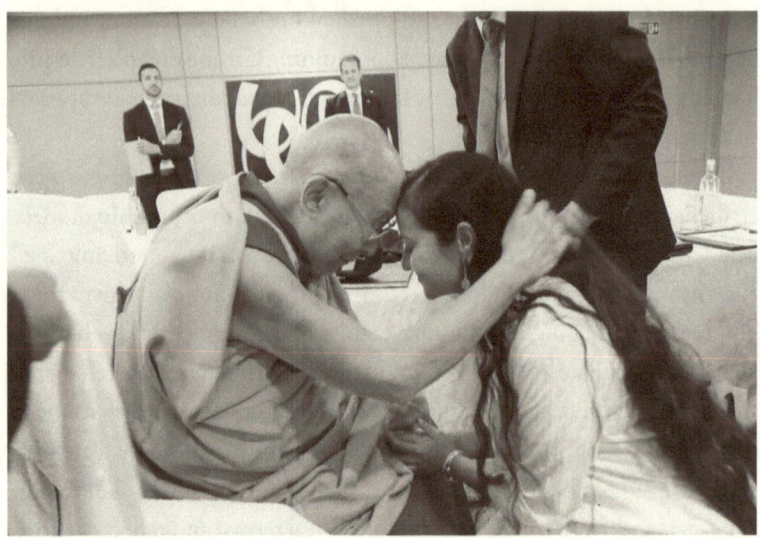

FIGURE 12.2. We must seek mentors who speak the truth when it comes to quitting—people like the Dalai Lama who sagely noted that "happiness doesn't always come from a pursuit." Courtesy of US Embassy New Delhi via Wikimedia Commons.

This brings us to the matter of choosing sagacious mentors—individuals who are able and willing to judge us or, even better, to draw us into a brutally and lovingly frank self-reflection on whether our quitting is principled and adroit. According to Mark Jenkins, a climber who summited Mount Everest, mountaineers possess but suppress an understanding that they have quit badly; their inclination is to shift responsibility (e.g., the weather was adverse or the maps weren't accurate). Existential authenticity means taking responsibility and having the integrity to explain—not to rationalize or absolve—a poorly executed quit.[20]

Contrary to Jenkins's view, Annie Duke—a former professional poker player turned business consultant and well-known quit proponent—contends that a climber can't fail. Either they summit or they implement the "kill criteria" (the preset time at which one turns back), and both constitute a win.[21] This is a fine strategy for building self-esteem, but if one quits an ascent because the turnaround time was triggered due to poor preparation, impractical planning, or cowardly pacing, then claiming victory is fatuous and even dangerous. Jenkins contends that to stay alive, let alone to succeed as an alpinist, one must fully grasp that "mountaineering is a long game, where self-honesty is crucial." The same can be said of life and the need for forthright judgment of one's quits. Given our capacity for exculpation and the psychological difficulty of accepting responsibility—a condition the existentialists well understand—the selection of a person who will aid in holding us accountable to ourselves can be crucial.

Consider Socrates. He was not interested in teaching others what he claimed to know but rather in encouraging his students to pursue self-knowledge through inquiry, including both questioning social norms and gaining self-awareness (what his enemies considered corrupting the youth). One can readily imagine a Socratic dialogue in which quitting is the topic of intense interrogation as the mentor demands of their interlocutor an account of the nature of quitting, the reasons for quitting, and the proper mode of quitting. The philosopher would neither abide excuses nor accept superficial expositions. Such is the value of a mentor who insists that a student, friend, or client engage in honest reflection.

A person can learn to function as their own constructively critical questioner. This is something like the way a writing teacher initially serves as external judge of a student's work while cultivating the young writer's ability to develop their internal editor. I often encourage students to put away a piece of writing for some time, so they can return to it with a more impartial, less defensive disposition. But when it comes to judging our intentions for taking action, such as quitting, research suggests that the passage of time may be problematic—or so it appears according to one interpretation of the data. Six to twelve months after some behavior, most people give different reasons for their action than they did at the time.[22] Researchers tend to presume that this later account is less accurate and involves greater rationalization; however, it's possible that the new reasons are more honest and objective (something like what we hope to achieve through the emotional distance of putting the essay in a drawer). While we may not be able to directly or objectively assess our intentions and actions, it does seem possible, upon sustained reflection, to know when we are providing a genuine reason for quitting versus making an excuse (i.e., a reason intended to avoid responsibility).

TRUE STORIES: GRIT AND QUIT

These aphorisms might seem a bit sententious and grim, but quitting is not something one ought to take lightly—or at least it should be done in proportion to the gravity of that which is being abandoned. However, recall that one of the fundamental qualities of quitting is hopefulness. An individual gives up in the belief that doing so will lead to greater well-being. We end a relationship in the hope of finding a better partner; we resign from a job with the aspiration of improving our career; we convert from a religion in the hope that another faith will resonate with our identity; we give up a harmful substance (alcohol, tobacco, soda, or meat) with the belief that we will thrive. Even an individual who decides to end their life might well think that nothingness (or some hoped-for afterlife) is superior to the misery of living.

For many people, quitting is the recognition that one's time and energy are zero-sum insofar as it may be necessary to do fewer things in order to do some things well. Or quitting may be needed to carve out the time for something closer to our unrealized potential. As such, quitting can be a potent precursor to creating a more authentic life that accords with both who one is and who one aspires to become. But again, given the human capacity for rationalization, it is crucial that we reflect deeply and honestly as to the nature of our decision to quit. And this leads to my final reflections in the form of personal stories that are intended to capture the complexity of grit-or-quit with respect to cultivating character and pursuing an exemplary life.

My son, Ethan, has been a climber, backpacker, and trail runner for years, during which he has learned a great deal about persevering and quitting.[23] As a college sophomore in 2012, he and his then-girlfriend decided to climb Pyramid Peak, the highest point in California's Desolation Wilderness, which requires a very arduous but non-technical ascent.[24] The final stretch necessitated scrambling over huge boulders, which made it difficult to see one's partner. Feeling an almost "magnetic pull" to reach the summit, Ethan clambered ahead, reached the top, and waited. When his girlfriend didn't arrive, he hurried back down and found her crying and scared. "I messed up," he told me. "She could've made it, but I violated the implicit agreement between climbers to stay together." Instead, "summit fever" had instilled an intense desire to keep going—and this selfish perseverance meant having abandoned his duty.

They pursued another peak with three friends a few months later. The notorious Cactus-to-Clouds trek is one of the hardest day hikes in the world, rising 10,300 feet in just 16 miles from Palm Springs, California, to San Jacinto Peak.[25] Along the way, Ethan developed a plan, a kind of penance through quitting. He stopped just minutes from the top and waited, reflecting on his earlier mistake and teaching himself a vital lesson about misguided perseverance. The others reached the summit, and upon their return nobody questioned his decision amid their jubilation.

Although he tries to avoid the cliché that "it's about the journey, not the destination," that's what he's come to understand. Even though the climbing community promotes keeping checklists of successful ascents, Ethan doesn't sign summit registers and avoids a scorecard measure of achievement. If quitting before the top means returning home safely (even if he figures that he probably could have soloed those last, risky moves), then he keeps his body healthy and his ego disciplined. And so, quitting is a tactic that allows him to persevere in the long game of his unfolding life in the outdoors.

In 2018, Ethan started—and quit, then didn't—his first 100-mile trail race. The 107 miles of the Idaho Mountain Trail Ultra Festival (IMTUF, a clever acronym) included more than 20,000 feet of gross vertical gain with a cutoff time of thirty-six hours. He'd trained for years, beginning with 2-mile cross-country races in high school, followed by 50-kilometer races in college, and then 50-mile races in graduate school (often finishing in the top ten and sometimes in first place). Ethan wanted to know what was possible; when would his body quit? He assembled a support crew, including a pair of pacers: his long-term partner, Molly (who would run through the night with him and co-hallucinate); and a close friend, James (who would run the last 19 miles with him). In the first half of the race, runners dropped out largely because they broke down physically; in the second half, the challenge was mental perseverance. During the latter, Ethan put on headphones to escape the pain, a tactic he came to regret.

Hoping to reach a key aid station in the middle of night, they arrived at dawn—and Ethan knew he'd fallen far behind his planned pace. Now 88 miles and 26 hours into the race, he was utterly exhausted and decided to call it quits. Then James showed up, full of unrelenting positivity and saying "c'mon, get up, let's go." Ethan rose, engaged his friend in a mantra (murmuring "catch the carnage" as they slowly reeled in other runners), took in the beauty of the mountains, and laughed at the sheer absurdity of the venture. He finished in 34:29:50.

My son started one other 100-miler before the pandemic; however, unable to keep food or drink down, his body quit after 50 miles. He plans to run another: "I physically finished one, but now I want to do it right." He wants to be fully present for all the brutal lows and ecstatic highs (no headphones). Virtuous perseverance, like good quitting, has to be done for the right reasons, in the right way.

——

Perhaps the most heartrending response to quitting is Dylan Thomas's "Do Not Go Gentle into That Good Night."[26] In this poem, a son pleads with his father not to give up but to "rage, rage against the dying of the light." An octogenarian friend views Thomas as selfish, not wanting to lose his father but lacking concern for what might be best for the old man. But I prefer to read this as a love poem, an expression of the son's desperate desire for one more day with the man who is so profoundly important to him.

Of course, Thomas knew that death is inevitable and natural: "Though wise men at their end know dark is right." However, I like to imagine that he is calling for his father to persevere not because he can prevail in the unwinnable contest against mortality but because raging in futile defiance can be a self-defining act. Even when loss is inevitable, one can retain dignity and strengthen character by not gently accepting an easy conclusion. The fact that one is beaten does not mean one is a loser, but perhaps the son must also understand that giving up has its proper time—and that quitting does not make one a quitter.

This poem has been the subject of extensive literary analysis and debate. I am not a scholar of Dylan Thomas or poetics, so I can't offer an authoritative interpretation. What I do understand is that sometimes "wise men know" certain things about living, persevering, and quitting. And sometimes, young men provide lessons that fathers might heed.

"Do Not Go Gentle into That Good Night"
DYLAN THOMAS

Do not go gentle into that good night,
Old age should burn and rave at close of day;
Rage, rage against the dying of the light.

Though wise men at their end know dark is right,
Because their words had forked no lightning they
Do not go gentle into that good night.

Good men, the last wave by, crying how bright
Their frail deeds might have danced in a green bay,
Rage, rage against the dying of the light.

Wild men who caught and sang the sun in flight,
And learn, too late, they grieve it on its way,
Do not go gentle into that good night.

Grave men, near death, who see with blinding sight
Blind eyes could blaze like meteors and be gay,
Rage, rage against the dying of the light.

And you, my father, there on the sad height,
Curse, bless, me now with your fierce tears, I pray.
Do not go gentle into that good night.
Rage, rage against the dying of the light.

Epilogue

I put this manuscript aside—a temporary quit—for four months in 2024 when my son, Ethan, was involved in a serious automobile accident caused by another driver crossing the center line and hitting him head-on. The crash ruptured his atrium. The doctors in the emergency room didn't quit despite a blood pressure of 40/20; a gifted surgeon repaired his heart just minutes before my son would have died.

And then began Ethan's long, grueling struggle. He suffered fifteen fractures and went through eight surgeries (including skin grafts), along with enduring a traumatic brain injury and several small strokes from vascular emboli. From July 13 to November 3, my wife and I stayed with him and his steadfast life partner, Molly (our leaving to return home was heartrending but a "good quit"). Amid tears, he gritted his way through long, painful weeks in intensive care, acute care, in-patient rehabilitation, and in-home therapies, along with countless hours of out-patient physical, occupational, speech-language, and psychological therapies.

As I write this in December 2024, Ethan refers to his walking as "a work in progress," but he's been hiking up to three miles in the foothills of Wenatchee, Washington, as well as riding his bike for fifteen miles along the Columbia River, carrying on complex conversations, playing strategic games, watching movies, sending emails, and reading books. His short-term memory and higher executive functions, as well as fine motor control in his right hand, are coming along. He still tires easily and has a way to go in terms of cognitive and physical stamina.

The bottom line is that Ethan and Molly were tenacious and courageous. They didn't quit—except. Except that the meaningful markers of recovery all involved quitting: the feeding tube, the catheter, the wheelchair, the walker, the cane, and—perhaps most hellish—the opiates that made his pain endurable during recovery. Tender visits from his loving sister, who brought touching artwork from his young nieces, were sources of strength. Time with aunts and uncles, along with kind and generous friends, surely made Ethan's journey less awful, but ultimately it was his to continue or abandon. The core of his remarkable progress (and the wellspring that sustained my days at his bedside) was an abiding sense of gratefulness, as he earnestly thanked family, friends, doctors, nurses, and therapists, as well as the custodians and orderlies (who delivered almost palatable hospital food). So, maybe I have one more book in me. Something about the nature and practice of gratitude, perhaps.

Notes

PREFACE

1. Concern for practical philosophy (as contrasted with theoretical philosophy) can be traced back to the ancient Greeks and their attention to how one led a good life. Around 250 years ago, Immanuel Kant distinguished between how we ought to behave (practical) versus how we come to know (conceptual). In modern times, the School of Practical Philosophy (https://www.practicalphilosopher.org/) was founded in 1937 and has expanded to more than seventy affiliates worldwide. The American Philosophical Practitioners Association was formed in 1999 and publishes a peer-reviewed journal. The goals of these enterprises largely overlap with those of more recent organizations devoted to public philosophy, including the Public Philosophy Network (https://www.publicphilosophynetwork.net/), which publishes the *Public Philosophy Journal*, and the American Philosophical Association's Committee on Public Philosophy (https://www.apaonline.org/group/public).
2. "W. C. Field Quotes," BrainyQuote, accessed February 12, 2025, https://www.brainyquote.com/quotes/w_c_fields_108002.
3. "Routledge Handbooks in Philosophy," accessed February 12, 2025, https://www.routledge.com/Routledge-Handbooks-in-Philosophy/book-series/RHP.

INTRODUCTION: CALL ME A QUITTER

1. "The Great Resignation Statistics," EDsmart, accessed February 12, 2025, https://www.edsmart.org/the-great-resignation-statistics/.

2. "I just chipped off all the stone that didn't look like David," Quote Investigator, accessed February 12, 2025, https://quoteinvestigator.com/2014/06/22/chip-away/.
3. "I wish I knew how to quit you," Schmoop Quotes, accessed February 12, 2025, https://www.shmoop.com/quotes/i-wish-i-knew-how-to-quit-you.html.
4. "Richard M. Nixon Quotes," BrainyQuote, accessed February 12, 2025, https://www.brainyquote.com/quotes/richard_m_nixon_116453.
5. "Douglas MacArthur Quotes," GoodReads, accessed February 12, 2025, https://www.goodreads.com/quotes/242252-americans-never-quit.
6. Douglas MacArthur, *Reminiscences of General of the Army Douglas MacArthur* (Annapolis, MD: Bluejacket Books, 1964), 101.
7. "Mike Ditka Quotes," BrainyQuote, accessed February 12, 2025, https://www.brainyquote.com/quotes/mike_ditka_357629.
8. Binesh Shrestha, "Former NFL's Mike Ditka's Successful Marriage with Wife Diana Ditka," SuperBhub, October 11, 2018, http://superbhub.com/entertainment/former-nfls-mike-ditkas-successful-marriage-wife-diana-ditka-married-since-1977/.
9. "Jack Nicklaus Quotes," BrainyQuote, accessed February 12, 2025, https://www.brainyquote.com/quotes/jack_nicklaus_159075; "Jack Nicklaus," Wikipedia, January 10, 2025, https://en.wikipedia.org/wiki/Jack_Nicklaus.
10. "Billie Jean King Quotes," BrainyQuote, accessed February 12, 2015, https://www.goodreads.com/quotes/209337-champions-keep-playing-until-they-get-it-right.
11. "Billie Jean King," Wikipedia, February 13, 2025, https://en.wikipedia.org/wiki/Billie_Jean_King.
12. "Chris Evert Quotes," A-Zquotes, accessed February 12, 2025, https://www.azquotes.com/quote/769188.
13. "Family Life: Marriage and Divorce," Centers for Disease Control and Prevention, March 13, 2024, https://www.cdc.gov/nchs/fastats/marriage-divorce.htm; "Chris Evert," Wikipedia, February 5, 2025, https://en.wikipedia.org/wiki/Chris_Evert.
14. Jennifer Hassan, "Naomi Osaka Hailed for Bravery, Pilloried for 'Diva Behavior' amid French Open Withdrawal," *Washington Post*, June 1, 2021, https://www.washingtonpost.com/world/2021/06/01/naomi-osaka-world-reacts-mental-health/.
15. "Ashleigh Barty: World Number One Makes Shock [sic] Call to Quit Tennis," BBC, March 23, 2022, https://www.bbc.com/news/world-australia-60843870.
16. Clem Samson, "Is Cowardice the New Courage?" The Haven, September 10, 2021, https://medium.com/the-haven/is-cowardice-the-new-courage-12a1257c3c40.
17. Stephen King, *On Writing: A Memoir of the Craft* (New York: Scribner, 2010), 39.
18. Javier Bernacer and Jose I. Murillo. "The Aristotelian Conception of Habit and Its Contribution to Human Neuroscience," *Frontiers in Human Neuroscience* 8 (2014): 883, doi.org/10.3389/fnhum.2014.00883.
19. Peg Streep and Alan B. Bernstein, *Quitting: Why We Fear It—and Why We Shouldn't—in Life, Love, and Work* (Boston: Da Capo, 2014), 213.
20. Christopher Peterson and Martin E. P. Seligman, *Character Strengths and Virtues: A Handbook and Classification* (New York: American Psychological Association and Oxford University Press, 2004), 234; Julia Keller, *Quitting: A Life Strategy* (New York: Balance/Hachette, 2023), 15.
21. Keller, *Quitting: A Life Strategy*, 5–13.

22. Julia Watzek and Sarah F. Brosnan, "Capuchin and Rhesus Monkeys Show Sunk Cost Effects in a Psychomotor Task," *Scientific Reports* 10 (2020): article number 20396.
23. Keller, *Quitting: A Life Strategy*, 40.
24. Watty Piper, *The Little Engine That Could: 90th Anniversary Edition* (New York: Grosset and Dunlap, 2020).
25. Suzanne Collins, *The Hunger Games* (New York: Scholastic, 2008).
26. Lynn Marie Morski, *Quitting by Design: Learn to Use Strategic Quitting as a Tool to Carve Out a Successful Life* (New York: Austin Macauley, 2018), 15. See also, Keller, *Quitting: A Life Strategy*, in which the author disparages self-help books but ironically devotes half of her own book to a section titled "Giving Up: A How-to Guide." The book enjoys a high Amazon ranking in the category "Motivational Self-Help" (https://www.amazon.com/Quitting-Strategy-Perseverance-Science-Giving-ebook/dp/B0B8YWVWN5, accessed February 12, 2015).
27. Keller, *Quitting: A Life Strategy*, xx.
28. "H. L. Mencken Quotes," BrainyQuote, accessed February 12, 2025, https://www.brainyquote.com/quotes/h_l_mencken_129796.
29. "All Science Is Either Physics or Stamp Collecting," Quote Investigator, accessed February 12, 2025, https://quoteinvestigator.com/2015/05/08/stamp/.
30. "Divorce Rates by Country, 2022," World Population Review, accessed February 12, 2025, https://worldpopulationreview.com/country-rankings/divorce-rates-by-country.
31. "Suicide Rates by Country, 2022," World Population Review, accessed February 12, 2025, https://worldpopulationreview.com/country-rankings/suicide-rate-by-country.
32. Jason Lalljee, "The Great Resignation Is Working for Women," Insider, March 22, 2022, https://www.businessinsider.com/great-resignation-women-pay-gap-quitting-jobs-to-make-more-2022-3.
33. Brooke Le Poer Trench, "Why Am I So Triggered When Women Quit Senior Roles for Their Families?" Allbright, June 30, 2021, https://www.allbrightcollective.com/edit/articles/why-am-i-so-triggered-when-women-quit-senior-roles-for-their-families.
34. Bernard C. K. Choi and Anita W. P. Pak. "Multidisciplinarity, Interdisciplinarity and Transdisciplinarity in Health Research, Services, Education, and Policy: 1. Definitions, Objectives, and Evidence of Effectiveness," *Clinical and Investigative Medicine* 29 (2006): 361–364. In this paper, the authors cogently define multidisciplinarity as "additive" by drawing on knowledge from different disciplines but staying within their boundaries; interdisciplinarity as "interactive" by analyzing, synthesizing, and harmonizing links among disciplines into a coordinated and coherent whole; and transdisciplinarity as "holistic" by integrating the natural, social, and health sciences in a humanities context that transcends their traditional boundaries.
35. Zoe Wynns, "Most People Never Finish Writing Their Book," Self Publishing US, February 2, 2023, https://www.selfpublishingus.com/post/most-people-never-finish-writing-their-book.
36. Thomas Umstattd Jr., "How to Hook Readers in the First 50 Pages," AuthorMedia, May 31, 2023, https://www.authormedia.com/the-power-of-first-impressions-how-to-hook-readers-in-the-first-50-pages/.

37 James Colley, "The Joy of Not Finishing Books: If You Don't Like It, Don't Read It," *The Guardian*, November 30, 2018, https://www.theguardian.com/commentisfree/2018/nov/30/the-joy-of-not-finishing-books-if-you-dont-like-it-dont-read-it.
38 "Taylor Swift Quotes," Twitter, May 23, 2015, https://twitter.com/quotetayswift/status/602324657249869824?lang=en.

CHAPTER 1: PERSONAL ENDINGS

1 "Why You Shouldn't Say 'Give Up for Adoption': The Importance of Positive Adoption Language," American Adoptions, accessed February 12, 2015, https://www.americanadoptions.com/pregnant/other-ways-to-say-give-up-for-adoption.
2 Lynn Marie Morski, *Quitting by Design: Learn to Use Strategic Quitting as a Tool to Carve Out a Successful Life* (New York: Austin Macauley, 2018), 62.
3 Robin Barry (psychologist and director of research in the Department of Family Medicine, University of Toledo), interview with the author, September 10, 2021.
4 Barry, interview, 2021.
5 Margaret Wilson (professor, Department of Theatre and Dance, University of Wyoming), interview with the author, April 13, 2022.
6 Barry, interview, 2021.
7 Karen Kayser, *When Love Dies: The Process of Marital Disaffection* (New York: Guilford, 1993).
8 Alison Clarke-Stewart and Cornelia Brentano, *Divorce: Causes and Consequences* (Current Perspectives in Psychology) (New Haven, CT: Yale University Press, 2007), 4–10.
9 Clarke-Stewart and Brentano, *Divorce*, 16–19.
10 Barry, interview, 2021.
11 Clarke-Stewart and Brentano, *Divorce*, 35–49.
12 Clarke-Stewart and Brentano, *Divorce*, 20–22.
13 Kayser, *When Love Dies*, 68.
14 Although the quote that indifference is the opposite of love is commonly attributed to Elie Wiesel, this notion appeared in print sixty-five years before Wiesel's statement in a book by prominent Austrian psychologist Wilhelm Stekel (https://quoteinvestigator.com/2019/05/21/indifference/February 15, 2025).
15 Morski, *Quitting by Design*, 68–69.
16 Clarke-Stewart and Brentano, *Divorce*, 22.
17 Clarke-Stewart and Brentano, *Divorce*, 25–26.
18 Clarke-Stewart and Brentano, *Divorce*, 89.
19 Eddy M. Zemach, "The Right to Quit," *Philosophical Quarterly* 23 (1973): 346–349.
20 Morksi, *Quitting by Design*, 28.
21 Søren Kierkegaard (Alastair Hannay, translator), *Fear and Trembling* (New York: Penguin Classics, 1986).
22 "Martyr," Wikipedia, February 14, 2025, https://en.wikipedia.org/wiki/Martyr.
23 Stuart A. Wright, "Disengagement and Apostasy in New Religious Movements," in *The Oxford Handbook of Religious Conversion*, ed. Lewis R. Rambo and Charles E. Farhadian (New York: Oxford University Press, 2014), 707.

24 Lewis R. Rambo and Charles E. Farhadian, "Introduction," in *The Oxford Handbook of Religious Conversion*, ed. Lewis R. Rambo and Charles E. Farhadian (New York: Oxford University Press, 2014), 5.
25 Quoted in Rambo and Farhadian, "Introduction," 5.
26 Quoted in Rambo and Farhadian, "Introduction," 5.
27 Diane Austin-Broos, "The Anthropology of Conversion: An Introduction," in *Anthropology of Religious Conversion*, ed. Andrew Buckser and Stephen D. Glazier (New York: Rowman and Littlefield, 2003), 1.
28 Thomas Kingsley Brown, "Mystical Experiences, American Culture, and Conversion to Christian Spiritualism," in *Anthropology of Religious Conversion*, ed. Andrew Buckser and Stephen D. Glazier (New York: Rowman and Littlefield, 2003), 142.
29 Todd M. Johnson, "Demographics of Religious Conversion," in *The Oxford Handbook of Religious Conversion*, ed. Lewis R. Rambo and Charles E. Farhadian (New York: Oxford University Press, 2014), 51.
30 Johnson, "Demographics of Religious Conversion," 52.
31 Heinz Streib, "Deconversion," in *The Oxford Handbook of Religious Conversion*, ed. Lewis R. Rambo and Charles E. Farhadian (New York: Oxford University Press, 2014), 280.
32 Michael Levitt, "These 2 Charts Show America's Christian Majority Is on Track to End," NPR, September 17, 2022, https://www.opb.org/article/2022/09/17/american-christian-majority-on-track-to-end/.
33 Streib, "Deconversion," 275–276.
34 Streib, "Deconversion," 275–276.
35 Mary Ann Reidhead and Van A. Reidhead, "From Jehovah's Witness to Benedictine Nun: The Roles of Experience and Context in a Double Conversion," in *Anthropology of Religious Conversion*, ed. Andrew Buckser and Stephen D. Glazier (New York: Rowman and Littlefield, 2003), 185.
36 Lewis Rambo, "Anthropology and the Study of Conversion," in *Anthropology of Religious Conversion*, ed. Andrew Buckser and Stephen D. Glazier (New York: Rowman and Littlefield, 2003), 213.
37 Raymond F. Paloutzian, "Psychology of Religious Conversion and Spiritual Transformation," in *The Oxford Handbook of Religious Conversion*, ed. Lewis R. Rambo and Charles E. Farhadian (New York: Oxford University Press, 2014), 222–223; Dan Smyer Yu, "Buddhist Conversion in the Contemporary World," in *The Oxford Handbook of Religious Conversion*, ed. Lewis R. Rambo and Charles E. Farhadian (New York: Oxford University Press, 2014), 467; Wright, "Disengagement and Apostasy," 709–710.
38 Wright, "Disengagement and Apostasy," 709–710.
39 Wright, "Disengagement and Apostasy," 709–710.
40 Streib, "Deconversion," 271.
41 Streib, "Deconversion," 272.
42 David W. Kling, "Conversion to Christianity," in *The Oxford Handbook of Religious Conversion*, ed. Lewis R. Rambo and Charles E. Farhadian (New York: Oxford University Press, 2014), 603.

43 "Americans' Complex Views on Gender Identity and Transgender Issues," Pew Research Center, June 28, 2022, https://www.pewresearch.org/social-trends/2022/06/28/americans-complex-views-on-gender-identity-and-transgender-issues/.
44 Kate Birdsall, *In Between: A Memoir* (independently published, 2021).
45 Michael Castleman, "Living Happily Ever After, and Never, Ever Having Sex," *Psychology Today*, September 1, 2016, https://www.psychologytoday.com/us/blog/all-about-sex/201609/living-happily-ever-after-and-never-ever-having-sex.
46 "Drug Abuse Statistics," National Center for Drug Abuse Statistics, accessed February 12, 2025, https://drugabusestatistics.org/.
47 Gene M. Heyman, "Quitting Drugs: Quantitative and Qualitative Features," *Annual Review of Clinical Psychology* 9 (2013): 38–39.
48 Heyman, "Quitting Drugs," 29, 31–32.
49 Alison Looby (professor, Department of Psychology, University of Wyoming), interview with the author, July 20, 2021.
50 American Psychiatric Association, *Diagnostic and Statistical Manual of Mental Disorders*, 5th ed.: *DSM-5* (Washington, DC: American Psychiatric Publishing, 2013).
51 Heyman, "Quitting Drugs," 53, 37, 32.
52 Craig Varnell (professional poker player with $1.2 million in winnings 2015–2022), interview with the author, February 4, 2022.
53 Tess Kilwein (licensed psychologist and director of Clinical Training, University of Wyoming, Counseling Center) and Looby, joint interview, 2021.
54 Kilwein, interview, 2021; Heyman, "Quitting Drugs," 48–51.
55 Heyman, "Quitting Drugs," 51, 53.
56 Kilwein, interview, 2021.
57 Kilwein and Looby, joint interview, 2021.
58 Dana A. V. Braner (medical doctor and professor of pediatrics, Division of Critical Care, School of Medicine, Oregon Health and Science University) and Paula Ann Vanderford (medical doctor and associate professor of pediatrics, Division of Critical Care, School of Medicine, Oregon Health and Science University), joint interview with the author, February 7, 2022.
59 Braner, interview, 2022.
60 Vanderford, interview, 2022.
61 Braner, interview, 2022.
62 Vanderford, interview, 2022.
63 Braner, interview, 2022.
64 Braner, interview, 2022.
65 Melissa Bailey and JoNel Aleccia, "Barbara Bush's End-Of-Life Decision Stirs Debate over 'Comfort Care,'" *Kaiser Health News*, April 17, 2018, https://khn.org/news/barbara-bushs-end-of-life-decision-stirs-debate-over-comfort-care/.
66 Lou Farley (spiritual director and licensed clinical psychologist, Hospice of Laramie), interview with the author, August 8, 2021.
67 Farley, interview, 2021.
68 Quoted in "Suicide," National Institute of Mental Health (NIMH), accessed February 12, 2025, https://www.nimh.nih.gov/health/statistics/suicide.

69 Kay Redfield Jamison, *Night Falls Fast: Understanding Suicide* (New York: Knopf, 1999), 27–28.
70 Jamison, *Night Falls Fast*, 34; "Death Wish," *American Psychological Association Dictionary of Psychology*, accessed February 12, 2025, https://dictionary.apa.org/death-wish.
71 Jamison, *Night Falls Fast*, 309; "Suicide," NIMH.
72 "Suicide," NIMH; Carolyn Pepper (professor and director of Clinical Training, Self-Injury, and Suicide, Department of Psychology, University of Wyoming), interview with the author, August 3, 2021.
73 Jamison, *Night Falls Fast*, 21.
74 Jamison, *Night Falls Fast*, 202–203.
75 "Suicide," NIMH.
76 "Suicide Mortality by State," Centers for Disease Control and Prevention, National Center for Health Statistics, accessed February 12, 2025, https://www.cdc.gov/nchs/pressroom/sosmap/suicide-mortality/suicide.htm.
77 Albert Camus, *The Myth of Sisyphus and Other Essays*, translated from the French by Justin O'Brien, 1955, https://people.brandeis.edu/~teuber, 4.
78 Sean Spoonts, "Jumping on a Grenade? Make Sure It's a German One," Special Operations Forces Report, November 8, 2021, https://sofrep.com/news/if-you-had-to-jump-on-a-grenade-make-it-a-german-one/.
79 Jennet Kirkpatrick, *The Virtues of Exit: On Resistance and Quitting Politics* (Chapel Hill: University of North Carolina Press, 2017), 106.
80 Kirkpatrick, *Virtues of Exit*, 106.
81 Monica Davey, "Kevorkian Speaks After His Release from Prison," *The New York Times*, June 4, 2007, https://www.nytimes.com/2007/06/04/us/04kevorkian.html.
82 "Physician-Assisted Suicide Fast Facts," *CNN Newsource*, June 1, 2021, https://abc17news.com/news/national-world/2021/06/01/physician-assisted-suicide-fast-facts/.
83 Lori Kogan (licensed psychologist and professor of psychology, Department of Clinical Sciences, Colorado State University, College of Veterinary Medicine and Biomedical Sciences), interview with the author, August 17, 2022.
84 Kogan, interview, 2002.
85 Susana Monsó, *Playing Possum: How Animals Understand Death* (Princeton, NJ: Princeton University Press, 2024).
86 Pepper, interview, 2022; Jamison, *Night Falls Fast*, 174–177.
87 Pepper, interview, 2022.
88 Jamison, *Night Falls Fast*, 81–96.
89 Jamison, *Night Falls Fast*, 199.
90 Pepper, interview, 2022.
91 Jamison, *Night Falls Fast*, 280–282.
92 Jamison, *Night Falls Fast*, 280–282.
93 Jamison, *Night Falls Fast*, 280–282.
94 Jamison, *Night Falls Fast*, 280–282.

CHAPTER 2: ENDING WORK

1. "Employment," Etymonline, accessed February 12, 2025, https://www.etymonline.com/search?q=employment.
2. Annie Duke, *Quit: The Power of Knowing When to Walk Away* (New York: Portfolio/Penguin, 2022), 167–168.
3. Thomas L. Dumm, "Resignation," *Critical Inquiry* 25 (1998): 63.
4. Carl P. Maertz Jr. and Michael A. Campion, "Profiles in Quitting: Integrating Process and Content Turnover Theory," *Academy of Management* 47 (2004): 566–582.
5. Guy Berger, "Will This Year's College Grads Job-Hop More than Previous Grads?" *Linkedin Official Blog*, April 12, 2016, https://blog.linkedin.com/2016/04/12/will-this-year_s-college-grads-job-hop-more-than-previous-grads.
6. Jeffrey R. Young, "How Many Times Will People Change Jobs? The Myth of the Endlessly-Job-Hopping Millennial," *EdSurge*, July 20, 2017, https://www.edsurge.com/news/2017-07-20-how-many-times-will-people-change-jobs-the-myth-of-the-endlessly-job-hopping-millennial.
7. Chris Kolmar, "Average Number of Jobs in a Lifetime [2022]," Zippia, January 11, 2023, https://www.zippia.com/advice/average-number-jobs-in-lifetime/.
8. Caroline Colvin, "Quits Rate Reaching Record High in 2021, BLS Data Shows," *HR Dive*, June 24, 2021, https://www.hrdive.com/news/quits-rate-reaching-record-high-in-2021-bls-data-shows/602371/.
9. Donald Sull, Charles Sull, and Ben Zweig, "Toxic Culture Is Driving the Great Resignation," *MIT Sloan Management Review*, January 11, 2022, https://sloanreview.mit.edu/article/toxic-culture-is-driving-the-great-resignation/.
10. Peg Streep and Alan B. Bernstein, *Quitting: Why We Fear It—and Why We Shouldn't—in Life, Love, and Work* (Boston: Da Capo, 2014), 82.
11. "United States Job Quits," *Trading Economics*, accessed February 12, 2025, https://tradingeconomics.com/united-states/job-quits; Austin Williams, "Fewer Americans Quitting Their Jobs—Here's Why," Fox26 Houston, accessed July 9, 2025, https://www.fox26houston.com/news/fewer-americans-quitting-jobs.
12. "Total Unfilled Job Vacancies for the United States," Federal Reserve Bank of St. Louis, accessed February 12, 2025, https://fred.stlouisfed.org/series/LMJVTTUVUSQ647S.
13. Jessica Stillman, "The Roots of the Great Resignation Stretch Back a Decade, Says Wharton's Adam Grant," *Inc.*, October 15, 2021, https://www.inc.com/jessica-stillman/adam-grant-great-resignation-roots.html.
14. Kolmar, "Average Number of Jobs."
15. Simon Sinek, "This Is Why You Don't Succeed—Simon Sinek on the Millennial Generation," YouTube, December 13, 2018, https://www.youtube.com/watch?v=xNgQOHwsIbg.
16. Juliana Kaplan and Andy Kiersz, "2021 Was the Year of the Quit: For 7 Months, Millions of Workers Have Been Leaving," *Business Insider*, December 8, 2021, https://www.businessinsider.com/how-many-why-workers-quit-jobs-this-year-great-resignation-2021-12.
17. Duke, *Quit*, 225.

18 Christian Edwards, "'Goblin Mode' Chosen as Oxford Word of the Year for 2022," CNN, December 6, 2022, https://amp.cnn.com/cnn/2022/12/05/world/oxford-word-goblin-mode-2022-intl-scli-wellness/index.html.
19 Amy Adkins, "Millennials: The Job-Hopping Generation," Gallup, accessed February 12, 2025, https://www.gallup.com/workplace/231587/millennials-job-hopping-generation.aspx.
20 Adkins, "Millennials."
21 Peter Anderson-Sprecher (CEO of Fox Robotics), interview with the author, July 30, 2021.
22 Sull, Sull, and Zweig, "Toxic Culture."
23 Lori Goler, Janelle Gale, Brynn Harrington, and Adam Grant, "Why People Really Quit Their Jobs," *Harvard Business Review*, January 11, 2018, https://hbr.org/2018/01/why-people-really-quit-their-jobs.
24 Bill Murphy Jr., "People Who Embrace This Controversial Word Have Very High Emotional Intelligence," *Inc.*, November 14, 2021, https://www.inc.com/bill-murphy-jr/people-who-embrace-this-controversial-word-have-very-high-emotional-intelligence.html; Lynn Marie Morski, *Quitting by Design: Learn to Use Strategic Quitting as a Tool to Carve Out a Successful Life* (New York: Austin Macauley, 2018); Duke, *Quit*, 225.
25 "Why Can We Not Perceive Our Own Abilities?" the Decision Lab, accessed February 12, 2025, https://thedecisionlab.com/biases/dunning-kruger-effect.
26 Angela Lee Duckworth, Christopher Peterson, Michael D. Matthews, and Dennis R. Kelly, "Grit: Perseverance and Passion for Long-Term Goals," *Journal of Personality and Social Psychology* 92 (2007): 1087–1101.
27 Duckworth et al., "Grit," 1094, 1097.
28 Colvin, "Quits Rate."
29 Francesca Coin, "On Quitting," *Ephemera* 17 (2017): 705–719.
30 Coin, "On Quitting," 713.
31 Peter Benson and Stuart Kirsch, "Capitalism and the Politics of Resignation," *Current Anthropology* 51 (2010): 459–486.
32 Len Gutkin, "Quit Lit for Senior Scholars," *Chronicle of Higher Education*, September 20, 2021, https://www.chronicle.com/newsletter/the-review/2021-09-20.
33 Coin, "On Quitting," 707.
34 Keguro Macharia, "On Quitting," *New Inquiry*, September 19, 2018, https://thenewinquiry.com/on-quitting/.
35 Coin, "On Quitting," 713.
36 Coin, "On Quitting," 707.
37 Ken Jacobs, Ian Perry, and Jenifer MacGillvary, "The High Public Cost of Low Wages," UC Berkeley Labor Center, Research Brief, 9 pp.
38 "Everything You Need to Know About the College Dropout Rate," *What to Become*, August 3, 2022, https://whattobecome.com/blog/college-dropout-rate/; Melanie Hanson, "College Dropout Rates," *Education Data Initiative*, August 16, 2024, https://educationdata.org/college-dropout-rates.
39 "Table 219.55," National Center for Education Statistics, accessed February 12, 2025, https://nces.ed.gov/programs/digest/d18/tables/dt18_219.55.asp?refer=dropout.

40 Aric Zion and Thomas Hollmann, "College Students Are Dropping Classes: How Often and Why," Z, accessed February 12, 2025, https://www.zionandzion.com/research/college-students-are-dropping-classes-how-often-and-why/; Katie Schoolov, "How Amazon Plans to Fix Its Massive Returns Problem," CNBC, April 10, 2022, https://www.cnbc.com/2022/04/10/how-amazon-plans-to-fix-its-massive-returns-problem.html.

41 David Leonhardt, "Trump's Refusal to Concede," *The New York Times*, November 12, 2020, https://www.nytimes.com/2020/11/12/briefing/ron-klain-jeffrey-toobin-tropical-storm-eta.html; Darragh Roche, "Did Donald Trump Concede? President's Statement Sparks Debate," *Newsweek*, January 7, 2021, https://www.newsweek.com/did-donald-trump-concede-president-statement-sparks-debate-1559597.

42 Carli Pierson, "When Al Gore Conceded, It Was Presidential; When Trump Concedes, It Will Be to Spite Nancy Pelosi," *The Independent*, December 12, 2020, https://www.independent.co.uk/voices/trump-concedes-electoral-college-votes-pelosi-al-gore-b1770312.html.

43 Pierson, "When Al Gore Conceded," 17–19.

44 Pierson, "When Al Gore Conceded," 4.

45 William F. Felice, *How Do I Save My Honor? War, Moral Integrity, and Principled Resignation* (New York: Rowman and Littlefield, 2009).

46 Edward Weisband and Thomas M. Franck, *Resignation in Protest: Political and Ethical Choices Between Loyalty to Team and Loyalty to Conscience in American Public Life* (New York: Grossman, 1975), 14–16.

47 Meridith McGraw and Daniel Lippman, "They Resigned in Protest Over Jan. 6—Then Never Went After Trump Again," *Politico*, January 3, 2022, https://www.politico.com/news/2022/01/03/trumpworld-jan-6-526291.

48 Weisband and Frank, *Resignation in Protest*.

49 Theo Barclay, *Fighters and Quitters: Great Political Resignations* (London: Biteback, 2018), xiii.

50 Evelyn Richards, "What Would Happen if the Queen Abdicated—and Why It's Not Likely," *Metro*, June 2, 2022, https://metro.co.uk/2022/02/06/what-would-happen-if-the-queen-abdicated-and-why-its-not-likely-16050151/.

51 Jennet Kirkpatrick, *The Virtues of Exit: On Resistance and Quitting Politics* (Chapel Hill: University of North Carolina Press, 2017), 48.

52 David Cortright, *Peace: A History of Movements and Ideas* (Cambridge, UK: Cambridge University Press, 2008), 164–165.

53 Cortright, *Peace*, 16.

54 Jeffrey A. Lockwood, *Behind the Carbon Curtain: The Energy Industry, Political Censorship, and Free Speech* (Albuquerque: University of New Mexico Press, 2017).

55 "History of Successful Boycotts," *Ethical Consumer*, December 19, 2024, https://www.ethicalconsumer.org/ethicalcampaigns/boycotts/history-successful-boycotts; Jeffrey Rindskopf, "The Biggest Retail Boycotts of All Time," *Cheapism*, January 18, 2024, https://blog.cheapism.com/biggest-boycotts/.

56 Jack Kelly, "CEOs Are Quitting and Joining the Great Resignation—Here's Why," *Forbes*, June 29, 2022, https://www.forbes.com/sites/jackkelly/2022/06/29/ceos-are-quitting-and-joining-the-great-resignation-heres-why/?sh=6737facf2303.

57 Kelly, "CEOs Are Quitting"; Joey Hadden, Debanjali Bose, and Laura Casado, "Groupon's CEO and COO Just Stepped Down, Joining a Slew of Executive Departures in 2020," *Business Insider*, March 26, 2020, https://www.businessinsider.com/bob-iger-keith-block-ceos-that-stepped-down-in-2020.
58 Anderson-Sprecher, interview, 2021.
59 Harriet Sherwood, "What Might a Pope Francis Retirement Mean for the Catholic Church?" *The Guardian*, August 5, 2022, https://www.theguardian.com/world/2022/aug/05/what-might-a-pope-francis-retirement-mean-for-the-catholic-church.
60 "Great Renunciation," Wikipedia, December 28, 2024, https://en.wikipedia.org/wiki/Great_Renunciation.
61 The term *quasi-quit* was used by Julia Keller in *Quitting: A Life Strategy* (New York: Balance/Hachette, 2023), 110–111, 132–133, to encompass a vaguely expansive range of possibilities, from quitting partially or temporarily (including a brief period of reflection) to any qualitative shift of an endeavor, which she also termed a "pivot." I'll pursue a much more precise explication of partial and incomplete quitting in chapter 7.
62 Lindsay Ellis and Angela Yang, "If Your Co-Workers Are 'Quiet Quitting,' Here's What That Means," *Wall Street Journal*, August 12, 2022, https://www.wsj.com/articles/if-your-gen-z-co-workers-are-quiet-quitting-heres-what-that-means-11660260608.
63 Maroosha Muzaffar, "An Entire Generation of Chinese Youth Is Rejecting the Pressures of Hustle Culture by 'Lying Flat,'" *The Independent*, June 9, 2021, https://www.independent.co.uk/asia/china/china-tang-ping-trend-work-culture-b1862444.html.
64 "Work-to-Rule," Wikipedia, February 14, 2025, https://en.wikipedia.org/wiki/Work-to-rule#Quiet_quitting.
65 Jim Harter, "Is Quiet Quitting Real?" Gallup, September 26, 2022, https://www.gallup.com/workplace/398306/quiet-quitting-real.aspx.
66 Amina Kilpatrick, "What Is 'Quiet Quitting,' and How It May Be a Misnomer for Setting Boundaries at Work," NPR, August 19, 2022, https://www.npr.org/2022/08/19/1117753535/quiet-quitting-work-tiktok.
67 Karla L. Miller, "Actually, We've Been 'Quiet Quitting' and 'Quiet Firing' for Years," *Washington Post*, September 8, 2022, https://www.washingtonpost.com/business/2022/09/08/quiet-quitting-quiet-firing-what-to-do/.
68 Ellis and Yang, "If Your Co-Workers Are 'Quiet Quitting.'"
69 Jeffrey A. Lockwood, *A Guest of the World* (Boston: Skinner House, 2006).
70 Viktor E. Frankl, *Man's Search for Meaning* (Boston: Beacon, 2006).
71 Dan Healing, "Husky Energy Vows to Boost Downstream Output if It Wins MEG Hostile Takeover," *Global News*, October 25, 2018, https://globalnews.ca/news/4596018/husky-energy-downstream-output-meg-hostile-takeover/.
72 Jon Decker, "'Nuclear Option': Gunstock Management Team Resigns," *Lanconia Daily Sun*, July 21, 2022, https://www.laconiadailysun.com/news/local/nuclear-option-gunstock-management-team-resigns/article_80fcd7ee-08ab-11ed-954f-43cbc30d5288.html.
73 Edward Russell, "United Airlines Throws in the Towel on San Francisco–Paine Field Route," the Points Guy, February 3, 2020, https://thepointsguy.com/news/united-airlines-san-francisco-everett-paine-field-route/.

74 Jay Lyman, "IBM Throws Knockout Punch at SCO," *Linux Insider*, March 31, 2004, https://www.linuxinsider.com/story/ibm-throws-knockout-punch-at-sco-58146.html.

75 Frank N. Wilner, "Union Boss May Have LIRR in Checkmate," *Railway Age*, May 23, 2014, https://www.railwayage.com/news/union-boss-may-have-lirr-in-checkmate/.

76 Philip Wen, "Poker-Faced Forrest Plays His Hand, but Market Calls Bluff," *Sydney Morning Herald*, September 14, 2012, https://www.smh.com.au/business/poker-faced-forrest-plays-his-hand-but-market-calls-bluff-20120913-25v36.html.

CHAPTER 3: QUITTING CONFLICTS AND CONTESTS

1 Adam R. Reddon, Tommaso Ruberto, and Simon M. Reader, "Submission Signals in Animal Groups," *Behaviour* 159 (2021): 1–20.

2 "George Cross for the Soldier Who Threw Himself on a Grenade," *The Independent*, July 24, 2008, https://www.independent.co.uk/news/uk/home-news/george-cross-for-the-soldier-who-threw-himself-on-a-grenade-875770.html#.

3 Jason R. Musteen (United States Army colonel and chief of military history, United States Military Academy), interview with the author, September 7, 2021.

4 Musteen, interview, 2021.

5 "Code of Conduct," Jackson State University, Department of Military Science, accessed February 12, 2025, https://www.jsums.edu/arotc/code-of-conduct/.

6 Geoffrey Roberts, *Stalin's Wars: From World War to Cold War, 1939–1953* (New Haven, CT: Yale University Press, 2006).

7 Robert McFadden, "Hiroo Onoda, Whose War Lasted Decades, Dies at 91," *The New York Times*, January 18, 2014, 18.

8 David Cortright, *Peace: A History of Movements and Ideas* (Cambridge, UK: Cambridge University Press, 2008), 164–165.

9 Blake Stillwell, "11 Ways People Dodged the Draft During the Vietnam War," *Business Insider*, January 5, 2020, https://www.businessinsider.com/11-ways-people-dodged-the-draft-during-the-vietnam-war-2020-1.

10 Zena Simmons, "The Execution of Pvt. Eddie Slovik," *Detroit News*, August 25, 1999, https://archive.ph/20120525211811/http://apps.detnews.com/apps/history/index.php?id=103#selection-1307.0-1319.16.

11 William F. Felice, *How Do I Save My Honor? War, Moral Integrity, and Principled Resignation* (New York: Rowman and Littlefield, 2009), 8.

12 "Benedict Arnold," Wikipedia, February 5, 2025, https://en.wikipedia.org/wiki/Benedict_Arnold.

13 Peter Finn and Sari Horwitz, "U.S. Charges Snowden with Espionage," *Washington Post*, June 21, 2013, https://www.washingtonpost.com/world/national-security/us-charges-snowden-with-espionage/2013/06/21/507497d8-dab1-11e2-a016-92547bf094cc_story.html.

14 Thomas L. Dumm, "Resignation," *Critical Inquiry* 25 (1998): 56–76.

15 Musteen, interview, 2021.

16 Holger H. Herwin, *The Marne, 1914: The Opening of World War I and the Battle That Changed the World* (New York: Random House, 2009).

17 Walter Lord, *The Miracle of Dunkirk: The True Story of Operation Dynamo* (New York: Open Road, 2017).
18 Musteen, interview, 2021.
19 Kilic Bugra Kanat, "The US Exit Strategy from Iraq to Syria," Foundation for Political, Economic and Social Research, January 2, 2019, https://setadc.org/us-exit-strategy-from-iraq-to-syria/.
20 Jill Kimball, "Costs of the 20-Year War on Terror: $8 Trillion and 900,000 Deaths," Brown University Costs of War Project, September 1, 2021, https://www.brown.edu/news/2021-09-01/costsofwar.
21 Robert Burns and Lolita C. Baldor, "Last Troops Exit Afghanistan, Ending America's Longest War," AP News, August 30, 2021, https://apnews.com/article/afghanistan-islamic-state-group-e10e038baea732dae879c111234507f81.
22 "U.S. Withdraws from Vietnam," *History*, accessed February 12, 2025, https://www.history.com/this-day-in-history/u-s-withdraws-from-vietnam.
23 Kanat, "US Exit Strategy."
24 Sydney D. Bailey, "Ceasefires, Truces, and Armistices in the Practice of the UN Security Council," *American Journal of International Law* 71 (1977): 461–473.
25 Robert O. Paxton, *Vichy France: Old Guard and New Order, 1940–1944* (New York: Columbia University Press, 2001).
26 Frank McLynn, *Genghis Khan: His Conquests, His Empire, His Legacy* (Cambridge: Da Capo, 2016).
27 "Operation Downfall," *New World Encyclopedia*, accessed February 12, 2025, https://www.newworldencyclopedia.org/entry/Operation_Downfall.
28 Quoted in "Throw in the Towel," Phrase Finder, accessed February 12, 2025, https://www.phrases.org.uk/meanings/throw-in-the-towel.html.
29 Joseph R. Svinth, "Death Under the Spotlight: The Manuel Velazquez Collection, 2011," October 2011, https://ejmas.com/jcs/velazquez/Death_Under_the_Spotlight_2011_Final.pdf.
30 Jason Burgos, "Has [sic] There Ever Been UFC Deaths? We Take a Look at the Darkside of Fighting Inside a Cage," *Ringside*, July 9, 2025, https://www.yardbarker.com/mma/articles/has_there_ever_been_ufc_deaths_we_take_a_look_at_the_darkside_of_fighting_inside_a_cage/s1_17358_40776375.
31 "Roberto Durán vs. Sugar Ray Leonard II," Wikipedia, January 5, 2025, https://en.wikipedia.org/wiki/Roberto_Dur%C3%A1n_vs._Sugar_Ray_Leonard_II.
32 David Christian, "The Thrilla in Manila Explained—Ali vs. Frazier 3 Breakdown," YouTube, accessed February 12, 2025, https://www.youtube.com/watch?v=4okggXa-ZQQ.
33 Thomas Hauser, "The Unforgiven," *The Guardian*, September 3, 2005, https://www.theguardian.com/sport/2005/sep/04/features.sport16.
34 Stephan Kesting, "37 Powerful BJJ Submissions for Grapplers," *Grapplearts*, June 18, 2016, https://www.grapplearts.com/37-powerful-bjj-submissions-for-grapplers/.
35 Flyin' Hawaiian, "Ultimate Fighting Championship: Crunching the Numbers," *Bleacher Report*, January 11, 2009, https://bleacherreport.com/articles/109873-ultimate-fighting-championship-crunching-the-numbers-updated.

36 Jad Semaan, "In MMA, Is Refusing to Submit Disrespectful?" *Bleacher Report*, August 29, 2008, https://bleacherreport.com/articles/52188-in-mma-is-refusing-to-submit-disrespectful.

37 Luis Aldea, "The History of Throwing in the Towel," *Sports Center Feature*, accessed February 12, 2025, https://www.youtube.com/watch?v=YITTvZo_eUI.

38 Thomas Erik Angerhofer (martial arts sensei), interview with the author, July 14, 2021.

39 Jack Longstaff, "Woman Ran Last 18 Miles of the London Marathon with a Broken Ankle," *Mirror*, May 1, 2019, https://www.mirror.co.uk/news/uk-news/woman-ran-last-18-miles-14977608.

40 Dan Wetzel, "How Simone Biles Saved Herself—and Her Teammates—at the Olympics," *Yahoo Sports*, July 27, 2021, https://sports.yahoo.com/how-simone-biles-saved-herself-and-her-teammates-at-the-olympics-171619025.html.

41 Madeline Coleman, "Simone Biles Explains the Twisties: 'Physical Health Is Mental Health,'" *Sports Illustrated*, July 30, 2021, https://www.si.com/olympics/2021/07/30/simone-biles-addresses-accusations-of-quitting-answers-questions-about-twisties; Claire Farrow, "Here's How Much It Costs US Athletes to Get to the Olympics," 10TampaBay, July 18, 2021, https://www.wtsp.com/article/sports/olympics/cost-of-being-an-olympian/67-7711bf2f-56bd-451f-ac8e-ac6afb5d5864.

42 Claire Farrow, "Simone Biles Mocked as a Coward by Candace Owens for Pulling Out of Olympics," *AceShowBiz*, July 28, 2021, https://www.aceshowbiz.com/news/view/00174503.html.

43 Bob Cook, "Football Coach Suspended for Violating Connecticut's No-Blowout Rule Was Wrong—but So Is the Rule," *Forbes*, October 25, 2012, https://www.forbes.com/sites/bobcook/2012/10/25/football-coach-suspended-for-violating-connecticuts-no-blowout-rule-was-wrong-but-so-is-the-rule/?sh=3b0e76706bc8.

44 Peter Sblendorio, "106–0 Blowout in High School Football Game Is Slammed as 'Classless,'" *Yahoo News*, October 31, 2021, https://news.yahoo.com/106-0-blowout-high-school-195100925.html.

45 David Astramskas, "Remembering When Lisa Leslie Scored 101 Points in 16 Minutes During a High School Game," *Ball Is Life*, July 7, 2016, https://ballislife.com/remembering-when-lisa-leslie-scored-101-points-in-16-minutes-during-a-high-school-game/.

46 Mark Jenkins (alpinist and foreign correspondent for *National Geographic Magazine*, *Smithsonian*, and *Outside Magazine*), interview with the author, August 5, 2021.

47 Annie Duke, *Quit: The Power of Knowing When to Walk Away* (New York: Portfolio/Penguin, 2022), 5.

48 "The Etiquette of Resigning," Chess.com Forums, January 25, 2010, https://www.chess.com/forum/view/general/the-etiquette-of-resigning#.

49 Yosha Iglesias, "The Ultimate Blunder: Resigning a Won Position," Chess24, December 21, 2019, https://chess24.com/en/read/news/the-ultimate-blunder-resigning-a-won-position; Yosha Iglesias, "The Ultimate Blunder: Unnecessary Resignation," Chess24, November 20, 2019, https://chess24.com/en/read/news/the-ultimate-blunder-unnecessary-resignation.

50 "Etiquette of Resigning," Chess.com Forums.

51 Annie Duke, "Why Quitting Is Underrated and Grit Is Not Always a Virtue," *The Atlantic*, September 27, 2022, https://www.theatlantic.com/ideas/archive/2022/09/why-quitting-is-underrated/671562/.
52 Craig Varnell (professional poker player with $1.2 million in winnings 2015–2022), interview with the author, February 4, 2022.
53 Andrei Marm, "How Law Is Like Chess," accessed February 12, 2015, https://gould.usc.edu/assets/docs/marmor.pdf; Chad Hansen, "The Law Language Game," *Philosophy of Law*, accessed February 12, 2015, https://philosophy.hku.hk/courses/law/Lawgame.htm.
54 Charles Pelkey (partner in the legal firm Neubauer, Pelkey, and Goldfinger LLP, Laramie, Wyoming), interview with the author, June 27, 2022.

CHAPTER 4: A TAXONOMY OF QUITTING

1 George Lakoff and Mark Johnson, *Metaphors We Live By* (Chicago: University of Chicago Press, 2003).
2 Christopher Peterson and Martin E. P. Seligman, *Character Strengths and Virtues: A Handbook and Classification* (New York: American Psychological Association and Oxford University Press, 2004), 6.
3 Ben G. Holt and Knud Andreas Jønsson, "Reconciling Hierarchical Taxonomy with Molecular Phylogenies," *Systematic Biology* 63 (2014): 1010–1017; Jerry A. Coyne and H. Allen Orr, *Speciation* (Sunderland, MA: Sinauer Associates, 2004).
4 Peterson and Seligman, *Character Strengths and Virtues*, 6.
5 Other traits are not unique to mammals and created confusion among early biologists. For example, a platypus lays eggs like a bird, and a whale has fins like a fish. Still other traits that distinguish mammals from reptiles and amphibians, such as an erect gait, are shared with other vertebrates such as birds.
6 Christina Szalinski, "10 Animals That Make 'Milk' and Aren't Mammals," *Discover Magazine*, June 24, 2021, https://www.discovermagazine.com/planet-earth/10-surprising-animals-that-make-milk-and-arent-mammals.
7 "Suicide Statistics," Suicide Awareness Voices of Education, accessed February 12, 2015, https://save.org/about-suicide/suicide-statistics/.
8 Iris D. Hartog, Margot L. Zomers, Ghislaine J. M. W. van Thiel et al., "Prevalence and Characteristics of Older Adults with a Persistent Death Wish Without Severe Illness: A Large Cross-Sectional Survey." *BMC Geriatrics* 20 (2020): 342–356.
9 Peg Streep and Alan B. Bernstein, *Quitting: Why We Fear It—and Why We Shouldn't—in Life, Love, and Work* (Boston: Da Capo, 2014), 190.
10 Christine M. Korsgaard, *The Sources of Normativity* (Cambridge, UK: Cambridge University Press, 1996).
11 Lynn Marie Morski, *Quitting by Design: Learn to Use Strategic Quitting as a Tool to Carve Out a Successful Life* (New York: Austin Macauley, 2018), 15; Julia Keller, *Quitting: A Life Strategy* (New York: Balance/Hachette, 2023).
12 Morski, *Quitting by Design*, 20.
13 "Names for the Human Species," Wikipedia, January 19, 2025, https://en.wikipedia.org/wiki/Names_for_the_human_species.

14. "Biles: I Didn't Quit, My Mind and Body Are Simply Not in Sync," *AS*, July 30, 2021, https://en.as.com/en/2021/07/30/olympic_games/1627673026_447174.html.
15. Annie Duke, *Quit: The Power of Knowing When to Walk Away* (New York: Portfolio/Penguin, 2022), xxii.
16. Streep and Bernstein, *Quitting: Why We Fear It*, 139.
17. Morski, *Quitting by Design*, 35; Keller, *Quitting: A Life Strategy*, 133.
18. Morski, *Quitting by Design*, 35 (quotation); Keller, *Quitting: A Life Strategy*, 133.
19. Robert E. Goodin, *On Settling* (Princeton, NJ: Princeton University Press, 2012), 29.
20. Morski, *Quitting by Design*, 9.
21. Morski, *Quitting by Design*, 59.
22. Thomas Erik Angerhofer (martial arts sensei), interview with the author, July 14, 2021.
23. Dana A. V. Braner (medical doctor and professor of pediatrics, Division of Critical Care, School of Medicine, Oregon Health and Science University) and Paula Ann Vanderford (medical doctor and associate professor of pediatrics, Division of Critical Care, School of Medicine, Oregon Health and Science University), joint interview with the author, February 7, 2022.
24. Jason R. Musteen (United States Army colonel and chief of military history, United States Military Academy), interview with the author, September 7, 2021.
25. Tess Kilwein (licensed psychologist and director of Clinical Training, Counseling Center, University of Wyoming) and Alison Looby (professor, Department of Psychology, University of Wyoming), joint interview with the author, July 20, 2021.
26. Mark Jenkins (alpinist and foreign correspondent for *National Geographic Magazine*, *Smithsonian*, and *Outside Magazine*), interview with the author, August 5, 2021.
27. Carolyn Pepper (professor and director of clinical training, self-injury and suicide, Department of Psychology, University of Wyoming), interview with the author, August 3, 2021.
28. Lou Farley (spiritual director and licensed clinical psychologist, Hospice of Laramie), interview with the author, August 8, 2021.
29. "Is There Such a Thing as a True Synonym?" Dictionary.com, January 17, 2020, https://www.dictionary.com/e/true-synonym/; "Who First Said That No Two Words Mean the Exact Same?" StackExchange Linguistics, accessed February 12, 2025, https://linguistics.stackexchange.com/questions/25625/who-first-said-that-no-two-words-mean-the-exact-same.
30. "Are There Two Words in English That Have the Exact Same Meaning and Use?" Quora, accessed February 12, 2025, https://www.quora.com/Are-there-two-words-in-English-that-have-the-exact-same-meaning-and-use.
31. Some of the difficulty in finding a synonym for quit might be reflected in an Anglophone's confusion with the French verbs *quitter*, *partir*, *sortir*, and *laisser*—which are all typically translated as "leave," which does not capture the nuanced differences in which *quitter* means to leave with an emphasis on the location one is leaving, the verb *partir* emphasizes the destination, *sortir* emphasizes the act of leaving, and *laisser* emphasizes what is left behind. See Dillon March, "What's the Difference Between *Partir*, *Sortir*, *Quitter*, and *Laisser*?" *Parler Français Blog*, February 2, 2015, https://parlefrancaisblog.wordpress.com/2015/02/02/whats-the-difference-between-partir-sortir-quitter-and-laisser/.

32 "Mikaela Shiffrin: I'm Going to Win Again," International Olympic Committee, accessed February 12, 2015, https://olympics.com/en/video/mikaela-shiffrin-interview-i-will-win-again.
33 "Vince Lombardi," BrainyQuote, accessed February 12, 2025, https://www.brainyquote.com/quotes/vince_lombardi_122285.
34 The Detroit Tigers won their first game of the 2019 baseball season 2–0 over the Toronto Blue Jays and then finished the year with one of the worst records in the modern era, posting 47 wins and 114 losses. Hardly a team fans would call "winners" even after one of their rare victories ("2019 Detroit Tigers Schedule," *Baseball Almanac*, accessed February 12, 2025, https://www.baseball-almanac.com/teamstats/schedule.php?y=2019&t=DET).
35 Morski, *Quitting by Design*, 11.
36 Tim Constantine, "Simone Biles Is No Hero, She Is a Quitter," *The Washington Times*, July 31, 2021, https://www.washingtontimes.com/news/2021/jul/31/simone-biles-no-hero-she-quitter/.
37 I thank my colleague Dr. Rob Colter in the Department of Philosophy and Religious Studies at the University of Wyoming for providing the quitting-versus-quitter distinction.
38 Duke, *Quit: The Power of Knowing*, xx.
39 "Featherless Biped," *Art and Popular Culture*, accessed February 12, 2025, http://www.artandpopularculture.com/Featherless_biped.

CHAPTER 5: THE PSYCHOLOGY OF QUITTING

1 Peg Streep and Alan B. Bernstein, *Quitting: Why We Fear It—and Why We Shouldn't—in Life, Love, and Work* (Boston: Da Capo, 2014), 190, 213.
2 Christopher Peterson and Martin E. P. Seligman, *Character Strengths and Virtues: A Handbook and Classification* (New York: American Psychological Association and Oxford University Press, 2004), 235.
3 Mark Jenkins (alpinist and foreign correspondent for *National Geographic Magazine*, *Smithsonian*, and *Outside Magazine*), interview with the author, August 5, 2021.
4 Annie Duke, *Quit: The Power of Knowing When to Walk Away* (New York: Portfolio/Penguin, 2022), 17.
5 Steven D. Levitt, "Heads or Tails: The Impact of a Coin Toss on Major Life Decisions," National Bureau of Economic Research Working Paper 22487, August 2016, http://www.nber.org/papers/w22487, https://doi.org/10.3386/w22487.
6 Duke, *Quit: The Power of Knowing*, 41.
7 Lisa A. Williams and David DeSteno, "Pride and Perseverance: The Motivational Role of Pride," *Journal of Personality and Social Psychology* 94 (2008): 1007–1017.
8 Williams and DeSteno, "Pride and Perseverance," 1007–1017.
9 Streep and Bernstein, *Quitting: Why We Fear It*, 53.
10 Dean B. McFarlin, Roy F. Baumeister, and Jim Blascovich, "On Knowing When to Quit: Task Failure, Self-Esteem, Advice, and Nonproductive Persistence," *Journal of Personality* 52 (1984): 138–155.
11 McFarlin et al., "On Knowing When to Quit," 138–155.

12 McFarlin et al., "On Knowing When to Quit," 138–155.
13 McFarlin et al., "On Knowing When to Quit," 153.
14 Peterson and Seligman, *Character Strengths and Virtues*, 232, 152.
15 Peterson and Seligman, *Character Strengths and Virtues*, 234.
16 Peterson and Seligman, *Character Strengths and Virtues*, 245.
17 Adam Himmelsbach, "Punting Less Can Be Rewarding, But Coaches Aren't Risking Jobs on It," *The New York Times*, August 19, 2012, https://www.nytimes.com/2012/08/19/sports/football/calculating-footballs-risk-of-not-punting-on-fourth-down.html.
18 Gregory E. Miller and Carsten Wrosch, "You've Gotta Know When to Fold 'Em: Goal Disengagement and Systemic Inflammation," *Adolescence: Psychological Science* 18 (2007): 773.
19 Jennet Kirkpatrick, *The Virtues of Exit: On Resistance and Quitting Politics* (Chapel Hill: University of North Carolina Press, 2017), 3.
20 Kirkpatrick, *Virtues of Exit*, 43.
21 Duke, *Quit: The Power of Knowing*, 32.
22 Lynn Marie Morski, *Quitting by Design: Learn to Use Strategic Quitting as a Tool to Carve Out a Successful Life* (New York: Austin Macauley, 2018), 19.
23 Streep and Bernstein, *Quitting: Why We Fear It*, 106.
24 Julia Keller, *Quitting: A Life Strategy* (New York: Balance/Hachette, 2023), 16.
25 Barry M. Staw, "Knee-Deep in the Big Muddy: A Study of Escalating Commitment to a Chosen Course of Action," *Organizational Behavior and Human Performance* 16 (1976): 27–44.
26 Streep and Bernstein, *Quitting: Why We Fear It*, 69.
27 Peterson and Seligman, *Character Strengths and Virtues*, 240.
28 Francesca Coin, "On Quitting," *Ephemera* 17 (2017): 705–719.
29 Matthew Posner, Kenneth L. Cameron, Jennifer M. Wold, Philip J. Belmont Jr, and Brett D. Owens, "Epidemiology of Major League Baseball Injuries," *American Journal of Sports Medicine* 39 (2011): 1676–1680, https://doi.org/10.1177/0363546511411700.
30 Greg King, "Expected Value Analysis (Economic Risk Analysis)," Penn State e-Education Institute, accessed February 12, 2025, https://www.e-education.psu.edu/eme460/node/730.
31 Duke, *Quit: The Power of Knowing*, 32.
32 Morksi, *Quitting by Design*, 51.
33 Duke, *Quit: The Power of Knowing*, 56.
34 Miller and Wrosch, "You've Gotta Know," 773–777.
35 Morksi, *Quitting by Design*, 18.
36 Peterson and Seligman, *Character Strengths and Virtues*, 240.
37 Richard Dawkins and T. R. Carlisle, "Parental Investment, Mate Desertion, and a Fallacy," *Nature* 262 (1976): 131–133, https://doi.org/10.1038/262131a0.
38 "Concorde," Wikipedia, February 13, 2025, https://en.wikipedia.org/wiki/Concorde.
39 Ralph Vartabedian, "How California's Bullet Train Went Off the Rails," *The New York Times*, October 9, 2022, https://www.nytimes.com/2022/10/09/us/california-high-speed-rail-politics.html.
40 Craig Varnell (professional poker player with $1.2 million in winnings 2015–2022), interview with the author, February 4, 2022.

41 William F. Felice, *How Do I Save My Honor? War, Moral Integrity, and Principled Resignation* (New York: Rowman and Littlefield, 2009), 180; Jason R. Musteen (United States Army colonel and chief of military history, United States Military Academy), interview with the author, September 7, 2021.

42 Keller, *Quitting: A Life Strategy*, 6.

43 Julia Watzek and Sarah F. Brosnan, "Capuchin and Rhesus Monkeys Show Sunk Cost Effects in a Psychomotor Task," *Scientific Reports* 10 (2020): article number 20396; Brian M. Sweis, Samanth V. Abram, Brandy J. Schmidt et al., "Sensitivity to 'Sunk Costs' in Mice, Rats, and Humans," *Science* 361 (2018): 178–181, https://doi.org/10.1126/science.aar8644; Fujimaki Shun and Sakagami Takayuki, "Experience That Much Work Produces Many Reinforcers Makes the Sunk Cost Fallacy in Pigeons: A Preliminary Test," *Frontiers in Psychology* 7 (2016), doi=10.3389/fpsyg.2016.00363; Anton D. Navarro and Edmund Fantino, "The Sunk Cost Effect in Pigeons and Humans," *Journal of Experimental Analysis of Behavior* 83 (2005): 1–13, https://doi.org/10.1901/jeab.2005.21-04.

44 Torben Ott, Paul Masset, Thiago S. Gouvea, and Adam Kepecs, "Apparent Sunk Cost Effect in Rational Agents," *Science Advances* 8 (2022), https://doi.org/10.1126/sciadv.abi7004; Hal R. Arkes and Peter Ayton, "The Sunk Cost and Concorde Effects: Are Humans Less Rational than Lower Animals?" *Psychological Bulletin* 125 (1999): 591–600.

45 Annie Duke, "Why Quitting Is Underrated and Grit Is Not Always a Virtue," *The Atlantic*, September 27, 2022, https://www.theatlantic.com/ideas/archive/2022/09/why-quitting-is-underrated/671562/; Barry M. Staw and Ha Hoang, "Sunk Costs in the NBA: Why Draft Order Affects Playing Time and Survival in Professional Basketball," *Administrative Science Quarterly* 40 (1995): 474–494; Quinn Keefer, "The Sunk-Cost Fallacy in the National Football League: Salary Cap Value and Playing Time," *Journal of Sports Economics* 18 (2015), https://doi.org/10.1177/1527002515574515.

46 Duke, *Quit: The Power of Knowing*, 94.

47 Morksi, *Quitting by Design*, 62.

48 Streep and Bernstein, *Quitting: Why We Fear It*, 19, 26.

49 Jenkins, interview, 2021; Duke, *Quit: The Power of Knowing*, 83.

50 Staw and Hoang, "Sunk Costs in the NBA," 29.

51 "George Ball Memo for Johnson on 'A Compromise Solution,'" *The New York Times*, June 15, 1971, https://www.nytimes.com/1971/06/15/archives/george-ball-memo-for-johnson-on-a-compromise-solution.html.

52 Duke, *Quit: The Power of Knowing*, 231.

53 Duke, *Quit: The Power of Knowing*, 140–143.

54 Streep and Bernstein, *Quitting: Why We Fear It*, 24.

55 Keith Chen, Venkat Lakshminarayanan, and Laurie R. Santos, "How Basic Are Behavioral Biases? Evidence from Capuchin Monkey Trading Behavior," *Journal of Political Economy* 114 (2006): 517–537.

56 Duke, *Quit: The Power of Knowing*, 141.

57 Duke, *Quit: The Power of Knowing*, 143.

58 Richard Foley, "Epistemic Conservatism," *Philosophical Studies* 43 (1983): 165–182.

59 William Samuelson and Richard J. Zeckhauser, "Status Quo Bias in Decision Making," *Journal of Risk and Uncertainty* 1 (1988): 7–59.

60 Fiona Woollard and Frances Howard-Snyder, "Doing vs. Allowing Harm," *Stanford Encyclopedia of Philosophy*, accessed February 12, 2025, https://plato.stanford.edu/archives/win2022/entries/doing-allowing/.
61 Duke, *Quit: The Power of Knowing*, 152.
62 Edward Weisband and Thomas M. Franck, *Resignation in Protest: Political and Ethical Choices Between Loyalty to Team and Loyalty to Conscience in American Public Life* (New York: Grossman, 1975), 96–97.
63 Weisband and Franck, *Resignation in Protest*, 174.
64 Alison Clarke-Stewart and Cornelia Brentano, *Divorce: Causes and Consequences* (Current Perspectives in Psychology) (New Haven, CT: Yale University Press, 2007), 76; Robin Barry (licensed psychologist and director of research in the Department of Family Medicine, University of Toledo), interview with the author, September 10, 2021.
65 Streep and Bernstein, *Quitting: Why We Fear It*, 95.
66 Robert Goodin, *On Settling* (Princeton, NJ: Princeton University Press, 2012), 37.
67 Streep and Bernstein, *Quitting: Why We Fear It*, 194–197.
68 Michael Bisping, *Quitters Never Win: My Life in UFC* (New York: Diversion Books, 2020), 357.
69 Bisping, *Quitters Never Win*, 371.
70 Lou Farley (spiritual director and licensed clinical psychologist, Hospice of Laramie), interview with the author, August 8, 2021.
71 Charles Pelkey (partner in the legal firm Neubauer, Pelkey, and Goldfinger LLP, Laramie, Wyoming), interview with the author, June 27, 2022.
72 Miller and Wrosch, "You've Gotta Know," 773.
73 Thomas L. Dumm, "Resignation," *Critical Inquiry* 25 (1998): 57.
74 Bill Murphy Jr., "People Who Embrace This Controversial Word Have Very High Emotional Intelligence," *Inc.*, November 14, 2021, https://www.inc.com/bill-murphy-jr/people-who-embrace-this-controversial-word-have-very-high-emotional-intelligence.html; Carl P. Maertz Jr. and Michael A. Campion, "Profiles in Quitting: Integrating Process and Content Turnover Theory," *Academy of Management* 47 (2004): 566–582; Streep and Bernstein, *Quitting: Why We Fear It*, 37.
75 Keller, *Quitting: A Life Strategy*, 18.
76 "Are You Experiencing Situational Depression?" University of Maryland Medical System, accessed February 12, 2025, https://health.umms.org/2021/08/31/situational-depression/; Streep and Bernstein, *Quitting: Why We Fear It*, 60.
77 "Blaise Pascal," AZ Quotes, accessed February 12, 2025, https://www.azquotes.com/quote/850001.
78 Mark Jenkins, "Die Another Day," *Backpacker Magazine*, September 7, 2012, https://www.backpacker.com/trips/die-another-day/.

CHAPTER 6: THE ROLE OF FREE WILL

1 "Meat Allergy," American College of Allergy, Asthma, and Immunology, accessed February 13, 2025, https://acaai.org/allergies/allergic-conditions/food/meat/.
2 Annie Duke, *Quit: The Power of Knowing When to Walk Away* (New York: Portfolio/Penguin, 2022), 206.

3   Julia Keller, *Quitting: A Life Strategy* (New York: Balance/Hachette, 2023), 140.
4   Many of the ideas and perspectives regarding free will/action are derived from conversations with Dr. Brad Rettler, Department of Philosophy and Religious Studies, University of Wyoming, whose generosity of time and expertise is deeply appreciated.
5   Ralph Barton Perry, *The Thought and Character of William James* (Boston: Little, Brown, 1936) vol. 1, 323.
6   Jennet Kirkpatrick, *The Virtues of Exit: On Resistance and Quitting Politics* (Chapel Hill: University of North Carolina Press, 2017), 9–10.
7   Kirkpatrick, *Virtues of Exit*, 9–10.
8   Timothy O'Connor and Christopher Franklin, "Free Will," *Stanford Encyclopedia of Philosophy*, accessed February 13, 2025, https://plato.stanford.edu/archives/win2022/entries/freewill/.
9   Carolyn Pepper (professor and director of clinical training, self-injury, and suicide, Department of Psychology, University of Wyoming), interview with the author, August 3, 2021.
10 Lou Farley (spiritual director and licensed clinical psychologist, Hospice of Laramie), interview with the author, August 8, 2021.
11 Robert Goodin, *On Settling* (Princeton, NJ: Princeton University Press, 2012), 67.
12 "Types of Harm," Ann Craft Trust, accessed February 13, 2025, https://www.anncrafttrust.org/resources/types-of-harm/; "Types of Harm: Adult Support and Protection (Scotland) Act 2007," Scottish Government, July 28, 2022, https://www.gov.scot/publications/adult-support-protection-scotland-act-2007-guidance-general-practice/pages/3/.
13 Scott Henkel (professor of English and director of the University of Wyoming Institute for Humanities Research), discussion with the author, February 9, 2022.
14 Henkel, discussion, 2022; "The Fugitive Slave Law of 1850," Constitutional Rights Foundation, accessed February 13, 2025, https://www.crf-usa.org/images/pdf/Fugitive-Slave-Law-1850.pdf.
15 "Why Don't Women Leave Abusive Relationships?" Women's Aid, accessed February 13, 2025, https://www.womensaid.org.uk/information-support/what-is-domestic-abuse/women-leave/.
16 Francesca Coin, "On Quitting," *Ephemera* 17 (2017): 705–719.
17 Louis CK, "Live Comedy Special: Reason for Women," accessed February 13, 2025, https://www.youtube.com/watch?v=tBbC2krBopw.
18 William F. Felice, *How Do I Save My Honor? War, Moral Integrity, and Principled Resignation* (New York: Rowman and Littlefield, 2009), 127.
19 "Roberto Durán vs. Sugar Ray Leonard II," Wikipedia, January 5, 2025, https://en.wikipedia.org/wiki/Roberto_Dur%C3%A1n_vs._Sugar_Ray_Leonard_II.
20 David Christian, "The Thrilla in Manila Explained—Ali vs. Frazier 3 Breakdown," YouTube, accessed February 12, 2025, https://www.youtube.com/watch?v=40kggXa-ZQQ.
21 TS Staff, "21 Brutal Times Martial Artists Refused to Tap Out," TheSportster, June 13, 2016, https://www.thesportster.com/mma/21-brutal-times-martial-artists-refused-to-tap-out/.

22 Lorrainne Murray, "Murder Most Horrid: The Grisliest Deaths of Roman Catholic Saints," Britannica, accessed February 13, 2025, https://www.britannica.com/list/murder-most-horrid-the-grisliest-deaths-of-roman-catholic-saints.
23 "Prayers for Offering Up Suffering," Our Catholic Prayers, accessed February 13, 2025, https://www.ourcatholicprayers.com/offering-prayers.html.
24 Felice, *How Do I Save*, 191.
25 Felice, *How Do I Save*, 104.
26 "Code of the United States Fighting Force," Wikipedia, February 11, 2025, https://en.wikipedia.org/wiki/Code_of_the_United_States_Fighting_Force.
27 Jason R. Musteen (United States Army colonel and chief of military history, United States Military Academy), interview with the author, September 7, 2021.
28 Buzz Bissinger, *The Mosquito Bowl: A Game of Life and Death in World War II* (New York: Harper, 2022).
29 Bissinger, *The Mosquito Bowl*, 324.
30 Bissinger, *The Mosquito Bowl*, 319–320.
31 Josephus B. Jimenez, "Supreme Court: Forced Retirement Before Age 65 Illegal," *The Freeman*, July 21, 2018, https://www.philstar.com/the-freeman/opinion/2018/07/21/1835453/supreme-court-forced-retirement-age-65-illegal.
32 "Mandatory Retirement," Wikipedia, February 13, 2025, https://en.wikipedia.org/wiki/Mandatory_retirement.
33 Julia Kagan, "Forced Retirement," Investopedia, July 10, 2024, https://www.investopedia.com/terms/f/forced-retirement.asp.
34 Sasha Cohen, "An Olympian's Guide to Retiring at 25," *The New York Times*, February 24, 2018, https://www.nytimes.com/2018/02/24/opinion/sunday/sasha-cohen-olympics-pyeongchang.html.
35 Alessandro Miglio, "For Quarterbacks, the NFL Is No Country for Old Men," *Bleacher Report*, July 15, 2013, https://bleacherreport.com/articles/1702238-for-quarterbacks-the-nfl-is-no-country-for-old-men.
36 Mark Sessler, "NFL QB Index: Ranking All 68 Starting Quarterbacks from the 2022 NFL Season," NFL+, February 15, 2023, https://www.nfl.com/news/nfl-qb-index-ranking-all-68-starting-quarterbacks-from-the-2022-nfl-season.
37 Theo Barclay, *Fighters and Quitters: Great Political Resignations* (London: Biteback, 2018), 279–301 (quotation on 301).
38 Lynn Marie Morski, *Quitting by Design: Learn to Use Strategic Quitting as a Tool to Carve Out a Successful Life* (New York: Austin Macauley, 2018), 29.
39 Morski, *Quitting by Design*, 68–69.
40 "Stress," *Mind*, March 2022, https://www.mind.org.uk/information-support/types-of-mental-health-problems/stress/signs-and-symptoms-of-stress/.
41 Pepper, interview, 2021.
42 "Top 8 Ultramarathon Pacer Do's and Don'ts," CTS, accessed February 14, 2025, https://trainright.com/ultramarathon-pacer-dos-and-donts/.
43 Alison Looby (professor, Department of Psychology, University of Wyoming), interview with the author, July 20, 2021.
44 Kay Redfield Jamison, *Night Falls Fast: Understanding Suicide* (New York: Knopf, 1999), 27–28.

45 Jamison, *Night Falls Fast*, 180, 190.
46 Jamison, *Night Falls Fast*, 186.
47 Jamison, *Night Falls Fast*, 192, 200.
48 Christopher Peterson and Martin E. P. Seligman, *Character Strengths and Virtues: A Handbook and Classification* (New York: American Psychological Association and Oxford University Press, 2004), 239.
49 "Divorce After Having an Affair," *Do Divorce Better*, accessed February 14, 2025, https://www.dodivorcebetter.com/blog/2018/divorce-after-having-an-affair.html.
50 Morski, *Quitting by Design*, 36.
51 Johanna H. Kordes-de Vaal, "Intention and the Omission Bias: Omissions Perceived as Nondecisions," *Acta Psychologica* 93 (1996): 161–172, https://doi.org/10.1016/0001-6918(96)00027-3.
52 Mark Jenkins, "Die Another Day," *Backpacker Magazine*, September 7, 2012, https://www.backpacker.com/trips/die-another-day/.
53 Dana A. V. Braner (medical doctor and professor of pediatrics, Division of Critical Care, School of Medicine, Oregon Health and Science University) and Paula Ann Vanderford (medical doctor and associate professor of pediatrics, Division of Critical Care, School of Medicine, Oregon Health and Science University), joint interview with the author, February 7, 2022.
54 Thomas L. Dumm, "Resignation," *Critical Inquiry* 25 (1998): 69–70.
55 Keller, *Quitting: A Life Strategy*, 153, 184.
56 Peg Streep and Alan B. Bernstein, *Quitting: Why We Fear It—and Why We Shouldn't—in Life, Love, and Work* (Boston, MA: Da Capo, 2014), 186.
57 Ingvild Lilleheie, Jonas Debesay, Asta Bye, and Astrid Berglanda, "The Tension Between Carrying a Burden and Feeling Like a Burden: A Qualitative Study of Informal Caregivers' and Care Recipients' Experiences After Patient Discharge from Hospital," *International Journal of Qualitative Studies on Health and Well-Being* 16 (2021), https://doi.org/10.1080/17482631.2020.1855751; Anna Vazeou Nieuwenhuis, Scott R. Beach, and Richard Schulz, "Care Recipient Concerns About Being a Burden and Unmet Needs for Care," *Innovation in Aging* 2 (2018): 1–10, https://doi.org/10.1093/geroni/igy026.
58 Kristin Beale, "The Burden Mindset," Christopher and Dana Reeve Foundation, accessed March 31, 2023, https://www.christopherreeve.org/blog/life-after-paralysis/the-burden-mindset.
59 Duke, *Quit: The Power of Knowing*, 15.
60 Morski, *Quitting by Design*, 25.
61 Morski, *Quitting by Design*, 26.
62 Streep and Bernstein, *Quitting: Why We Fear It*, 180.
63 Streep and Bernstein, *Quitting: Why We Fear It*, 181.
64 Isadora Baum, "9 Men Reveal Why They Regret Breaking up with Their Exes," *Men's Health*, February 13, 2019, https://www.menshealth.com/sex-women/a26325897/regret-breaking-up/.
65 Mike Morrison and Neal J. Roese, "Regrets of the Typical American: Findings from a Nationally Representative Sample," *Social Psychological and Personality Science* 2 (2011): 576–582, https://doi.org/10.1177/1948550611401756.

66 Mark Prigg, "Break-ups Hurt Women More in the Short Term but Men Never Recover, Researchers Claim," *Daily Mail*, August 6, 2015, https://www.dailymail.co.uk/sciencetech/article-3187416/Breakups-hurt-women-short-term-men-NEVER-recover-researchers-claim.html.

67 Mark Jenkins (alpinist and foreign correspondent for *National Geographic Magazine*, *Smithsonian*, and *Outside Magazine*), interview with the author, August 5, 2021.

68 Felice, *How Do I Save*, 39.

69 Keller, *Quitting: A Life Strategy*, 5–13.

70 Perran Ross, "When a Mosquito Can't Stop Drinking Blood, the Result Isn't Pretty," *Entomology Today*, March 19, 2020, https://entomologytoday.org/2020/03/19/when-a-mosquito-cant-stop-drinking-blood-the-result-isnt-pretty/; Robert W. Gwadz, "Regulation of Blood Meal Size in the Mosquito," *Journal of Insect Physiology* 15 (1969): 2039–2042.

71 Alina L. Evans, Navinder J. Singh, Andrea Friebe et al., "Drivers of Hibernation in the Brown Bear," *Frontiers in Zoology* 13 (2016): 7, https://doi.org/10.1186/s12983-016-0140-6; Mark J. Biel and Kerry A. Gunther, "Denning and Hibernation Behavior," Information Paper no. BMO-10 (2006), Yellowstone National Park, WY.

72 Konrad Lorenz, *On Aggression* (New York: Harper, 1974).

73 Rudolf Schenkel, "Submission: Its Features and Function in the Wolf and Dog," *American Zoologist* 7 (1967): 319–329.

74 Peterson and Seligman, *Character Strengths and Virtues*, 230.

75 Talia Y. Moore and Andrew A. Biewener, "Outrun or Outmaneuver: Predator-Prey Interactions as a Model System for Integrating Biomechanical Studies in a Broader Ecological Context," *Integrative and Comparative Biology* 55 (2015): 1188–1197, https://doi.org/10.1093/icb/icv074.

76 "Antagonism in Nature: Intraspecific Fights," Animal Ethics, accessed February 14, 2025, https://www.animal-ethics.org/intraspecific-fights/.

77 Henrique Cardoso Delfino, "Individual Features Influence the Choice to Attack in the Southern Lapwing *Vanellus chilensis*, but the Opponent Type Dictates How the Interaction Goes," *Acta Ethologica* 26 (2023): 93–107, https://doi.org/10.1007/s10211-023-00416-6; Henry R. Hermann, *Dominance and Aggression in Humans and Other Animals: The Great Game of Life* (Cambridge, MA: Academic Press, 2016).

78 Paul A. Stevenson and Jan Rillich, "The Decision to Fight or Flee—Insights into Underlying Mechanism in Crickets," *Frontiers in Neuroscience* 6 (2012), https://doi.org/10.3389/fnins.2012.00118.

79 Jamison, *Night Falls Fast*, 175.

CHAPTER 7: QUASI-QUITTING

1 American Psychiatric Association, *Diagnostic and Statistical Manual of Mental Disorders*, 5th ed.: *DSM-5* (Washington, DC: American Psychiatric Publishing, 2013).

2 Tess Kilwein (licensed psychologist and director of clinical training, Counseling Center, University of Wyoming), interview with the author, July 20, 2021.

3 Alison Looby (professor, Department of Psychology, University of Wyoming), interview with the author, July 20, 2021.

4. Lynn Marie Morski, 2018, *Quitting by Design: Learn to Use Strategic Quitting as a Tool to Carve Out a Successful Life* (New York: Austin Macauley, 2018), 68–69; Thomas L. Dumm, "Resignation," *Critical Inquiry* 25 (1998): 56–76.
5. Dumm, "Resignation," 63.
6. Peg Streep and Alan B. Bernstein, *Quitting: Why We Fear It—and Why We Shouldn't—in Life, Love, and Work* (Boston: Da Capo, 2014), 194.
7. Philip W. Anderson, "More Is Different: Broken Symmetry and the Nature of the Hierarchical Structure of Science," *Science* 177 (1972): 393–396, https://doi.org/10.1126/science.177.4047.393.
8. Franz-Peter Griesmaier and Jeffrey A. Lockwood, *This Is Philosophy of Science* (Hoboken, NJ: Wiley-Blackwell, 2022), chapter 14.
9. James B. MacKinnon, *The Day the World Stops Shopping: How Ending Consumerism Saves the Environment and Ourselves* (New York: Ecco, 2021).
10. Neil Levy, "Downshifting and Meaning in Life," *Ratio* 18 (2005): 176–189.
11. Levy, "Downshifting," 176–189.
12. Levy, "Downshifting," 176–189.
13. Excerpt from "The Lone Striker" by Robert Frost from *The Poetry of Robert Frost*, edited by Edward Connery Lathem (© 1969 by Henry Holt and Company; © 1964 by Lesley Frost Ballantine; © 1936 by Robert Frost); reprinted by permission of Henry Holt and Company; all rights reserved.
14. Jennet Kirkpatrick, *The Virtues of Exit: On Resistance and Quitting Politics* (Chapel Hill: University of North Carolina Press, 2017), 49–50.
15. Craig Varnell (professional poker player with $1.2 million in winnings 2015–2022), interview with the author, February 4, 2022.
16. Mark Jenkins (alpinist and foreign correspondent for *National Geographic Magazine*, *Smithsonian*, and *Outside Magazine*), interview with the author, August 5, 2021.
17. Morski, *Quitting by Design*, 33.
18. "Sugar Ray Leonard," Wikipedia, February 4, 2025, https://en.wikipedia.org/wiki/Sugar_Ray_Leonard.
19. Streep and Bernstein, *Quitting: Why We Fear It*, 82.
20. "Sugar Ray Leonard," Wikipedia, February 4, 2025.
21. Streep and Bernstein, *Quitting: Why We Fear It*, 5.
22. Robin Barry (licensed psychologist and director of research in the Department of Family Medicine, University of Toledo), interview with the author, September 10, 2021.
23. Barry, interview, 2021.
24. Michael Chaiton, Lori Diemert, Joanna E. Cohen et al., "Estimating the Number of Quit Attempts It Takes to Quit Smoking Successfully in a Longitudinal Cohort of Smokers," *British Medical Journal Open* 6(6):e011045 (June 9, 2016), doi:10.1136/bmjopen-2016-011045.
25. Gene M. Heyman, "Quitting Drugs: Quantitative and Qualitative Features," *Annual Review of Clinical Psychology* 9 (2013): 29–59.
26. Marta Jimenez, "Aristotle on Becoming Virtuous by Doing Virtuous Actions," *Phronesis* 61 (2016): 3–32, doi 10.1163/15685284-12341297.

27 Phillippa Lally, Cornelia H. M. van Jaarsveld, Henry W. W. Potts, and Jane Wardle, "How Are Habits Formed: Modelling Habit Formation in the Real World," *European Journal of Social Psychology* 40 (2009): 998–1009.
28 Mary Cuadrado and Louis Lieberman, "The Virgin of Guadalupe as an Ancillary Modality for Treating Hispanic Substance Abusers: Juramentos in the United States," *Journal of Religion and Health* 50 (2011): 922–930.
29 "Who's the Boss? You Are!" Alcohol Change UK, accessed February 14, 2025, https://alcoholchange.org.uk/get-involved/campaigns/dry-january.
30 Richard de Visser, "Evaluation of Dry January 2019," School of Psychology, University of Sussex, https://www.drugsandalcohol.ie/32647/1/R-de-Visser-Dry-January-evaluation-2019.pdf.
31 Henry David Thoreau, *Walden or Life in the Woods* (New York: Thomasy Crowell, 1899), 84, https://dn790008.ca.archive.org/0/items/cu31924021445741/cu31924021445741.pdf.
32 "Pete Buttigieg," Wikipedia, February 11, 2025, https://en.wikipedia.org/wiki/Pete_Buttigieg; "Tony Blair," Wikipedia, February 9, 2025, https://en.wikipedia.org/wiki/Tony_Blair.
33 Claudia Willen, "16 Celebrities That Have Converted or Practiced Different Religions," *Insider*, August 4, 2020, https://www.insider.com/celebrities-religions-converted-different-belief-systems-practices.
34 Stuart A. Wright, "Disengagement and Apostasy in New Religious Movements," in *The Oxford Handbook of Religious Conversion*, ed. Lewis R. Rambo and Charles E. Farhadian (New York: Oxford University Press, 2014), 707–710.
35 Heinz Streib, "Deconversion," in *The Oxford Handbook of Religious Conversion*, ed. Lewis R. Rambo and Charles E. Farhadian (New York: Oxford University Press, 2014), 272.
36 This strategy for assessing the authenticity of quitting has an analogous case with the famous thought experiment "The Ship of Theseus" (http://classics.mit.edu/Plutarch/theseus.html, accessed February 14, 2025), in which Plutarch imagines a ship that has its decaying planks replaced over a period of time and then asks if the restored ship is the same as the original and, if not, at what point it was no longer its old self. I manage to avoid the messy metaphysical question by being able to rely on the incrementally changed person (rather than a ship) to tell us when it subjectively feels changed.
37 Looby, interview, 2021.
38 Alison Clarke-Stewart and Cornelia Brentano, *Divorce: Causes and Consequences* (Current Perspectives in Psychology) (New Haven, CT: Yale University Press, 2007), 213.
39 Morski, *Quitting by Design*, 34.
40 Morski, *Quitting by Design*, 41.
41 Kirkpatrick, *The Virtues of Exit*, 96.
42 Kirkpatrick, *The Virtues of Exit*, 96.
43 Jason R. Musteen (United States Army colonel and chief of military history, United States Military Academy), interview with the author, September 7, 2021.
44 Streib, "Deconversion," 272.

45 Christina Capatides, "The Difference Between Being Not Racist and Being Antiracist," CBS News website, June 25, 2020, https://www.cbsnews.com/news/antiracist-not-racist-difference/.
46 William F. Felice, *How Do I Save My Honor? War, Moral Integrity, and Principled Resignation* (New York: Rowman and Littlefield, 2009), 2.
47 Theo Barclay, *Fighters and Quitters: Great Political Resignations* (London: Biteback, 2018), 34–35.
48 Evan Thomas, "George H. W. Bush Warned Iraq War Would 'Not Be Another Vietnam': Relive Newsweek's 1990 Cover Story," *Newsweek*, December 5, 2018, https://www.newsweek.com/george-hw-bush-iraq-war-vietnam-newsweek-1241896.
49 Thomas, "George H. W. Bush Warned."
50 Bobby Franklin, "'No Mas' Revisited: Duran vs Leonard II Why Did Duran Quit?" *Boxing over Broadway*, accessed February 14, 2025, https://www.boxingoverbroadway.com/no-mas-revisted-leonard-vs-duran-2/; Thomas Hauser, *Thomas Hauser on Boxing: Another Year Inside the Sweet Science* (Fayetteville: University of Arkansas Press, 2014).
51 Yosha Iglesias, "The Ultimate Blunder: Resigning a Won Position," Chess24, December 21, 2019, https://chess24.com/en/read/news/the-ultimate-blunder-resigning-a-won-position.
52 Streep and Bernstein, *Quitting: Why We Fear It*, 183, 186.
53 Streep and Bernstein, *Quitting: Why We Fear It*, 183, 189.
54 Ian McLaughlin, John A Dani, and Mariella De Biasi, "Nicotine Withdrawal," *Current Topics in Behavioral Neurosciences* 24 (2015): 99–123, https://doi.org/10.1007/978-3-319-13482-6_4; "Getting Past Alcohol Cravings When You're in Recovery," Maryland Recovery, April 30, 2020, https://www.marylandrecovery.com/blog/getting-past-alcohol-cravings-when-youre-in-recovery.
55 Ayoola Adetayo, "7 Ways to Deal with Sexual Urges in a Celibate Relationship," Pulse.ng, September 19, 2020, https://www.pulse.ng/lifestyle/relationships-weddings/7-ways-to-deal-with-sxual-urges-in-a-celibate-relationship/hsl867v.
56 Streep and Bernstein, *Quitting: Why We Fear It*, 193.
57 "Why You Shouldn't Say 'Give Up for Adoption': The Importance of Positive Adoption Language," American Adoptions, accessed February 12, 2015, https://www.americanadoptions.com/pregnant/other-ways-to-say-give-up-for-adoption.
58 Susan M. Henney, Susan Ayers-Lopez, Ruth G. McRoy, and Harold D. Grotevant, "Evolution and Resolution: Birthmothers' Experience of Grief and Loss at Different Levels of Adoption Openness," *Journal of Social and Personal Relationships* 24 (2007): 875–889, https://doi.org/10.1177/0265407507084188; Susie Books, "Birth Mother Regrets: Learning to Let Go," Adoption Network, accessed February 14, 2025, https://adoptionnetwork.com/birth-mother-regrets-learning-to-let-go/.
59 Arnold van Gennep, *The Rites of Passage*, 2nd ed. (Chicago: University of Chicago Press, 2019).
60 Victor Turner, *The Ritual Process: Structure and Anti-Structure* (New York: Routledge, 1995); Bjørn Thomassen, "The Uses and Meaning of Liminality," *International Political Anthropology* 2 (2009): 5–28.

CHAPTER 8: DEFINING QUITTING

1. "Water Is Not H₂O," *Philosophy Now*, accessed February 14, 2025, https://forum.philosophynow.org/viewtopic.php?t=39844.
2. *Collins English Dictionary*, https://www.collinsdictionary.com/us/; *MacMillan Dictionary*, https://www.macmillandictionary.com/; *Merriam-Webster English Dictionary*, https://www.merriam-webster.com/; *Oxford English Dictionary*, https://www.oed.com/.
3. Annie Duke, *Quit: The Power of Knowing When to Walk Away* (New York: Portfolio/Penguin, 2022), xxii. Duke's use of "choice" conflicts with her later reference to "forced quitting" (206), so it's not clear if she means to include or exclude coerced acts as quits—a rather important conceptual matter.
4. Juan Piñeros Glasscock and Sergio Tenenbaum, "Action," *Stanford Encyclopedia of Philosophy*, January 11, 2023, https://plato.stanford.edu/archives/spr2023/entries/action/; Caroline Leaf, "How Are the Mind and the Brain Different? A Neuroscientist Explains," mindbodygreen, March 8, 2021, https://www.mindbodygreen.com/articles/difference-between-mind-and-brain-neuroscientist; David Hunter. "Is Thinking an Action?" *Phenomenology and the Cognitive Sciences* 2 (2003): 133–148.
5. The view of Julia Keller (*Quitting: A Life Strategy* [New York: Balance/Hachette, 2023, 5–13, 21]) appears to be that any change from one activity to another, as well as any change of mind, constitutes quitting. As such, every moment in life is characterized either by persisting or quitting, which reduces these important decisions to triviality.
6. Ludwig Wittgenstein (Gertrude E. M. Anscombe, translator), *Philosophical Investigations* (London: Pearson, 1973).
7. Jack Kelly, "'Bare Minimum Monday' Is the Newest TikTok Trend of Quiet Quitting and Cyberloafing Throughout the Work Day," *Forbes*, February 22, 2023, https://www.forbes.com/sites/jackkelly/2023/02/22/bare-minimum-monday-is-the-newest-tiktok-trend-of-quiet-quitting-and-cyberloafing-throughout-the-work-day/?sh=70c715be522b.

CHAPTER 9: QUALITY QUITTING

1. Lynn Marie Morski, *Quitting by Design: Learn to Use Strategic Quitting as a Tool to Carve Out a Successful Life* (New York: Austin Macauley, 2018), 68–69; Thomas L. Dumm, "Resignation," *Critical Inquiry* 25 (1998): 28; Bill Murphy Jr., "People Who Embrace This Controversial Word Have Very High Emotional Intelligence," *Inc.*, November 14, 2021, https://www.inc.com/bill-murphy-jr/people-who-embrace-this-controversial-word-have-very-high-emotional-intelligence.html.
2. Annie Duke, *Quit: The Power of Knowing When to Walk Away* (New York: Portfolio/Penguin, 2022), 29.
3. William F. Felice, *How Do I Save My Honor? War, Moral Integrity, and Principled Resignation* (New York: Rowman and Littlefield, 2009), 91.
4. Duke, *Quit: The Power of Knowing*, 39.
5. Edward Weisband and Thomas M. Franck, *Resignation in Protest: Political and Ethical Choices Between Loyalty to Team and Loyalty to Conscience in American Public Life* (New York: Grossman, 1975), 163; Felice, *How Do I Save*, 20, 113, 117.

6 Quoted in Felice, *How Do I Save*, 57.
7 Morski, *Quitting by Design*, 28 (original emphasis).
8 Alison Clarke-Stewart and Cornelia Brentano, *Divorce: Causes and Consequences* (Current Perspectives in Psychology) (New Haven, CT: Yale University Press, 2007), 101.
9 Duke, *Quit: The Power of Knowing*, 39.
10 "George Burns," Wikipedia, February 5, 2025, https://en.wikipedia.org/wiki/George_Burns.
11 Julia Keller, *Quitting: A Life Strategy* (New York: Balance/Hachette, 2023).
12 Keller, *Quitting: A Life Strategy* (Keller's book is essentially a series of anecdotes intended to establish the value of quitting); Morski, *Quitting by Design*, 34.
13 Duke, *Quit: The Power of Knowing*, 35.
14 Scott Henkel (professor of English and director of the Institute for Humanities Research, University of Wyoming), discussion with the author, February 9, 2022.
15 Peg Streep and Alan B. Bernstein, *Quitting: Why We Fear It—and Why We Shouldn't—in Life, Love, and Work* (Boston: Da Capo, 2014), 106.
16 "Soren Kierkegaard Quotes," BrainyQuote, accessed February 14, 2025, https://www.brainyquote.com/quotes/soren_kierkegaard_105030.
17 Jennet Kirkpatrick, *The Virtues of Exit: On Resistance and Quitting Politics* (Chapel Hill: University of North Carolina Press, 2017), 50.
18 Henry David Thoreau, *Civil Disobedience* (New York: G. P. Putnam, 1849), 8, https://archive.org/details/civil-disobedience/page/n3/mode/2up.
19 Robin Barry (licensed psychologist and director of research in the Department of Family Medicine, University of Toledo), interview with the author, September 10, 2021.
20 Eddy M. Zemach, "The Right to Quit," *Philosophical Quarterly* 23 (1973): 346–349.
21 Larry Alexander and Michael Moore, "Deontological Ethics," *Stanford Encyclopedia of Philosophy*, October 30, 2020, https://plato.stanford.edu/archives/win2021/entries/ethics-deontological/.
22 B. Sharon Byrd and Joanchim Hruschka, "Kant on 'Why Must I Keep My Promise?'" *Chicago-Kent Law Review* 81, article 5, December 2005, https://scholarship.kentlaw.iit.edu/cgi/viewcontent.cgi?article=3521&context=cklawreview.
23 Anthony Skelton, "William David Ross," *Stanford Encyclopedia of Philosophy*, March 2, 2022, https://plato.stanford.edu/archives/spr2022/entries/william-david-ross/.
24 Thomas Carson, *Lying and Deception: Theory and Practice* (New York: Oxford, 2010), 67–88.
25 "Wyoming Puts 'Cowboy Ethics' into Law," *Denver Post*, March 3, 2010, https://www.denverpost.com/2010/03/03/wyoming-puts-cowboy-ethics-into-law/.
26 Felice, *How Do I Save*, 4, 16, 119.
27 Felice, *How Do I Save*, 126.
28 Weisband and Franck, *Resignation in Protest*, 20.
29 Streep and Bernstein, *Quitting: Why We Fear It*, 9–10.
30 Christopher Peterson and Martin E. P. Seligman, *Character Strengths and Virtues: A Handbook and Classification* (New York: American Psychological Association and Oxford University Press, 2004), 5; Weisband and Franck, *Resignation in Protest*, 1.
31 Peterson and Seligman, *Character Strengths and Virtues*, 19.

32 Kirkpatrick, *Virtues of Exit*, 27.
33 Streep and Bernstein, *Quitting: Why We Fear It*, 11.
34 Streep and Bernstein, *Quitting: Why We Fear It*, 212; Peterson and Seligman, *Character Strengths and Virtues*, 24. Duke (*Quit: The Power of Knowing*, 21) makes a rather incoherent case in this regard, asserting: "This is a fundamental truth about grit and quit: The opposite of a great virtue is also a great virtue." More sensibly, the opposite of every great vice is another great vice; hence, the Doctrine of the Mean.
35 Jason R. Musteen (United States Army colonel and chief of military history, United States Military Academy), interview with the author, September 7, 2021.
36 Morski, *Quitting by Design*, 30.
37 Dorothea Frede and Mi-Kyoung Lee, "Plato's Ethics: An Overview," *Stanford Encyclopedia of Philosophy*, February 1, 2023, https://plato.stanford.edu/archives/spr2023/entries/plato-ethics/.
38 Duke, *Quit: The Power of Knowing*, 239.
39 Keller, *Quitting: A Life Strategy*, 144, 147.
40 Robert Goodin, *On Settling* (Princeton, NJ: Princeton University Press, 2012), 4; Peterson and Seligman, *Character Strengths and Virtues*, 240; Streep and Bernstein, *Quitting: Why We Fear It*, 4.
41 Richard Kraut, "Aristotle's Ethics," *Stanford Encyclopedia of Philosophy*, July 2, 2022, https://plato.stanford.edu/archives/fall2022/entries/aristotle-ethics/; Jessica Moss, "'Virtue Makes the Goal Right': Virtue and Phronesis in Aristotle's Ethics," *Phronesis* 56 (2011): 204–261, doi:10.1163/156852811X575907; Giles Pearson, "Phronesis as a Mean in the Eudemian Ethics," *Oxford Studies in Ancient Philosophy* 32 (2007): 273–296; C. D. C. Reeve, *Aristotle on Practical Wisdom: Nicomachean Ethics VI* (Cambridge, MA: Harvard University Press, 2013).
42 Streep and Bernstein, *Quitting: Why We Fear It*, 213; Angela Lee Duckworth, Christopher Peterson, Michael D. Matthews, and Dennis R. Kelly, "Grit: Perseverance and Passion for Long-Term Goals," *Journal of Personality and Social Psychology* 92 (2007): 1090.
43 Duke, *Quit: The Power of Knowing*, 21 (makes exactly this mistake).
44 Lou Farley (spiritual director and licensed clinical psychologist, Hospice of Laramie), interview with the author, August 8, 2021.
45 Peterson and Seligman, *Character Strengths and Virtues*, 231.

CHAPTER 10: THE TRIFECTA OF QUITTING

1 Craig Varnell (professional poker player with $1.2 million in winnings 2015–2022), interview with the author, February 4, 2022.
2 Varnell, interview, 2022.
3 Jeffrey A. Lockwood, *Grasshopper Dreaming: Reflections on Killing and Loving* (Boston: Skinner House, 2002); Jeffrey A. Lockwood, *Prairie Soul: Finding Grace in the Earth Beneath My Feet* (Boston: Skinner House, 2004).
4 Meredith A. Addicott, "Caffeine Use Disorder: A Review of the Evidence and Future Implications," *Current Addiction Reports* 1 (2014): 186–192, https://doi.org/10.1007/s40429-014-0024-9.

5   Michael Bisping, *Quitters Never Win: My Life in UFC* (New York: Diversion Books, 2020), 97.
6   Lynn Marie Morski, *Quitting by Design: Learn to Use Strategic Quitting as a Tool to Carve Out a Successful Life* (New York: Austin Macauley, 2018), 13.
7   Dana A. V. Braner (medical doctor and professor of pediatrics, Division of Critical Care, School of Medicine, Oregon Health and Science University) and Paula Ann Vanderford (medical doctor and associate professor of pediatrics, Division of Critical Care, School of Medicine, Oregon Health and Science University), joint interview with the author, February 7, 2022.
8   Francesca Coin, "On Quitting," *Ephemera* 17 (2017): 705–719.
9   Edward Weisband and Thomas M. Franck, *Resignation in Protest: Political and Ethical Choices Between Loyalty to Team and Loyalty to Conscience in American Public Life* (New York: Grossman, 1975), 14.
10 Theo Barclay, *Fighters and Quitters: Great Political Resignations* (London: Biteback, 2018), 102, 279.
11 Peg Streep and Alan B. Bernstein, *Quitting: Why We Fear It—and Why We Shouldn't—in Life, Love, and Work* (Boston: Da Capo, 2014), 183.
12 Jason R. Musteen (United States Army colonel and chief of military history, United States Military Academy), interview with the author, September 7, 2021.
13 Musteen, interview, 2021.
14 Fred Shapiro, "How I Discovered I Was Wrong About the Origin of the Serenity Prayer," *US Catholic*, May 15, 2014, https://uscatholic.org/news_item/commentary-how-i-discovered-i-was-wrong-about-the-origin-of-the-serenity-prayer/.
15 Barclay, *Fighters and Quitters*, 34–35.
16 Robert Goodin, *On Settling* (Princeton, NJ: Princeton University Press, 2012), 68.
17 Braner, interview, 2022.
18 Musteen, interview, 2021.
19 Carolyn Pepper (professor and director of clinical training, self-injury, and suicide, Department of Psychology, University of Wyoming), interview with the author, August 3, 2021.
20 Lou Farley (spiritual director and licensed clinical psychologist, Hospice of Laramie), interview with the author, August 8, 2021.
21 Morski, *Quitting by Design*, 40; Barclay, *Fighters and Quitters*, 113–116.
22 Julia Keller, *Quitting: A Life Strategy* (New York: Balance/Hachette, 2023), 186.
23 Keller, *Quitting: A Life Strategy*, 151, 186; Streep and Bernstein, *Quitting: Why We Fear It*, 212.
24 Carl P. Maertz Jr. and Michael A. Campion, "Profiles in Quitting: Integrating Process and Content Turnover Theory," *Academy of Management* 47 (2004): 566–582.
25 Annie Duke, *Quit: The Power of Knowing When to Walk Away* (New York: Portfolio/Penguin, 2022), 5.
26 "Caffeine's Side Effects," Aurora Health Care, accessed February 14, 2025, https://www.aurorahealthcare.org/services/gastroenterology-colorectal-surgery/caffeine-side-effects.
27 Duke, *Quit: The Power of Knowing*, xix.
28 Morski, *Quitting by Design*, 41.

29 LeAnne Lagasse, "5 Reasons Your Employees Hate Their Jobs," *Medium*, October 11, 2018, annelagasse.medium.com/5-reasons-your-employees-hate-their-jobs-ac662ae29305.
30 Daniela Zamudio, "A Millennial's Unexpected Secret to Success," TED, November 2017, https://www.ted.com/talks/daniela_zamudio_a_millennial_s_unexpected_secret_to_success#t-463544.
31 Streep and Bernstein, *Quitting: Why We Fear It*, 82.
32 Maertz and Campion, "Profiles in Quitting," 579.
33 Maertz and Campion, "Profiles in Quitting," 578.
34 James Wharton, "Myth Busting the French Surrender of 1940," ForcesNet, July 13, 2021, https://www.forces.net/heritage/wwii/myth-busting-french-surrender-1940.
35 Barclay, *Fighters and Quitters*, 189.
36 Barclay, *Fighters and Quitters*, 189.
37 Varnell, interview, 2022.
38 Angela Lee Duckworth, Christopher Peterson, Michael D. Matthews, and Dennis R. Kelly, "Grit: Perseverance and Passion for Long-Term Goals," *Journal of Personality and Social Psychology* 92 (2007): 1087–1101.
39 Goodin, *On Settling*, 49–50.
40 Tess Kilwein (licensed psychologist and director of clinical training, Counseling Center, University of Wyoming), interview with the author, July 20, 2021.
41 "What Do You Know About Addiction?" University of Rochester Medical Center, accessed February 14, 2025, https://www.urmc.rochester.edu/encyclopedia/content.aspx?ContentTypeID=40&ContentID=AddictQuiz&CustomAnswers_AddictQuiz=q2a1_c. Addiction can weaken with time, as argued by Maia Szalavitz, "Most People with Addiction Simply Grow Out of It: Why Is This Widely Denied?" New Zealand Drug Foundation, November 1, 2014, https://www.drugfoundation.org.nz/matters-of-substance/archive/matters-of-substance-november-2014/ageing-out-of-addiction/.
42 Duke, *Quit: The Power of Knowing*, 30.
43 Pepper, interview, 2021; Farley, interview, 2021.
44 Robin Barry (licensed psychologist and director of research in the Department of Family Medicine, University of Toledo), interview with the author, September 10, 2021.
45 Lori Kogan (licensed psychologist and professor of psychology, Department of Clinical Sciences, Colorado State University, College of Veterinary Medicine and Biomedical Sciences), interview with the author, August 17, 2022.
46 Thomas Erik Angerhofer (martial arts sensei), interview with the author, July 14, 2021.
47 Barclay, *Fighters and Quitters*, 82.
48 Bisping, *Quitters Never Win*, 371.
49 Pepper, interview, 2021.
50 Malcolm Gladwell, "Complexity and the Ten-Thousand-Hour Rule," *New Yorker*, August 21, 2013, https://www.newyorker.com/sports/sporting-scene/complexity-and-the-ten-thousand-hour-rule.
51 Braner and Vanderford, joint interview, 2022.
52 Angerhofer, interview, 2021.

CHAPTER 11: HOW TO QUIT

1. Carlotta Pavese, "Knowledge How," *Stanford Encyclopedia of Philosophy*, April 20, 2021, https://plato.stanford.edu/entries/knowledge-how/.
2. Pavese, "Knowledge How."
3. "50 Ways to Leave Your Lover Lyrics," A-ZLyrics, accessed February 14, 2025, https://www.azlyrics.com/lyrics/paulsimon/50waystoleaveyourlover.html.
4. Gholamreza Heydari, Mohammadreza Masjedi, Arezoo Ebn Ahmady et al., "A Comparative Study on Tobacco Cessation Methods: A Quantitative Systematic Review," *International Journal of Preventive Medicine* 5 (2014): 673–678.
5. Mayo Clinic Staff, "Quit Smoking," Mayo Clinic, May 28, 2022, https://www.mayoclinic.org/healthy-lifestyle/quit-smoking/in-depth/nicotine-craving/art-20045454.
6. Wynne Armand, "What's the Best Way to Quit Smoking?" *Harvard Health Publishing*, July 8, 2016, https://www.health.harvard.edu/blog/whats-best-way-quit-smoking-201607089935.
7. Edward Weisband and Thomas M. Franck, *Resignation in Protest: Political and Ethical Choices Between Loyalty to Team and Loyalty to Conscience in American Public Life* (New York: Grossman, 1975), 55.
8. Lynn Marie Morski, *Quitting by Design: Learn to Use Strategic Quitting as a Tool to Carve Out a Successful Life* (New York: Austin Macauley, 2018), 53.
9. Weisband and Franck, *Resignation in Protest*, 47, 153–155.
10. Weisband and Franck, *Resignation in Protest*, 158.
11. Weisband and Franck, *Resignation in Protest*, 15.
12. William F. Felice, *How Do I Save My Honor? War, Moral Integrity, and Principled Resignation* (New York: Rowman and Littlefield, 2009), 22.
13. Felice, *How Do I Save*, 164.
14. Felice, *How Do I Save*, 22.
15. Weisband and Franck, *Resignation in Protest*, 28–29.
16. Felice, *How Do I Save*, 34–36.
17. Robin Barry (psychologist and director of research in the Department of Family Medicine, University of Toledo), interview with the author, September 10, 2021.
18. Julia Keller, *Quitting: A Life Strategy* (New York: Balance/Hachette, 2023), 168.
19. Meridith McGraw and Daniel Lippman, "They Resigned in Protest Over Jan. 6—Then Never Went After Trump Again," *Politico*, January 3, 2022, https://www.politico.com/news/2022/01/03/trumpworld-jan-6-526291; Felice, *How Do I Save*, 3.
20. Susan Harmeling, "Virtue Signaling on Race Relations Only Hurts the Cause," *Forbes*, January 16, 2023, https://www.forbes.com/sites/susanharmeling/2023/01/16/virtue-signaling-on-race-relations-only-hurts-the-cause/?sh=672bd59e52f7.
21. Theo Barclay, *Fighters and Quitters: Great Political Resignations* (London: Biteback, 2018), 189.
22. Richard Kraut, "Aristotle's Ethics," *Stanford Encyclopedia of Philosophy*, July 2, 2022, https://plato.stanford.edu/archives/fall2022/entries/aristotle-ethics/.
23. Weisband and Franck, *Resignation in Protest*, 112–113.
24. Barclay, *Fighters and Quitters*, 82.

25 Weisband and Franck, *Resignation in Protest*, 21.
26 Barclay, *Fighters and Quitters*, 113–116.
27 Peg Streep and Alan B. Bernstein, *Quitting: Why We Fear It—and Why We Shouldn't—in Life, Love, and Work* (Boston: Da Capo, 2014), 37–42.
28 Jason R. Musteen (United States Army colonel and chief of military history, United States Military Academy), interview with the author, September 7, 2021.
29 Barclay, *Fighters and Quitters*, 39; "John Stonehouse," Wikipedia, February 5, 2025, https://en.wikipedia.org/wiki/John_Stonehouse.
30 Eddy M. Zemach, "The Right to Quit," *Philosophical Quarterly* 23 (1973): 346–349.
31 Marta Jimenez, "Aristotle on Becoming Virtuous by Doing Virtuous Actions," *Phronesis* 61 (2013): 3–32.
32 Joe Sachs, "Aristotle: Ethics," *Internet Encyclopedia of Philosophy*, accessed February 14, 2025, https://iep.utm.edu/aristotle-ethics/#:~:text=Virtue%20has%20the%20aspect%20of,can%20have%20their%20full%20development; Morski, *Quitting by Design*, 17.
33 Christopher Peterson and Martin E. P. Seligman, *Character Strengths and Virtues: A Handbook and Classification* (New York: American Psychological Association and Oxford University Press, 2004), 27.
34 "Key Statistics from the National Survey of Family Growth," Centers for Disease Control and Prevention, accssed November 8, 2021, https://www.cdc.gov/nchs/nsfg/key_statistics/n-keystat.htm.
35 Chris Kolmar, "Average Number of Jobs in a Lifetime 2023," Zippia, January 11, 2023, https://www.zippia.com/advice/average-number-jobs-in-lifetime/.
36 "Most Reported Substance Use Among Adolescents Held Steady in 2022," National Institute on Drug Abuse, December 15, 2022, https://nida.nih.gov/news-events/news-releases/2022/12/most-reported-substance-use-among-adolescents-held-steady-in-2022.
37 Douglas Gentile, "Pathological Video-Game Use Among Youth Ages 8 to 18: A National Study," *Psychological Science* 20 (2009): 594–602, https://doi.org/10.1111/j.1467-9280.2009.02340.x.
38 Jeanne Ricci, "The Growing Case for Social Media Addiction," California State University, June 28, 2018, https://www.calstate.edu/csu-system/news/Pages/Social-Media-Addiction.aspx.
39 Sandy Cohen, "Suicide Prevention," UCLA Health, February 23, 2023, https://www.uclahealth.org/news/suicide-rate-highest-among-teens-and-young-adults.
40 Carolyn Pepper (professor and director of clinical training, self-injury, and suicide, Department of Psychology, University of Wyoming), interview with the author, August 3, 2021.
41 Tess Kilwein (licensed psychologist and director of clinical training, Counseling Center, University of Wyoming), interview with the author, July 20, 2021; Tim Lancaster and Lindsay F. Stead, "Individual Behavioural Counselling for Smoking Cessation," *Cochrane Database Systematic Reviews* 3 (2017): CD001292, https://doi.org/10.1002/14651858.CD001292.pub3.
42 Barry, interview, 2021.
43 Lou Farley (spiritual director and licensed clinical psychologist, Hospice of Laramie), interview with the author, August 8, 2021.

CONCLUSION: A FEW LAST WORDS BEFORE I QUIT

1. Julia Keller, *Quitting: A Life Strategy* (New York: Balance/Hachette, 2023), 159.
2. "Confucius," AZ Quotes, accessed February 25, 2025, https://www.azquotes.com/quote/62125.
3. "Gautama Buddha," AZ Quotes, accessed February 25, 2025, https://www.azquotes.com/quote/1462975.
4. "Babe Ruth," AZ Quotes, accessed February 25, 2025, https://www.azquotes.com/quote/255401.
5. "Vince Lombardi," BrainyQuote, accessed February 25, 2025, https://www.brainyquote.com/quotes/vince_lombardi_122285.
6. Peg Streep and Alan B. Bernstein, *Quitting: Why We Fear It—and Why We Shouldn't—in Life, Love, and Work* (Boston: Da Capo, 2014), 144.
7. David L. Levy, "Applications and Limitations of Complexity Theory in Organization Theory and Strategy," in *Handbook of Strategic Management*, ed. Jack Rabin, Gerald J. Miller, and W. Bartley Hildreth (New York: Marcel Dekker, 2000), 67–87.
8. Robert E. Goodin, *On Settling* (Princeton, NJ: Princeton University Press, 2012), 63.
9. Clara Lieu, "Ask the Art Professor: How Does a Visual Artist Know When to Stop Working on an Artwork?" Clara Lieu, December 5, 2013, https://claralieu.wordpress.com/2013/12/05/ask-the-art-professor-how-do-you-know-when-to-stop-working/.
10. Aristotle, *Nicomachean Ethics* 4.3, Boston University, accessed February 14, 2025, https://people.bu.edu/bobl/Aristotle.htm.
11. Kevin Aho, "Existentialism," *Stanford Encyclopedia of Philosophy*, January 6, 2023, https://plato.stanford.edu/archives/sum2023/entries/existentialism/.
12. Psychiatric Medical Care Communications Team, "The Difference Between Empathy and Sympathy," Psychiatric Medical Care, accessed February 14, 2025, https://www.psychmc.com/blogs/empathy-vs-sympathy.
13. Keller, *Quitting: A Life Strategy*, xxvii, 145.
14. Annie Duke, *Quit: The Power of Knowing When to Walk Away* (New York: Portfolio/Penguin, 2022), 188.
15. Duke, *Quit: The Power of Knowing*, 189.
16. Scott Mautz, "6 Ways to Stop Being So Hard on Yourself, According to Science," *Inc.*, July 27, 2019, https://www.inc.com/scott-mautz/6-ways-to-stop-being-so-hard-on-yourself-according-to-science.html; "'I'm My Worst Critic' How to Combat Self-Defeating Thoughts," Embracing You Therapy, accessed February 14, 2025, https://embracingyoutherapy.com/im-my-worst critic how to combat-self-defeating-thoughts/; Preston Schlueter, "Stop Being Your Own Worst Critic! 6 Self-Improvement Tips," *Gentleman's Gazette*, accessed February 14, 2025, https://www.gentlemansgazette.com/self-criticism-tips/.
17. John Boitnott, "4 Ways to Capitalize on Being Your Own Worst Critic," *Entrepreneur*, October 21, 2022, https://www.entrepreneur.com/living/4-ways-to-capitalize-on-being-your-own-worst-critic/436009.
18. Jason R. Musteen (United States Army colonel and chief of military history, United States Military Academy), interview with the author, September 7, 2021.
19. Thomas Erik Angerhofer (martial arts sensei), interview with the author, July 14, 2021.

20 Mark Jenkins (alpinist and foreign correspondent for *National Geographic Magazine*, *Smithsonian*, and *Outside Magazine*), interview with the author, August 5, 2021.
21 Duke, *Quit: The Power of Knowing*, 242.
22 "Do We Know Our True Intentions?" Big Think, January 27, 2011, https://bigthink.com/surprising-science/do-we-know-our-true-intentions/.
23 Ethan Lockwood, interview with the author's son, August 1, 2023.
24 "Pyramid Peak (California)," Wikipedia, December 7, 2024, https://en.wikipedia.org/wiki/Pyramid_Peak_(California).
25 Cris Hazzard, "Cactus to Clouds Hike," *Hiking Guy*, accessed February 14, 2025, https://hikingguy.com/hiking-trails/los-angeles-hikes/cactus-to-clouds-hike/.
26 Dylan Thomas, "Do Not Go Gentle into That Good Night," from *The Poems of Dylan Thomas*, by Dylan Thomas (© 1952 by Dylan Thomas); reprinted by permission of New Directions Publishing Corp.

Index

Page numbers followed by *f* indicate a figure.

abdication, 50, 76
abortion, 34, 73
Abu Ghraib prison, 49, 60
addiction, 13, 18, 29–31, 125, 152, 185, 219; and partial quitting, 127–128; as personal quit, 75–77; as socially sanctioned quit, 6–7, 20; and stigma, 80; and when to quit, 195
adoption, 20, 73, 140, 145
Adorno, Theodor, 51
Afghanistan, 60, 62, 71, 97, 120, 208, 223
Al-Hussan, Razak, 113
alcoholism, 22, 30, 152, 202; and partial quitting, 127–128, 136; and suicide, 118
Ali, Muhammed, 65, 187
Anderson, Philip W., 129
Anderson-Sprecher, Peter, 241*n*21, 243*n*58
Angerhofer, Thomas Erik, 66, 196
Arendt, Hannah, 51
Aristotle: and definition, 127, 162; and virtue, 10, 136, 176, 178–180, 195–196, 205, 211, 219

armistice, 61, 63
Arnold, Benedict, 60–61
associations, 19, 20
atheism, 27, 60
attachment theory, 24
availability heuristic, 93

bad habit. *See* vice
Ball, George, 99
Ballinger, Richard, 48*f*
Barbados, 15
Barry, Robin, 16
Barty, Ashleigh, 9
behavior use disorder (BUD), 30; gambling, 30, 70, 157; social media, 77, 157, 179, 213; video games, 213
Bentham, Jeremy, 166
Bezos, Jeff, 51
Biden, Joe, 63
Biles, Simone, 3, 66–67, 78, 79*f*, 82, 143
Bisping, Michael, 103, 186, 196
Blair, Tony, 138, 203

boxing, 10, 64, 77, 103, 113, 133; No Mas Fight, 64, 113; Thrilla in Manila, 64, 113
boycott, 51
Brady, Tom, 116
Brandt, Willy, 51
Braner, Dana A. V., 238*n58*, 238*n59*, 238*n61*, 238*n63*, 238*n64*, 248*n23*, 255*n53*, 263*n7*, 263*n17*, 264*n15*
breakup, 19, 21, 122, 140, 191, 212
Brokeback Mountain, 7
Bryan, William Jennings, 204
Buckner, Simon, 115
Buddha, Gautama, 52, 217
Buddhism, 26, 52
Burns, George, 170
burnout, 45
Bush, Barbara, 33
Bush, George W., 49
Buttigieg, Pete, 138

Camus, Albert, 34
Cantwell, Steve, 113
career, 18, 21, 40–55, 152, 204, 226; and coercion, 107, 116; and consequentialism, 166; and cost-benefit analysis, 102; and identity, 129; and partial quitting, 134, 146; and phronesis, 210, 214, 219; and sunk cost effect, 95, 97; and the author, 184, 192, 197, 222; and virtue, 178, 187, 200
Carmouche, Liz, 3
Carnegie Hall, 10
ceasefire. *See* truce
celibacy, 11, 29, 75, 107, 157
Chao, Elaine, 50
character, 7, 9, 16, 78, 146; of the author, 198; change in, 77, 128–129, 139, 17; cultivation of, 205, 215, 218, 221, 226; and virtue theory, 181, 187, 189, 220, 223, 229. *See also* virtue ethics
character flaw, 10, 69, 82, 177, 206, 208
character traits. *See* virtue ethics
Chapelle, Dave, 138
chess, 3, 56, 75, 152, 160; and partial quitting, 126; and phronesis, 212; and public quitting, 143, 203; and resignation, 68–70, 144, 150

Christianity, 3, 25–26, 85, 114, 137–138, 186; Catholicism, 4, 6, 26, 27–28, 52, 60, 129, 138, 152, 155, 184, 190, 198; Protestant, 26
Churnin, Nancy, 91
CK, Louis, 112
Clinton, Chelsea, 91
code of conduct, 58, 115
coercion, 110–119, 125, 151, 154, 172, 208
Cohen, Sasha, 116
collective quitting, 51, 61
Colter, Rob, 249*n37*
combat sports, 18, 55, 64, 66, 67, 113, 124
commitments, 12, 19, 58, 159, 192; and identity, 55, 102, 141, 158; and resignation, 68
Confucius, 217
Concorde fallacy, 96
consequentialism, 166, 168, 170, 172, 175, 181
Coolidge, Calvin, 91
cost-benefit analysis, 11, 22, 85, 87, 94; as a rational tool, 102–105, 218; and utilitarianism, 168
counterfactual, 120, 122, 144, 168
Covid-19, 42
cowboy ethics, 175
Cox, Archibald, 50
Cruise, Tom, 3

Darwin, Charles, 17–18, 72
death, 7, 76*f*, 228. *See also* free will; marriage; military surrender; mortality; omission-commission bias; phronesis; religious conversion; suicide; war
Declaration of Independence, 61
decision justification theory, 144
delay of gratification, 42, 92
Delgado, Aidan, 60
Denham, John, 203
deontology, 166, 172, 175, 176, 180–181
desertion, 59–60, 162, 173, 187
DeVos, Betsy, 50
DiMaggio, Joe, 23*f*
disengagement, 151; romantic, 21–24; goal, 134–138, 151
Ditka, Mike, 9
divine judgement, 117

divorce, 3, 13–15, 103–104, 135, 160, 169, 222–223; and stigma, 78, 111, 117. *See also* Declaration of Independence; Edward VIII; marriage
doctrine of the mean, 178, 195, 211
domestic abuse, 110
downshifting, 130–131
drop out, 47, 80, 150
Dry January, 137, 138, 151
Duke, Annie, 224, 260*n3*
Dumm, Thomas L., 40, 129
Dunning-Kruger effect, 44
Durán, Roberto, 3, 64, 113, 143
duty, 44, 60, 172–176, 180, 227

Eat Pray Love, 22
Edward VIII, 3, 50, 76
Edison, Thomas, 93
Einstein, Albert, 51
emotional harm, 186
employment, 18, 39, 40–42, 73, 140, 153; and identity, 129; and phronesis, 192, 212; and suicide, 38; and virtue, 179. *See also* Great Resignation, The
endowment effect, 100
escalating commitment, 99, 196
ethics, 40, 162, 165, 175–177; and the author, 5, 184, 192
eudaimonia, 221
euthanasia, 20, 35, 37, 75
Everest, Mount, 68, 71, 186, 224
Evert, Chris, 9
evolution, 5; and free will, 125; and persistence, 10, 88, 91–92, 123; and submission, 57; and taxonomy, 73
existentialism, 221, 225
expected value, 94–105, 155, 168, 170
expressive exits, 51

Farley, Lou, 33, 81, 215
Fitzgerald, F. Scott, 129
flourishing, 43, 105, 137, 179, 181, 189, 208, 213, 218
Frankl, Viktor, 55
Frazier, Joe, 65, 71, 113
free action, 107, 115, 124

free will, 86, 105, 107–109, 113–125, 150, 154; determinism, 107–108
friendship, 129, 131, 167, 120, 193
Frost, Robert, 131
Futch, Eddie, 65, 71

gambler's fallacy, 98
Gates, Bill, 51, 93, 170
Gautama, Prince Siddhārtha, 52. *See also* Buddha, Gautama
Geneva Convention, 115
Gen Z, 54, 193
grit, 9, 11, 44–47, 78, 91, 195, 231; in sport, 65
goblin mode, 43
good quit, 14, 33, 68, 86, 128, 146, 162–182, 231; and phronesis, 183–199, 202, 228
Goodin, Robert, 102, 218
Gorbachev, Mikhail, 3
Gore, Al, 49
Great Renunciation, The, 52
Great Resignation, The, 4, 15, 41–46
Gurgel, Jorge, 66

Hadrian, 63
Hamlet, 34
hardships, 186
Haz, Rachid, 65*f*
Hemingway, Ernest, 34, 129
Henkel, Scott, 253*n13*, 253*n14*, 261*n14*
Henry VIII, 162
Hinduism, 26
Holmes, Katie, 138
Holmes, Sherlock, 18
hospice, 18, 33, 103, 110, 147; and relationship therapy, 22; and virtue, 181, 188. *See also* Farley, Lou

Ickes, Harold, 49
Imanari, Masakazu, 66
investment, 91, 97–99, 195, 200
Islam, 26, 60

James, William, 26, 109
Jamison, Kay, 118
Jenkins, Mark, 68, 81, 186, 224
Jobs, Steve, 93

Johnson, Harold, 122
Johnson, Lyndon, 99
Jordan, Michael, 93
judgement, 68, 88, 121, 125, 138, 166, 205, 220–225; and character, 78; and gender, 15, 28, 111, 194; and suicide, 35, 38. *See also* character flaw
Juramentos, 137

Kabul, 3
Kahn, Genghis, 63, 70
Kahneman, Daniel, 223
Kant, Immanuel, 174–175
Kevorkian, Jack, 35, 36*f*
Kierkegaard, Søren, 25, 171
King, Billy Jean, 9
King, Stephen, 10
Kirkpatrick, Jennet, 109
Kilwein, Tess, 238*n*53, 238*n*54, 238*n*56, 238*n*57, 248*n*25, 256*n*2, 264*n*40, 266*n*41
Kogan, Lori, 239*n*83–84, 264*n*45

law, 34, 70, 108, 175, 202
Leonard, Sugar Ray, 64, 113, 133, 134, 143
Lent, 25, 137, 211. *See also* practice quit
Leslie, Lisa, 67
Levitt, Steven, D., 89
Levy, Neil, 131
Lieu, Clara, 219
Lockwood, Ethan, 226–228, 231, 232, 268*n*23
Lombardi, Vince, 82, 217
Looby, Allison, 238*n*49, 238*n*54, 238*n*57, 248*n*25, 254*n*43, 256*n*3, 258*n*37
loss aversion, 100, 196

MacArthur, Douglas, 8, 16
marriage, 9, 10, 18, 19–26, 73, 77, 119, 158, 208, 209, 219, 220; and goal disengagement, 135; and deontology, 176; and identity, 117; and partial quitting, 140–144; and virtue, 219–220; as a state, 152–153
martial arts, 13, 56, 75, 93, 167, 223; and athletic quits, 64–66; and coercion, 111, 113; and identity, 103; and rights, 173; and virtue, 186, 196, 199

martyr, 25–26, 35, 58, 75, 111, 114
Marx, Karl, 129
Mencken, H. L., 12
Methbyterian, 85–86
Michelangelo, 7
military conflict, 58, 60, 61, 63, 144, 220; and draft dodging, 51, 60, 187
military surrender, 13, 70, 186
Mill, John Stuart, 167, 167*f*
millennials, 42–43
Mir, Frank, 66
Monroe, Marilyn, 23*f*
moral luck, 171
mortality, 37, 147, 196, 228; and work, 43, 45
mountaineering, 68–70, 99, 122, 186, 225
Moskovitz, Dustin, 52
Musteen, Jason R., 244*n*3, 244*n*4, 244*n*15, 245*n*18, 248*n*24, 251*n*41, 254*n*27, 258*n*43, 262*n*35, 263*n*12, 263*n*13, 263*n*18, 266*n*28, 267*n*18

Nicklaus, Jack, 9
Nicomachean Ethics, The, 10, 127, 178
Nixon, Richard, 3, 8, 8*f*, 16, 50, 161, 203
Nock, Arthur Darby, 26
normativity, 165, 175, 176, 180

Obama, Barack, 63
O'Keeffe, Siobhan, 66
omission-commission bias, 101
opportunity costs, 92
organizational abuse, 111
Osaka, Naomi, 9
Onada, Hiroo, 59, 194

palliative care, 33
partners, 19, 20, 68, 163, 207, 212
Pascal, Blaise, 104
Pauley, Edwin, 49
Pelkey, Charles, 247*n*54, 252*n*71
Pence, Mike, 4
Pepper, Carolyn, 38, 81
persistence, 44, 60, 88, 95–97; and biology, 11–12, 88, 90–91; and free will, 119, 123; myth of, 93; and phronesis, 182,

196, 220; and regret, 144; and virtue, 178, 179
Petain, Henri-Phillippe, 63
phronesis, 180–183, 187, 192–194, 198–199, 203, 208, 223; and dying, 215; and meaning in life, 201; and public quits, 204; and practice, 211–212; and shaping a life, 219; and the author, 189, 192, 217
physician-assisted death, 20, 35
Piper, Watty, 91
Plath, Sylvia, 34
Plato, 83, 176, 179
poker, 18, 95–96, 129, 151, 160, 183, 224; and addiction, 30; and partial quitting, 133; and phronesis, 193; and practice quitting, 213; and resignation, 69, 71
politics of resignation, 45
Pope Benedict XVI, 52, 53
Pope Francis, 52
Powell, Colin, 49, 169
practical wisdom, 164, 196–197, 202, 209, 214–219, 221–222. *See also* phronesis
practice quit, 137, 147, 213
promising, 25, 174
protest resignation, 205–207
psychological harm, 111
psychology, 14, 22, 26–27, 44, 85–87, 130, 223

Qatar, 14
Queensbury Rules, 64
quiet quitting, 54–55, 128
quit lit, 12, 46
quitter, 4, 10–11, 82–83, 91, 164, 217, 229, 248*n*31, 249*n*37; and evolution, 91; and gender, 28; and partial quitting, 132, 140; and work, 41, 44–45, 189, 194; as a character flaw, 177

Ramadan, 25, 137, 211
rationalization, 92–93, 193, 225–226; and consequentialism, 169
regret, 37, 120–122, 144–145, 223, 228
relativism, 165, 168, 176, 181, 220
religious conversion, 13, 26–29, 114, 160, 219; and abandonment, 60; and partial

quitting, 138; and deconversion, 27, 141
resignation, 33, 39, 55, 68–70, 77–78, 150; political resignation, 13, 49–50, 142; and consequentialism, 171; and cost-benefit analysis, 101; and family resemblance, 160–162; the myth of, 93; and partial quitting, 133, 142, 147; and phronesis, 187, 193, 204–208, 213; and well-being, 104, 120. *See also* Great Resignation, The
retreat, 70, 120, 124, 207; as a euphemism for quitting, 80–81; military, 61, 62; and partial quitting, 141; political, 50
retirement, 21, 52, 116, 134, 153, 210
Rice, Condoleezza, 3
Richardson, Elliot, 50, 203
Roberts, Julia, 138
Roddenberry, Gene, 104
Rogers, Kenny, 193
Romeo and Juliet, 34
Roosevelt, Franklin, 9
Ross, William David, 174
Ruckelshaus, William, 50
rule utilitarianism, 171
Rumsfeld, Donald, 62
Ruth, Babe, 217
Rutherford, Ernest, 13

Saigon, 3, 35, 62
Saint Cassian, 114
Saint Paul, 3, 27
Santa Claus, 6
Schelling, Friedrich Wilhelm Joseph von, 160
Scientology, 3
Schopenhauer, Arthur, 160
Sedaka, Neil, 24
self-esteem, 90–91, 224
selfhood, 7, 14, 55
sense of self, 14, 128, 157, 158, 186
Serenity Prayer, 187
settling, 80, 118
Shakespeare, William, 34, 167
Shiffrin, Mikaela, 82
Short, Clare, 195
Sinek, Simon, 42

Singer, Peter, 169
Slovik, Eddie, 60, 162
Smith, Jaqui, 116
Snowden, Edward, 61
Socrates, 34, 176, 178, 180, 225
Soviet Union, 59
Stalin, Joseph, 59
status quo bias, 100
Stonehouse, John, 209
submission. *See* martial arts
substance use disorder (SUD), 30–31, 128, 213–214; and alcohol, 7, 29–31, 75, 128, 137, 151, 226; and nicotine, 29, 31, 129, 139, 201, 213; and opiates, 29, 75, 232
suicide, 33–39, 77, 81, 110, 118–119, 213; ritual suicide, 35, 116, 165; suicide mission, 35, 58; suicide rate, 15, 24, 38, 196
Sullivan, John, 49
sunk cost fallacy, 95–100
Swift, Taylor, 16
Sylvia, Tim, 66

Texas Hold 'Em. *See* poker
Thatcher, Margaret, 207
transformation, 5, 27, 129, 131, 132, 145
Thomas, Dylan, 228–229
Thompson, Hunter S., 34
Thoreau, Henry David, 51, 132, 138, 172
transgender, 29
trolley problem, 101
Truman, Harry, 49
Toastmasters, 10
Tokyo Bay, 3
truce, 63
Trump, Donald, 48, 50, 63, 205
turnaround time, 68, 71, 189, 197, 224

Under the Tuscan Sun, 22
Unitarian Universalism, 28, 47, 138, 145, 190, 193, 198

United States Armed Forces, 58, 115
United States Special Forces, 58–59
Ushijima, Mitsuru, 115
USS *Missouri*, 3, 4f
utilitarianism, 166–169, 176, 180
University of Wyoming, 5, 38, 191, 215

van Gogh, Vincent, 34
Varnell, Craig, 69–70, 183, 195
veganism, 28, 75
vegetarian, 28, 106, 132, 136, 145, 173
Verde, Susan, 91
vice, 10, 137, 179, 195–196, 207, 211
virtue ethics, 176–182

Wallace, David Foster, 34
war, 18, 49, 55, 57–63, 70, 152; and coercion, 115; culture war, 10; Iraq War, 112, 114, 169, 203, 205; Korean War, 63; Mexican-American War, 51; and partial quitting, 142–144; Revolutionary War, 60, 188; and sunk cost fallacy, 96, 99; US Civil War, 51; Vietnam, 51, 60, 62, 99, 122, 142, 169, 187; World War I, 62, 204; World War II, 4, 22, 35, 59–60, 62–63, 115, 166, 194
Washington, George, 48
Watada, Ehren, 60, 112
well-being, 33, 168, 221, 226; of others, 158, 207; harm to, 104, 186, 202
Williams, Robin, 162
Wittgenstein, Ludwig, 160–161
Woolf, Virginia, 34
Wright, Ann, 114–115

Zeigarnik effect, 144
Zemach, Eddy M., 24–25, 210
Zuckerberg, Mark, 52, 93, 170

About the Author

Jeffrey A. Lockwood is professor of natural sciences and humanities at the University of Wyoming. He is the author of seven nonfiction books, three works of fiction, and numerous essays and the co-author of *This Is Philosophy of Science: An Introduction*. His writing has been honored with a Pushcart Prize, the John Burroughs award, inclusion in the *Best American Science and Nature Writing*, and a silver medal from the Independent Book Publishers Association.

www.ingramcontent.com/pod-product-compliance
Lightning Source LLC
Chambersburg PA
CBHW060552080526
44585CB00013B/540